CITIZENSHIP AND INDIGENOUS AUSTRALIANS
Changing Conceptions and Possibilities

For most of Australia's colonial history Aboriginal people and Torres Strait Islanders have been denied full membership of Australian society. This book examines the history of indigenous peoples' citizenship status and asks, 'It is possible for indigenous Australians to be members of a common society on equal terms with others?' Leading commentators from a range of disciplines examine historical conceptions of indigenous civil rights, consider issues arising from recent struggles for equality and consider possibilities for multicultural citizenship that recognise difference. Topics include self-determination, the 1967 referendum, resource development, whether Australian Aborigines *and* white Australians can belong, the international law context, and sovereignty. This book makes a crucial intervention in current debates by providing the context for understanding struggles over distinctive indigenous rights.

Nicolas Peterson is a reader in anthropology at the Australian National University. He has had a long-term involvement with land rights issues, beginning with his work as research officer for the Woodward Royal Commission into Aboriginal Land Rights. He has taught at universities in the USA and Canada and, apart from publishing widely in key journals, is the author or editor of five books on Aboriginal issues. Will Sanders is a research fellow at the Centre for Aboriginal Economic Policy Research at the Australian National University. He has published widely, and edited *Mabo and Native Title: Origins and Institutional Implications*.

RESHAPING AUSTRALIAN INSTITUTIONS

Series editors: Geoffrey Brennan and Francis G Castles, Research School of Social Sciences, Australian National University.

Published in association with the Research School of Social Sciences, Australian National University.

This program of publications arises from the School's initiative in sponsoring a fundamental rethinking of Australia's key institutions before the centenary of Federation in 2001.

Published in this program will be the work of scholars from the Australian National University and elsewhere who are researching and writing on the institutions of the nation. The scope of the program includes the institutions of public governance, intergovernmental relations, Aboriginal Australia, gender, population, the environment, the economy, business, the labour market, the welfare state, the city, education, the media, criminal justice and the Constitution.

Brian Galligan *A Federal Republic*
  0 521 37354 9 hardback 0 521 37746 3 paperback
Patrick Troy (ed.) *Australian Cities*
  0 521 48197 X hardback 0 521 48437 5 paperback
Ian Marsh *Beyond the Two Party System*
  0 521 46223 1 hardback 0 521 46779 9 paperback
Elim Papadakis *Environmental Politics and*
  Institutional Change
  0 521 55407 1 hardback 0 521 55631 7 paperback
Chilla Bulbeck *Living Feminism*
  0 521 46042 5 hardback 0 521 46596 6 paperback
John Uhr *Deliberative Democracy in Australia*
  0 521 62458 4 hardback 0 521 62465 7 paperback
Mitchell Dean and Barry Hindess (eds)
  Governing Australia
  0 521 58357 8 hardback 0 521 58671 2 paperback

CITIZENSHIP AND INDIGENOUS AUSTRALIANS

Changing Conceptions and Possibilities

EDITED BY

NICOLAS PETERSON

AND

WILL SANDERS

CAMBRIDGE
UNIVERSITY PRESS

PUBLISHED BY THE PRESS SYNDICATE OF THE UNIVERSITY OF CAMBRIDGE
The Pitt Building, Trumpington Street, Cambridge, United Kingdom

CAMBRIDGE UNIVERSITY PRESS
The Edinburgh Building, Cambridge CB2 2RU, UK http://www.cup.cam.ac.uk
40 West 20th Street, New York, NY 10011–4211, USA http://www.cup.org
10 Stamford Road, Oakleigh, Melbourne 3166, Australia

First published 1998

Printed in Australia by Brown Prior Anderson

Typeset in New Baskerville 10/12 pt

A catalogue record for this book is available from the British Library

National Library of Australia Cataloguing in Publication data

Citizenship and indigenous Australians: changing
conceptions and possibilities.
Bibliography.
Includes index.
ISBN 0 521 62195 X.
ISBN 0 521 62736 2 (pbk).
1. Aborigines, Australian – Citizenship. 2. Aborigines,
Australian – Legal status, laws, etc. 3. Citizenship –
Australia. I. Peterson, Nicolas, 1941– . II. Sanders,
Will. (Series: Reshaping Australian institutions).
323.60899915

ISBN 0 521 62195 X hardback
ISBN 0 521 62736 2 paperback

Contents

Contributors

BAIN ATTWOOD is a senior lecturer in the Department of History at
Monash University.

GEOFFREY GRAY is a research fellow at the Australian Institute of
Aboriginal and Torres Strait Islander Studies.

ANDREW MARKUS is an associate professor in the Department of History,
Monash University.

RICHARD MULGAN is a professor in the Public Policy Program, Faculty of
Arts, Australian National University.

GARTH NETTHEIM is Chair of the Indigenous Law Centre and of the
Australian Human Rights Information Centre and Visiting Professor
in the Faculty of Law at the University of New South Wales.

NICOLAS PETERSON is a reader in the Department of Archaeology and
Anthropology, Australian National University.

PETER READ is an ARC fellow in the Department of History at the
Australian National University.

HENRY REYNOLDS is Professor of History in the Department of History
and Politics, James Cook University.

TIM ROWSE is a research fellow in the Department of Government and
Public Administration at the University of Sydney.

WILL SANDERS is a research fellow at the Centre for Aboriginal
Economic Policy Research at the Australian National University.

DAVID TRIGGER is a senior lecturer in the Department of Anthropology, University of Western Australia.

MARILYN WOOD is a postgraduate research student in the Department of Archaeology and Anthropology, Australian National University.

Preface

This book arose from a conference on citizenship and indigenous Australians. When we originally started thinking about that conference, we imagined a small workshop in which there would be only limited interest. As it turned out, there was much greater interest than we had expected – in part, we believe, because citizenship provides a focus for people with diverse interests in Aboriginal studies and can energise interdisciplinary discussion. It enables academics, indigenous people and policy makers to meet on common ground because it brings together, within a single framework, theoretical debates, political issues and practical concerns. It also provides a key focus for reconciliation and dialogue between indigenous and other Australians.

The conference was sponsored by three bodies from within the Australian National University: the Reshaping Australian Institutions project of the Research School of Social Sciences; the Centre for Aboriginal Economic Policy Research; and the Department of Archaeology and Anthropology. Participation was sought from numerous indigenous and non-indigenous people and organisations. Yet, disappointingly, very few indigenous people eventually took part. One reason for this was that the Aboriginal and Torres Strait Islander Commission (ATSIC) called, at short notice, a major meeting of indigenous organisations to be held at the same time as the conference, and several people who had planned to attend our citizenship conference felt compelled to go to the meeting.

We would like to thank Jon Altman for his unfailingly generous support for the whole project; Jack Barbalet and Barry Hindess for helpful advice; and Richard Eves and Rebecca Morphy for invaluable help in organising the conference and subsequently in preparing the manuscript for publication.

N P & W S

Abbreviations

AA	Australian Archives
ABM	Australian Board of Missions
ALP	Australian Labor Party
AGPS	Australian Government Publishing Service
ANRC	Australian National Research Council
APNR	Association for the Protection of Native Races
ATSIC	Aboriginal and Torres Strait Islander Commission
AWB	Aborigines Welfare Board
CAR	Council for Aboriginal Reconciliation
CDEP	Community Development Employment Projects
DAA	Department of Aboriginal Affairs
DEIP	Department of Employment and Industrial Relations
DSS	Department of Social Security
EP	Elkin Papers
FCAATSI	Federal Council for the Advancement of Aborigines and Torres Strait Islanders
HALT	Healthy Aboriginal Life Team
HREOC	Human Rights and Equal Opportunity Commission
ICCPR	International Covenant on Civil and Political Rights
ICERD	International Convention on the Elimination of all Forms of Racial Discrimination
JSA	Job Search Allowance
NAC	National Aboriginal Conference
NACC	National Aboriginal Consultative Committee
NMC	National Missionary Council
NPY	Ngaanyatjarra, Pitjantjatjara and Yankunytjara
NRMA	National Roads and Motorists Association

NSA	Newstart Allowance
NTA	Native Title Act
RDA	Racial Discrimination Act
UB	unemployment benefit

CHAPTER 1

Introduction

Citizenship defines the membership of a common society and the rights and duties of that society's members. 'Citizenship' is usually used for 'membership' in a state society where there is a strong emphasis on individual rights as a result of the development of commoditisation and the economy. Throughout this book the word 'citizenship' is sometimes used in the looser sense of full membership in any society.

For most of Australia's colonial history the great majority of Aboriginal people and Torres Strait Islanders have been denied full membership of Australian society and consequently the rights and equal treatment that other Australians take for granted. Further, the settler society has, since the earliest decades of colonisation, ignored the existence in Australia of indigenous societies or social orders,[1] which have provided, and continue to provide, the first locus of social membership and identity for most Aboriginal people. The fact that, after a long hard struggle, indigenous people finally secured full formal equal rights within the encapsulating settler society in the 1960s, gaining access to the same set of citizenship rights as non-indigenous Australians, was a vital step, but the question of the recognition of membership in their own indigenous social orders remains unaddressed.

The failure of the colonists to recognise, at the outset of colonisation, the rights of the people who were here first has left not only a moral and legal taint on the nation's title to the country but also many unanswered questions about the articulation of settler and indigenous societies. Among these questions are: how is it possible for people from different cultural and historical backgrounds to be members of a common society on equal terms? What is a fair and equitable relationship between indigenous Australians and non-indigenous Australians? How much difference in rights between citizens can (or will) other citizens tolerate?

1

And, if indigenous citizens have distinctive rights, what will hold the Australian nation and society together?

These questions, which are being faced because of the persistence of indigenous social orders, are now unavoidable in Australia, because of the Mabo and Wik judgments, trends in international law, the growing demand by indigenous people for the right to self-determination internationally, and the process of globalisation itself. The questions raise broad theoretical issues related to notions of justice, equality, equity, difference and fairness, and the changing relationship between nation and state, all of which find expression within the idea of citizenship. The questions also raise issues that are emotive and contentious in everyday political life, particularly where they are seen to confer advantage and to be dependent on redistribution by the state. How do equal rights, indigenous rights, compensation and restoration fit together in the context of Australian political life, mateship, the 'fair go' and a growing emphasis on economic rationalism and the market?

The liberal democratic principles on which Australian citizenship is based may seem to be challenged by demands for recognition of the existence of indigenous social orders through an additional set of distinctive indigenous rights – broadly called self-determination. Under those principles both equity and equality may seem to be formally achieved when every citizen is treated in the same way and has the same rights. For indigenous Australians to have additional rights, where they are not special rights to facilitate catching up to other citizens, may seem to fly in the face of the fundamental principles of citizenship. Yet, over the last twenty-five years, and particularly following the High Court Mabo decision in June 1992, indigenous Australians have already been successful in having some such distinctive rights recognised by the state, and the same process is going on elsewhere in the world.

The history of modern citizenship in western societies is a history of social and political struggle arising out of class relations in state formations. T H Marshall's analysis of modern citizenship distinguished three components – civil rights, political rights and social rights – which emerged sequentially with the development of capitalism.[2] Given the impact of commoditisation and the growth of the market-place it became essential for property rights to be formalised and protected by law so that trade and the economy could expand. By the eighteenth century these pressures had given rise to formal civil rights, which covered not only property rights and the rights of contract (both integral to the market-place), but freedoms of speech, religious practice and assembly. These freedoms prevent the state interfering in people's everyday lives.[3]

Political rights were granted by the British elites in response to demands by the emergent working class political movements of the nineteenth century, in what might be broadly seen as a containment strategy.[4] These rights were granted to adult males in the middle of the century and only extended to women early in the twentieth century.

Social rights finally started to emerge in the twentieth century. Marshall argues that these were largely to reduce class conflict further; but war, with its full employment, need for national solidarity and the common purpose resulting from external threat, also played a part (although, as Barbalet argues, its contribution can be over drawn).[5] While social rights emerged well before the welfare state, they received their maximum expression during its flowering after World War II. Social rights differ from civil and political rights in that they are provided by the state to ensure that people achieve a minimum standard of living.[6]

These ideas about citizenship developed in the heyday of nationalism, when state and nation were closely identified and were under the influence of liberal political theory, with its concern for formal political and legal equality. But now, at the end of the twentieth century, there is a decline in the identity of state and nation. World-wide those who feel that existing states and current concepts of citizenship have a cultural and gender bias are starting to demand the recognition of differences and to test the extent to which such differences can be accommodated within the liberal democratic framework.[7] The strongest challenge comes from those first-citizens, first nations or national minorities, as they are variously called, in settler societies. Their loyalty is usually primarily to their own communities, which often, but by no means always, have quite distinct cultural and social practices; and only secondarily to the encapsulating settler society.

In this introduction we examine the ways in which ideas about the citizenship status of indigenous Australians have been shaped and reshaped over the last two centuries and the influences likely to shape and reshape them in the coming decades. These changing ideas have been institutionalised in ordinances, state and federal legislation, the Constitution and the many rules, regulations and structures that have affected and still do affect the treatment of different classes of citizens, whether they be war veterans, elderly members of the armed forces, women, children or indigenous people.

Central to this history is an attitude of ambivalence and inconsistency towards formally incorporating Aboriginal people into a common Australian society and a failure by the settler society to come to grips with the persistence of indigenous identities and social orders.

The first part of this book (chapters 2 and 3) considers historical conceptions of indigenous people's civil rights; the second part (chapters 4 to 8) examines issues arising out of the more recent struggle to achieve equal rights; the third part (chapters 9 to 12) considers issues relating to the recognition of indigenous rights, and emerging possibilities for the development of multicultural citizenship.

Becoming colonial subjects, 1788–c1836

It took nearly fifty years from first settlement for the settler state to fully encompass Aboriginal people as colonial subjects. The main reason for this was that, in the early days of the colony, the area occupied by Europeans was quite circumscribed and Aboriginal people were able to continue a fully independent life, appearing and disappearing at will. Indeed settlers had no direct contact with Aboriginal people outside the Port Jackson area for the first three years.[8] Aboriginal people clearly had their own autonomous way of life, as well as radically different social and cultural practices barely glimpsed by the Europeans, and they were beyond the fledgling colony's control. It is not surprising, therefore, that there was an initial acceptance by the settlers of the separate existence of indigenous societies. However, Aboriginal people were soon treated inconsistently as this acceptance began to falter.

In the early days of colonial settlement, official correspondence frequently drew a distinction between British subjects and 'Natives', treating the two groups differently and separately. However, as interaction between the groups increased, Aboriginal people came to be treated as if they were British subjects for some purposes. In a Governor's proclamation of 1802, for example, British subjects were forbidden to commit:

> any act of injustice or wanton Cruelty towards the Natives, on pain of being dealt with in the same manner as if such act of Injustice or wanton Cruelty should be committed against the Persons and Estates of any of His Majesty's Subjects.[9]

As the victims of settlers' crimes, then, indigenous Australians were to be treated as the equals of British subjects, without actually being British subjects, in order to allow the Governor some semblance of control over actual British subjects. As the perpetrators of crimes – or rather what the settlers saw as crimes – they were treated somewhat differently. This same Governor's proclamation went on to state that, while settlers were not to 'suffer' their 'property to be invaded' or their 'existence endangered', they should observe 'a great degree of forbearance and plain dealing with the Natives' as this offered the 'only means ... to avoid future attacks'.[10] Natives, then, were not to be dealt with under the law applying to British subjects, but rather were to be treated as external third parties, for this purpose.

The official tolerance of this initial period lasted until May 1816, when Aboriginal ways for settling disputes among themselves, which often involved much loss of blood, were prohibited on the grounds that they were a 'barbarous custom repugnant to British Laws, and strongly militating against the Civilization of the Natives which is an Object of the highest Importance to effect'.[11] Yet, despite this, the New South Wales Supreme Court, established in 1823, continued to decline to hear charges involving only Aboriginal people. It was not until 1836, in the case of R v. Jack Congo Murrell, that an authoritative statement was made by the court that there was no difference between an offence committed by an Aboriginal person on a European and one committed on another Aboriginal person.[12] This case is sometimes cited as marking the end of 'legal pluralism' in Australia,[13] or as the end of British settler recognition of distinct and separate status for indigenous peoples. However, as Reynolds has recently pointed out, some of Australia's supreme court judges continued to ponder the question of whether it was in fact within their jurisdiction to hear cases of crimes alleged to have been 'committed by Natives against other Natives' well into the 1840s.[14]

The racialised attitudes that permeated the thinking of the vast majority of the members of colonial society, allied with economic self-interest, made it easy and convenient for them to overlook the shared status of colonial subject or even the shared humanity of Aboriginal people. The difference was constructed as dramatic inferiority, and their social practices as barbaric, releasing those at the frontier from the normal moral constraints on behaviour towards other human beings.

The section of the population that was broadly committed to a notion of common humanity were the missionaries.[15] But even in their eyes a recovery of the equal relations implied by recognising the humanity of Aboriginal people was only possible if these people acquired the cultural and social competencies of the colonisers and if difference was erased. In effect, assimilation has long been the principal term on which Aboriginal people could redeem themselves and become citizens of the settler society.

Significantly, as early as 1815 the government set about making this assimilation possible with the establishment of the Native Institution at Parramatta. This institution, which was founded by a former member of the London Missionary Society, was for children between the ages of four and seven who, like their predecessors at the turn of the century, were mostly taken from their parents without consent.[16]

Thus, during the first half of the nineteenth century, there was a tendency for the settlers gradually to discount, ignore or simply forget the membership of indigenous people in their own societies and to regard them instead as just another group of colonial subjects.[17]

Exclusion and the loss of rights as colonial subjects, c1836–1901

The history of the extension of settlement, of the process of Aboriginal dispossession, of the marginalisation and of the ensuing social relations established between Aboriginal people and the colonisers is enormously varied and complex. However, during the second half of the century, as the colonies became self-governing and the influence of the Colonial Office and others in London declined, Aboriginal people were increasingly set apart, legally and physically, as a distinct class of colonial subjects. Where legislation was introduced it tended to reduce Aboriginal people's rights as colonial subjects – such as limiting their access to firearms (New South Wales 1840), restricting their access to alcohol (Victoria 1862) or prohibiting them from doing particular jobs (Queensland 1867).[18] Much of the early exclusion was done by regulation, administrative practice or piecemeal legislation. Towards the end of the nineteenth century, however, all-encompassing legislation in the form of various Aboriginal protection acts was being introduced.

In Chapter 2, on settler construction of indigenous identities in nineteenth century New South Wales, Marilyn Wood captures many of these changes from the later eighteenth to the late nineteenth centuries. She argues that there was an early period of 'relatively fluid' relations and 'indigenous autonomy' during which some settlers, like Watkin Tench, did try to learn about and, to some extent accommodate, indigenous ways. However, relations soon deteriorated as an ever wider area was settled and the executive government began to lose control of violent exchanges between the races. The indigenous people's rights to continued occupation of their lands became conceptually invalidated by the settlers, through their increasing adoption of the doctrine of *terra nullius*, and the autonomy of the indigenous social systems was rapidly undermined.

The new marginal status of indigenous people in relation to the settler society could be seen, Wood argues, in naming practices and birth and death registration procedures. While Aboriginal people were encouraged to (and did willingly) adopt some European naming practices, these often implied illegitimacy and low social status. Birth registration was also not fully open to Aboriginal people, first because it was the province of the church and later, once civil registration was established, through bureaucratic neglect and failure to adopt a consistent and inclusive approach. One effect of the exclusion of Aboriginal people from the registration procedures was, Wood argues, to support the proposition that they were a disappearing race. Yet some indigenous people, particularly those of lighter appearance, were being conditionally included in these official settler records, either with or without a 'distinguishing comment' which marked them as 'different'. This complex of bureaucratic practices reflected, Wood argues, a wider social belief that conspicuously Aboriginal people could not be accepted into the wider community. The few who were included 'passed' as Anglo-Celts and were divided off from the many who were excluded. Either social difference was erased or the bearers of it were excluded. There was no acceptance of indigenous difference as an element of colonial citizenship.

Significantly, during the latter half of the nineteenth century some Aboriginal people did, in theory, have the political rights of citizenship. In Victoria, New South Wales, South Australia and Tasmania, Aboriginal men were allowed to vote, although in Queensland, and Western Australia after it gained colonial self-government in 1890, they were not able to do so unless they were freeholders.[19]

The formal citizenship status ascribed to Aboriginal people in the late nineteenth century is a difficult terminological issue. Chesterman and Galligan use the phrase 'citizens without rights', although it has been conventionally held that Aboriginal people were simply not citizens during this period.[20] Certainly Aboriginal people were not full and equal members of the colonial societies. An alternative is to describe Aboriginal people in this period as having been subjects but not citizens of the colonial societies. Yet this terminology, too, has its problems, since the term 'subject' was formally used to describe the full members of these colonial societies: the settler British subjects. So the term 'subjects' is clear only if it is understood that they were *indigenous* subjects with a highly restricted set of rights in comparison with those of other citizen subjects.

Federation and the development of a Commonwealth approach

The federation debates in Australia in the 1890s were primarily concerned with developing the institutions of the proposed Commonwealth government and specifying the new government's relationships with the existing governments of the colonies, which were to become the States. A move for the Commonwealth Constitution to include a positive statement of citizens' rights was defeated fairly early on in the debates and reference to Aboriginal people was minimal. As a result, the Commonwealth Constitution of 1901 had only two minor exclusionary references to Aboriginal people, which were to be the focus of the 1967 referendum, and no references at all to citizens or citizenship.

The references to Aboriginal people were at section 51(xxvi) and section 127. Section 51 listed the powers of the Commonwealth and, at subsection xxvi, included a power with respect to: 'The people of any race, other than the aboriginal race in any State, for whom it is deemed necessary to make special laws.' The federation debates suggested that the concern of this subsection was to give the Commonwealth a power to deal with matters such as the bringing to (and presence in) Australia of indentured labourers of particular races – a nineteenth century practice that was significantly contested at the time of federation.[21] Subsection xxvi was, as such, seen to be an adjunct to and reinforcement of the Commonwealth's 'immigration and emigration' power at subsection xxvii and was not intended to apply to Aboriginal people.

The second reference to Aboriginal people was at section 127 and stated that: 'In reckoning the numbers of the people of the Common-wealth, or of a State or other part of the Commonwealth, aboriginal natives shall not be counted.' Though this sounds exclusionary and draconian, its purpose, as revealed in the federation debates, was not so entirely unreasonable. The issue at stake related to how the surplus finances of the new Commonwealth government would be divided between the States. Division was proposed to be in proportion to pop-ulation, and section 127 was seen as adjunct to such division, ensuring that States with larger Aboriginal populations but few financial com-mitments to them did not benefit financially.[22]

Underlying these sparse references to Aboriginal people in the Constitution was a clear assumption that dealing with Aboriginal people was to be primarily left to the States. The Commonwealth might need to legislate with respect to Aboriginal people for the purposes of its own powers but dealing with them would not specifically be one of those powers. The lack of any reference to citizens or citizenship in the Con-stitution can be similarly understood. The people of the Commonwealth were designated in the Constitution simply as 'subjects', without specified rights or obligations, and it was left to the Commonwealth and the States, within their respective spheres of jurisdiction, to enunciate their rights and obligations through normal legislation.

The Commonwealth's approach to the rights and obligations of indigenous Australians soon became evident. In 1902, after some heated debate, the Commonwealth passed a Franchise Act which replicated the Queensland and Western Australian approaches of excluding Aboriginal people from the right to vote. This set the pattern for Commonwealth legislation for many years to come, despite some continuing opposition. The term 'aboriginal native' quickly became a standard exclusionary reference in many pieces of Commonwealth legislation establishing both rights and obligations for Australian people. The 1908 Invalid and Old Age Pensions Act excluded 'aboriginal natives' from qualifying for its benefits – as, too, did the 1912 Maternity Allowance Act, to name just two of the more important pieces of Commonwealth legislation. Indeed it was not just 'aboriginal natives' of Australia who were often excluded from the rights and obligations created by Commonwealth legislation, but also 'aboriginal natives' of Asia, Africa and the Islands of the Pacific.[23]

These exclusionary references to Aboriginal people in early Commonwealth legislation were not always consistently expressed. The Defence Act of 1909 and 1910, for example, adopted a converse terminology, exempting from an obligation to undertake military training and active service those 'not substantially of European origin or descent'.

Commonwealth and State approaches fed on and reinforced each other, and this process of elaboration and reinforcement continued well into the twentieth century. In 1911, for example, when the Commonwealth took over the Northern Territory from South Australia, it incorporated South Australia's existing Aboriginal legislation into its new Northern Territory ordinance governing Aboriginal people. When rewritten by the Commonwealth in 1918, the new Northern Territory Aboriginals Ordinance still maintained a vast array of restrictive rules applying only to Aboriginal people. Under the new ordinance:

> The Northern Territory Chief Protector of Aborigines was vested with all the powers held by Chief Protectors in other jurisdictions. He had the power to provide for the custody and education of Aboriginal children, over whom he was the legal guardian, and he could force Aborigines not 'lawfully employed' to reside on reserves [...] Female Aborigines could not marry non-Aborigines without special permission, and it was an offence for a non-Aboriginal to have 'carnal knowledge' of a female Aboriginal.[24]

Across the continent State Aboriginal protection agencies were generally applying more severe restrictions to Aboriginal people during these early years of the twentieth century and in 1904 the Torres Strait Islanders were brought under the Queensland State legislation.[25] The result was that, by the time of World War I, indigenous people had suffered a loss of rights in settler society that was legally entrenched at State, Territory and federal levels.

Struggling for equal rights as Commonwealth and State citizens, c1914–c1970

Reaction against these growing regimes of exclusion and restriction of Aboriginal and Torres Strait Island people was always evident. In Western Australia, William Harris protested consistently about the lack and loss of rights around the turn of the century.[26] Another form of opposition, which became evident during World War I, was that some Aboriginal men tried to camouflage their Aboriginality in order to enlist for military service. Other Aboriginal men protested more openly about their lack of a right to fight and in 1917, when the need for reinforcements was growing, the provisions of the Defence Act, which barred those 'not substantially of European origin or descent', were reinterpreted so as to allow 'half-castes' to be accepted into the defence forces. As a result over three hundred men of Aboriginal descent served in the war on an equal footing with other soldiers.[27] Their motivations for enlisting were obviously complex but crucial among these must have been the desire to demonstrate their equality, the pay and the expectation that wartime service would give them full citizenship rights.[28] Yet, on their return, they were re-confronted with all the racial ambiguities of their status.[29] Some successfully applied for exemption from their State Aboriginal acts so that they had the rights of other citizens, but the cost was a prohibition on association with their Aboriginal relatives.

Because some Aboriginal men who served did receive 'exemption certificates' from the various State Aboriginal protection regimes, on their return some received Commonwealth repatriation and social security benefits but they were only a tiny handful, and only one Aboriginal soldier is known to have received a soldier-settlement block of land.[30]

As a result of the wartime experience the first formal attempts initiated by Aboriginal people to recover citizenship rights materialised with Frederick Maynard's establishment of the Australian Aboriginal Progressive Association at the end of 1923.[31] Maynard's immediate demands were for freehold land for farming and for the cessation of the removal of children from their families.

In the 1930s a prominent Aboriginal campaigner was William Cooper, of the Melbourne-based Australian Aborigines League, who had lost a son to World War I.[32] Cooper was a major force behind the 'Day of Mourning' conference which Aboriginal activists Jack Patten and William Ferguson organised expressly for Aboriginal people on 26 January 1938, to mark 'the 150th Anniversary of the Whiteman's seizure of our country', and which passed a resolution calling for 'a new policy which will raise our people to full citizen status and equality within the community'.[33]

In Chapter 3 of this book Geoff Gray examines the call for a new policy in the 1930s from a quite different perspective: that of A P Elkin, Professor of Anthropology at the University of Sydney from 1934, ordained Anglican priest and influential advisor to governments of the time. Elkin was campaigning strongly for 'full citizenship' for Aborigines by the late 1930s but, Gray argues, his conception of citizenship was quite different from that of the Aboriginal activists. Whereas the Aboriginal activists demanded unconditional recognition of Aboriginal citizenship rights, Elkin had a more conditional view. Elkin's citizenship was to be earned by Aboriginal people through a process of training and moral 'uplift', a movement from nomadism to civilisation. Through this conditional citizenship discourse, Elkin also became involved in distinctions made at that time between Aboriginal people of 'full' and 'part' descent. He identified people of 'part' descent as more likely to be receptive to the moral uplift of training for citizenship. Aboriginal people of full descent, on the other hand, were unlikely, in Elkin's view, to be ready for such full citizenship for two or three generations to come. Gray notes, however, that Elkin advocated the granting of citizenship to people of 'full' descent somewhat earlier than this as a symbolic gesture that would have 'significant value [. . .] in the eyes of the world'.

Elkin's conception of citizenship for Aboriginal people may now seem somewhat dated; but for its time his thinking was, in many ways, reformist and progressive. He did, Gray argues, put 'moral pressure on white Australia' by providing a more positive view of the Aboriginal future than had been common in the past and he also argued strongly that the Commonwealth should accept some 'national responsibility' for them. This last aspect of Elkin's advocacy put him in agreement with the Aboriginal activists who were also demanding Commonwealth control of Aboriginal affairs – although, Gray argues, Elkin did not have a great deal to do with these activists.

An Aboriginal delegation from the 'Day of Mourning' conference, led by Jack Patten, met with Prime Minister Lyons five days after the conference. Patten presented Lyons with a ten point plan for a new long-range national policy towards Aboriginal people which included Commonwealth control of Aboriginal affairs.[34] The response of Lyons, and of other United Australia Party Commonwealth ministers of the late 1930s, to this and other demands for Commonwealth control of Aboriginal affairs policy was twofold. One line of argument was that Commonwealth control had been considered at a conference of State and Commonwealth ministers in 1936 and had been rejected as 'undesirable and impracticable'.[35] Another was that such control was not possible without alteration of the Commonwealth Constitution at section 51(xxvi).[36] This last line of argument cast section 51(xxvi) in a very different role from that envisaged by the founding fathers. However, this now became the dominant interpretation of section 51(xxvi), and removal of the exclusionary reference to Aboriginal people was consequently seen as the *sine qua non* of a greater Commonwealth role in Aboriginal affairs.

With war threatening in Europe in 1938 and 1939, the issue of Aboriginal military service as a citizenship right or obligation once again became a matter of debate. Both Jack Patten of the Aborigines' Progressive Association and William Cooper of the Australian Aborigines

League advocated during 1938 the formation of Aboriginal units within the military. Both linked their advocacy to the struggle for citizens' rights, with Cooper suggesting the name 'Aboriginal citizens corps' for the units. By early 1939, Cooper had gone one step further. Citing the death of his son in World War I and the poor treatment of Aboriginal servicemen after that war, he argued for 'no enlistment without citizenship'. Aboriginal people, in their current position, he argued, had 'no status, no rights, no land [...] no country and nothing to fight for'. To give them something to fight for, he argued, 'the enlistment of natives should be proceeded by the removal of all disabilities'.[37]

The demands fell on deaf ears. When enlistment began in September 1939, Aboriginal men and women joined up in considerable numbers. Indeed, later in the war Patten himself enlisted. This successful enlistment was, at one level, quite surprising since the provisions of the Defence Act still barred from service those 'not substantially of European origin or descent', as they had during World War I. However, in the early days of World War II, there seemed to be little consciousness of these provisions among recruiting officers. During 1940 the higher echelons of the services did turn their attention to this bar and tried to provide some authoritative interpretation of how it should be applied to Aboriginal people. They tried at first to substantiate an interpretation that barred the further recruitment of any Aboriginal men or women, except under special conditions. However, this was quickly seen to be untenable, partly because of inequities between those Aboriginal people already enlisted and those wanting to enlist. A modified interpretation was then developed at senior level that suggested 'half-castes' could enlist but 'full-bloods' could not. This distinction in treatment was never, however, made public and the reality was that many Aboriginal and Torres Strait Island people, of varying degrees of descent, continued to enlist successfully, although some were knocked back.[38]

Hall has estimated that, by the end of World War II, probably more than 3000 Aborigines and Torres Strait Islanders had enlisted, with another 150 to 200 serving as 'de facto servicemen' and a third group of up to 3000 providing defence support services as 'civilian labourers'. This level of contribution to the war effort from a population of indigenous Australians which was estimated in 1944 to be 76,000 was, in Hall's view, 'a remarkable achievement'. The contribution of Torres Strait Islanders was, Hall argues, 'even more impressive' with 'one in every four Islanders having given formally enlisted military service by the end of the war'.[39] This higher Islander contribution was probably in part due to the fact that, from June 1941, distinct Islander service units were formed in Torres Strait.[40] Aboriginal service units, on the other hand, never eventuated.

Hall has also argued that this level of Aboriginal and Torres Strait Islander service in World War II probably led to 'a change in attitudes' – both amongst the large numbers of serving Aboriginal people and Islanders and amongst those they served alongside. Horizons were considerably expanded by the war and indigenous people experienced a form of social relations in the military that was quite different from what they had known in pre-war civil society. On the contrast between pre-war and army employment Hall quotes Oodgeroo Noonuccal (Kath Walker) as saying, 'all of a sudden the colour line disappeared'; and Reg Saunders, an Aboriginal commissioned officer, as saying that white soldiers with whom he served 'were not colour conscious towards the Aboriginal'.[41] This experience, Hall goes on to argue, while 'not revolutionary [...] did establish a new model of inter-racial behaviour by which Aboriginal people could judge post-war relations'.[42]

The new model of inter-racial behaviour and change in attitudes was not, however, greatly evidenced in the actions of Commonwealth Labor governments, which were in power during and directly after the war. These governments passed a number of pieces of legislation providing for new services and benefits, or rights, which could have been extended to indigenous as well as other Australians. However, replicating practices from the early years of the century, the Child Endowment Act of 1941, the Widows' Pensions Act of 1942 and the Unemployment and Sickness Benefits Act of 1944 all contained provisions which specifically excluded 'aboriginal natives of Australia' from qualifying for these benefits, although they did now permit Aboriginal eligibility in certain limited or exceptional circumstances.[43] The one concession that the Commonwealth Labor governments of the war years did make to the demands of Aboriginal activists was the inclusion in the 1944 constitutional alteration referendum of a proposed new power of the Commonwealth to make laws for 'the people of the Aboriginal race'.[44] This was, however, only one of a dozen changes to Commonwealth powers put to the 1944 referendum as a single package and, along with the others, it was not passed.

In the post-war years, pressure continued for both a greater Commonwealth role in Aboriginal affairs and for equal rights for Aboriginal people and Torres Strait Islanders through Commonwealth and State legislation which would apply equally to all Australians. Some Commonwealth legislation enacted in 1948 and 1949 did suggest that change was beginning to take place.

In 1948 the Commonwealth parliament passed a Nationality and Citizenship Act. This Act created for the first time the formal legal category of Australian 'citizen', replacing the earlier formal legal category of British 'subject'. The new category applied equally to indigenous and other Australians but, like that of British subject before it, was an empty vessel to which virtually no rights and obligations were attached. These had to be spelt out in other Commonwealth and State legislation, and in 1948 the myriad of earlier legislation with exclusionary references to 'aboriginal natives', and the restrictive acts pertaining to Aboriginal people and Torres Strait Islanders, all remained in place. Although Aboriginal people were now formally regarded by the Commonwealth as citizens, they still had restricted rights in comparison with other Commonwealth citizens and so they were not on an equal footing with other members of the Australian community.

In 1949 the Defence Act was rewritten in a way that deleted the bar from service of those 'not substantially of European origin or descent' and the Commonwealth Electoral Act was amended to give a right to vote in Commonwealth elections to both Aboriginal people who had served in the military and those who had the right to vote in State elections (that is, those in New South Wales, Victoria, Tasmania and South Australia).

The 1950s and 1960s facilitated a period of quite considerable change in the legislative approaches of Australian governments to indigenous Australians. It was the heyday of the assimilation policy, and the economic assimilation of a stream of migrants made it easy to overlook the persistence of indigenous social orders. The push to rid much general legislation of exclusionary provisions came to fruition. Commonwealth social security legislation had most references to Aboriginal people expunged from it in 1959, and a couple of final references expunged in 1966. Following a House of Representatives Select Committee report in 1961, the Commonwealth Electoral Act was amended in 1962 to give Aboriginal people in all States and Territories the right to vote in Commonwealth elections.[45] The Western Australian State franchise was extended to Aboriginal people in 1963 and the Queensland State franchise to both Aboriginal people and Torres Strait Islanders in 1965. Also in the early 1960s, the States and the Commonwealth in the Northern Territory significantly reviewed their acts relating to Aboriginal people and Torres Strait Islanders and in so doing began to make them considerably less inhibiting. Restrictions on matters such as where Aboriginal people could live, who they could marry and associate with and their access to alcohol began to be revised and lessened, even in some instances abolished. In 1965 the Northern Territory pastoral award was amended to phase in equal wages for indigenous stockmen over three years. Thus century-old restrictive regulation which had reduced Aboriginal people and Torres Strait Islanders to jural minors was being quickly eliminated.[46]

This legislative change and policy review was undertaken in the name of equal rights, a term that still has positive connotations today. However, it was also undertaken in the name of assimilation, a term that was first used by governments in relation to policy for Aboriginal people of mixed descent in the 1940s and became the central term of government policies towards all indigenous people in the 1950s.[47] Unlike 'equal rights', 'assimilation' today has strong negative connotations. It is seen as indicating cultural arrogance, even racism. Yet ideas about assimilation were, in their time, closely associated with ideas about citizenship and equal rights. Tim Rowse asks, in Chapter 4 of this book, whether we can write a history of both these aspects of the policy of assimilation. Can we, he asks, 'honour the emancipatory intentions and effects of "assimilation", while fully registering the cultural arrogance which looms large in indigenous memory?' His answer is not only that we can, but that we should. Nothing less will do justice to the complexity of 'assimilation'.

Rowse's chapter examines the shift from 'rationing', or 'managed consumption', to cash in the Aboriginal welfare systems of central Australia which flowed from the 'equal rights' and 'assimilation' policy era. According to some accounts this transition was an emancipation, but according to others it was a crisis. The crisis narrative, Rowse argues, rivals the plausibility of the emancipation narrative. It helps bring back into view the idea that Aboriginal people, rather than being just a collection of individuals, are a 'surviving social order' which is owed some duty of support by the Australian state. Rowse goes on to identify how this idea of a 'surviving social order' has re-established itself in government policy in more recent years and to explore the 'problem of shared responsibility' that has been raised by this re-establishment. The great weakness of the assimilation policy was that it lost sight of the possibility of a 'surviving social order'. It focused on acultural individuals whose social and cultural life was seen to be in ruins. Under the assimilation policy only Commonwealth and State citizenship mattered for indigenous Australians, not membership in indigenous societies.

Nicolas Peterson's chapter (Chapter 5) resonates strongly with Rowse's. He is interested in the 'radical change' that took place in remote Aboriginal communities after 'social' citizenship rights were granted in the 1960s and the transition to a cash economy was made. He wonders, along with welfare colonialism analysts, whether this change may unintentionally have been as debilitating as it was beneficial. Using the Arnhem Land Trust area as an example, he argues that Aboriginal societies in remote Australia in the 1960s were not in ruins, but in fact maintained a high degree of independence and autonomy. Earlier policies and practices that had attempted to limit and mediate the impact of settler society on indigenous society in remote areas had maintained 'two different social and moral regimes' between which Aboriginal people could move. In so doing, indigenous people moved between being 'full citizens' and 'wards' in Australian society. A vast social gap had been maintained between these two regimes, which resulted in a considerable degree of ongoing autonomy for the indigenous people and society.

Peterson argues that the granting of the social rights of citizenship and the rapid integration into a cash economy provoked a transformation with which Aboriginal people in remote areas are still coming to terms today. This transformation lessened the gap and created a 'double citizenship', the dilemmas of which are now constantly before indigenous people. It increased indigenous people's reliance on the settler state and perhaps lessened their autonomy. The concept of 'welfare colonialism' does not, Peterson argues, adequately capture the nature of this new dependence. It obscures complex economic and cultural issues in favour of a 'political analysis of dependency'.

Having equal rights and benefiting from them are two different things. In New South Wales the extent to which the entrenched discrimination, exclusion and segregation that was particularly evident in rural areas was preventing Aboriginal people benefiting from the removal of discriminatory legislation became evident during the 1965 Freedom Ride. The ride was organised by Student Action for Aborigines, with membership drawn from the Humanist Society, Abscol and the Labor Club at Sydney University and modelled directly on the American civil rights movement. Of the thirty people involved, only one, Charles Perkins, was an Aboriginal person, reflecting the fact that the struggle for Aboriginal rights was still substantially in the hands of sympathetic non-Aboriginal people (mainly from church groups) and the left, and that a widespread Aboriginal political consciousness was only weakly developed.[48]

The ride both reflected the growing momentum for rights and helped build the momentum for amending the two exclusionary references to Aboriginal people in the Commonwealth Constitution of 1901.

From the late 1930s Aboriginal activists and their non-Aboriginal supporters had come to see these references as a major impediment to change in Aboriginal affairs. The campaign for their removal from the Commonwealth Constitution was gathering force, spearheaded by the Federal Council for the Advancement of Aborigines and Torres Strait Islanders (FCAATSI). Chapter 6, by Bain Attwood and Andrew Markus, begins by examining the reactions to this campaign of the Menzies and Holt Commonwealth Coalition Government. Both Robert Menzies and Harold Holt unequivocally supported the repeal of section 127. Menzies, though, was unconvinced of the merits of amending section 51(xxvi) by deleting the phrase referring to Aborigines. Holt, on the other hand, who took over from Menzies as prime minister in January 1966, was convinced that any referendum to alter the Constitution had to cover both references. However, the Holt Government's decision to put the deletion of the two references to a constitutional alteration referendum on 27 May 1967 was, Attwood and Markus argue, still 'a rather un-interested, even cynical one'. Yet the decision was made and activists for the change made much of it.

Attwood and Markus argue that the importance of the 1967 referendum lay not in the changes that were being sought to the words but rather in the 'representations' of those changes that were being put forward. FCAATSI, they argue, talked up the constitutional alterations, making them an issue of 'Aboriginal Citizenship Rights' and of national pride and identity for all Australia. Supporters also talked up the idea that the changes would create a 'reasonable expectation' of far greater Commonwealth involvement in Aboriginal and Torres Strait Islander affairs. Once the referendum was passed, the 90.77 per cent vote in favour of the amendments did itself become part of this talking-up representation. There was, however, another representation of the referendum which, Attwood and Markus argue, still had some currency in the Commonwealth Coalition governments of the late 1960s and early 1970s, and which allowed these governments to do less in Aboriginal and Torres Strait Islander affairs nationally than the pro-amendment activists would have liked.

Attwood and Markus argue that the representation of the pro-amendment campaigners did eventually facilitate change, but not until the Whitlam Labor Government used it after December 1972 to legitimise a more substantial reform agenda in Aboriginal and Torres Strait Islander affairs. Hence Attwood and Markus argue that the link between the 1967 referendum and the Commonwealth assuming a greater role in Aboriginal affairs was 'implied', rather than 'necessary'. The linkage process needed a government with 'the authority and the will to tie the two narratives of the referendum together'.

Attwood and Markus conclude by arguing that it was not the literal meaning of the 1967 referendum that mattered but its interpretation. For indigenous Australians it is now seen as 'getting the rights' which has since been conveniently and mythically 'condensed into a single moment in time'. In fact, as we have seen, the process of indigenous Australians gaining equal rights as Commonwealth and State citizens was far more complex and extended.

Access, equity and indigenous rights

After 1967 the push for equal rights as Commonwealth and State citizens was quickly superseded as the focus of Aboriginal and Torres Strait Islander political activity – first by the demand that equal rights have a much greater impact on the material circumstances and life chances of indigenous people; and second, and more importantly, by the demand for land rights.

The Coalition governments of the late 1960s and early 1970s attempted to tackle the first matter by establishing a new national Office and Council of Aboriginal Affairs and by making grants to the States in the areas of Aboriginal health, housing, education, employment and training.[49] They were forced to confront the second issue by Mr Justice Blackburn. His decision in the 1971 Gove land rights case (*Milirrpum and Others* v. *NABALCO and the Commonwealth of Australia*) declared that Australian common law did not recognise any native title to land. This precipitated a huge outcry, and not just from indigenous people.

It was in response to the obviously unsatisfactory nature of the legal fiction that Australia was *terra nullius*, and in the light of Blackburn's recognition that Aboriginal people had a complex system of laws, that the McMahon Coalition Government made a major policy statement on Aboriginal affairs on Australia Day, 26 January, 1972. This foreshadowed 'a greater awareness of Aboriginal wishes', the recognition of Aboriginal 'culture, language, tradition and arts' as 'living elements in the diverse culture of the Australian society' and 'a new form of lease for land on Aboriginal reserves' in the Northern Territory.[50] While this recognition of Aboriginal culture was welcomed, the offer to deal with land rights by leasing land back to the Aboriginal people was ridiculed. It precipitated a defining moment in Aboriginal political history in which Aboriginal people started setting the political agenda in Aboriginal affairs by establishing a tent embassy outside (what is now old) Parliament House in Canberra.

Land rights were to dominate indigenous affairs during the 1970s. They were an issue that bridged the matter of equal civil rights in Australian society and the emergence of the demand for indigenous rights. The lobby groups for Aboriginal rights in the late 1960s, which were dominated by non-Aboriginal people, phrased the demand for land rights in terms of property rights and equity law – the land had been taken without consent or compensation – but over the next decade this emphasis was to change.[51] The link to specifically indigenous rights began with the election in December 1972 of Gough Whitlam's Commonwealth Labor government, which had a policy of 'self-determination' in Aboriginal and Torres Strait Islander affairs.[52]

To implement land rights the Whitlam Government established a royal commission. This began its work in the Northern Territory, where the complication of a State jursidiction over land was not present, but its ultimate intention was to extend the principles of land rights recognition to the States. The royal commission resulted in the landmark *Aboriginal Land Rights (Northern Territory) Act 1976* – actually enacted by the Fraser

Government, in slightly amended form, after the dismissal of the Whitlam Government.

To further self-determination the Whitlam Government established a national elected Aboriginal and Torres Strait Islander consultative body, the National Aboriginal Consultative Committee (NACC). It also established a new Commonwealth Department of Aboriginal Affairs (DAA), which began funding incorporated indigenous organisations for the delivery of various services and the organisation of community affairs. The new DAA incorporated the small national Office and Council of Aboriginal Affairs and the somewhat larger and longer established NT (Aboriginal) Welfare Branch. Within two years it had also taken over from all the States, except Queensland, the remnants of their disintegrating Aboriginal welfare authorities. This enlarged DAA clearly established the pre-eminence of the Commonwealth over the States in indigenous affairs, except in Queensland.

In Queensland the State Government was attempting to maintain an old style, restrictive Aboriginal and Torres Strait Islander policy regime, which strained Commonwealth–State relations. Gough Whitlam wrote to Joh Bjelke-Petersen seeking amendments to aspects of Queensland's 1968 Aboriginal and Torres Strait Islander Affairs Act, which the Commonwealth regarded as discriminatory. Whitlam argued that this was necessary in order for the Commonwealth to ratify the 1965 International Convention on the Elimination of all Forms of Racial Discrimination (ICERD), which it wished to do. When amendments passed by the Queensland parliament in November 1974 were still viewed by the Whitlam Government as discriminatory, the Commonwealth parliament in early 1975 passed an Aboriginal and Torres Strait Islanders (Queensland Discriminatory Laws) Act. This would override the Queensland Act to the extent of any inconsistency. Later in 1975 this was followed by the Commonwealth parliament passing the Racial Discrimination Act, which incorporated the ICERD into Australian domestic law.[53]

Despite these diverse and concerted reform efforts, relations between the indigenous community and the Whitlam Government were not without tension.[54] The National Aboriginal Consultative Committee wanted executive power rather than an advisory role; indigenous people outside the Northern Territory felt let down over the failure to extend land rights to the States; and the Torres Strait Islanders were apprehensive that changes to the border might be made in the process of granting independence to Papua New Guinea, resulting in some populated islands changing countries.

Despite its anti-Whitlam Government origins and rhetoric, Malcolm Fraser's Commonwealth Coalition government did not greatly undo what Whitlam had done in indigenous affairs. It reformed the NACC rather slightly into a National Aboriginal Conference (NAC) and split an Aboriginal Development Commission off from the DAA. But otherwise policy continued as under Whitlam.

However, one telling semantic change, which reflected some resistance to the growing pressure for indigenous rights, was the replacement of the term 'self-determination' by 'self-management' – although in practice this did not make a great difference to what actually happened.

Chapter 7, by Will Sanders, deals with one of the Fraser Government's most enduring initiatives in indigenous affairs, the Community Development Employment Projects (CDEP) scheme. This scheme arose out of the inclusion of Aboriginal people in the Commonwealth social security system and, in particular, the issue of whether Aboriginal people in remote communities should be eligible for unemployment benefit. During the late 1960s and early 1970s eligibility had been restricted by the Department of Social Security (DSS). However, by the mid-1970s, this restriction of eligibility was breaking down. An unemployment benefit 'epidemic' was threatening in remote Aboriginal communities with few employment opportunities, and this was viewed with considerable concern. The Fraser Government's solution, pushed along by H C Coombs and others, was an unemployment benefit-equivalent employment grants scheme. Aboriginal people in participating communities would work for their local Aboriginal community council for the equivalent of unemployment benefit. Sanders points out the popularity of the CDEP scheme with Aboriginal community councils and describes its expansion over a period of twenty years. He also identifies a more difficult and contested process of program development involving the interplay of ideas about equal rights and difference. He argues that these two somewhat divergent sets of ideas have co-existed within the CDEP scheme and have been mediated or balanced through ideas about appropriateness.

The Fraser Coalition Government's approach to the recognition of indigenous land rights outside the NT was to leave legislation to the States. Some States were gradually taking up this challenge. South Australia passed its Pitjantjatjara Land Rights Act in 1981 and New South Wales passed its Aboriginal Land Rights Act in 1983. Other States, however, were more reluctant to recognise indigenous rights to land, and the Fraser Government was unwilling to be seen to push them. The Labor Opposition of the early 1980s saw in this an opportunity to set itself apart from the Fraser Government and committed itself to uniform national recognition of indigenous land rights.

When Bob Hawke's Commonwealth Labor government came to power in 1983 it tried to introduce uniform national land rights. But this initiative fell foul of State rights (especially in Western Australia) and a fear on the part of Northern Territory Aboriginal people that it would lead to a watering down of their rights, and nothing happened. The NAC vigorously criticised the Hawke Government for this backdown, and it was eventually disbanded.[55] However, the government did commit itself to replacing the NAC with another body and it attempted to retrieve relations with the indigenous constituency through a number of policies giving greater substantive effect to equal rights. Of note was a new employment policy, the Aboriginal Employment Development Policy, which aimed to achieve equality in employment and income measures by the year 2000.[56] A second initiative was a royal commission into Aboriginal deaths in custody, established in 1987.

The replacement for the NAC was a national statutory commission, the Aboriginal and Torres Strait Islander Commission (ATSIC). Created in March 1990, it incorporated elected regional councils and national commissioners and took over the administrative functions of the Department of Aboriginal Affairs, thus combining some executive authority over government programs and expenditure with indigenous representation.

The Hawke Government's other major initiative of relevance to indigenous Australians was the establishment in 1991 of a Council for Aboriginal Reconciliation. This was an attempt to recreate some bi-partisanship in Commonwealth policy after the Coalition had disagreed strongly with Labor's establishment of ATSIC. The council's twenty-five members were divided between indigenous and other Australians and its work was to focus on national unity and nation building in the ten year lead-up to the centenary of federation, rather than on indigenous affairs policy per se.

Paul Keating's Commonwealth Labor government, established in late 1991, soon found itself in a situation very different from its predecessors in relation to the recognition of indigenous rights to land. In June 1992, in the Mabo case, the High Court of Australia recognised for the first time common law indigenous rights to land. This placed land rights back on the national political agenda, and this time there was no escaping the issue. In late 1993, the Keating Government passed legislation recognising the common law of native title, but also validating past interests in land which might now be held to have contravened native title rights. The Native Title Act also established a quasi-judicial regime for dealing with native title claims and future acts on land subject to native title claim. Two other elements of the Keating Government's response to the Mabo decision were the establishment of a national indigenous land fund, which could acquire land for indigenous people who would not benefit directly from native title, and the foreshadowing of a wider ranging 'social justice package'.

This final element of the Keating Government's response to the Mabo decision resonated strongly with another reform of late 1992: the creation of a new position on the Commonwealth's Human Rights and Equal Opportunity Commission for an Aboriginal and Torres Strait Island social justice commissioner. The creation of this new position was one of the Commonwealth's responses to the report of the royal commission into Aboriginal deaths in custody, released in 1991. The 'major function' of the new position was to be the preparation of yearly reports on the 'enjoyment and exercise of human rights by Aboriginal and Torres Strait Islander people'.[57] When the Native Title Act was passed at the end of 1993, the Social Justice Commissioner was further required to report annually on the operation of the Native Title Act and prepare a submission to the Commonwealth Government on the proposed social justice package. ATSIC and the Council for Aboriginal Reconciliation were also asked to prepare submissions on the social justice package.

The submissions on the social justice package by the Social Justice Commissioner, ATSIC and the Council for Aboriginal Reconciliation all used the language of citizens and citizenship in making their cases for further reform and emphasised that two kinds of rights were involved: citizenship or equality rights, and indigenous rights.

The Social Justice Commissioner's submission spoke of 'indigenous rights' and 'citizenship rights' and also of 'citizenship services'. Of the latter it noted:

> Many Aboriginal and Torres Strait Islander people have not benefitted in any substantive way from government efforts to improve basic community infrastructure and the delivery of citizenship services. Infrastructure and services that are taken for granted in the capital cities or regional centres do not yet exist in many areas where relatively large numbers of Aboriginal and Torres Strait Islander people live.[58]

It went on to argue that, because of this, many indigenous organisations had taken on 'de facto responsibility for a relatively wide range of citizenship services', particularly in remote areas, and that as a consequence these organisations needed to be funded by some method that provided an 'alternative' to the current discretionary 'grants based approach'.[59] It suggested a 'comprehensive review of funding arrangements' conducted by the Commonwealth Grants Commission that would apply principles of 'fiscal equalisation' to Aboriginal communities and hence place funding of indigenous community organisations for the delivery of 'citizenship services' on a footing similar to current Commonwealth general-purpose funding of States, Territories and local governments.[60]

All three of these submissions confirmed that ideas of recognising indigenous rights and giving greater effect to equal rights had become

central to recent indigenous political activity. They also demonstrated
how the language of citizens and citizenship could be used to advantage
in calls for further reform. Yet, as David Trigger shows in Chapter 8 of
this book, the language of citizenship can also be used by other political
actors in ways that attempt to marginalise or discredit indigenous
interests.

Trigger is interested in large-scale mining developments and how
protagonists for these developments, such as State premiers and mining
industry representatives, often appeal to notions of the national interest
and shared citizenship commitments in their pro-development stances.
Aboriginal people in the Gulf Country, he argues, do not share this
unequivocal commitment to large-scale resource development. Their
attitudes towards such developments are more ambiguous and contingent. They have apprehensions about the integrity of their 'country' and
environmental pollution. They also have different expectations about
what might constitute a fair trade of material benefits if mining did
proceed. But the predominant notions of citizenship, civic virtue and
social responsiblity in Australia are, Trigger argues, inscribed with pro-
development values and so Aboriginal people remain peripheral and
marginalised. To overcome this marginalisation Trigger suggests a
notion of 'cultural citizenship for encapsulated minorities'. This 'would
imply that real moral weight should be accorded to world views and
practices that are at times inconsistent with predominant sentiments'.

With this final suggestion Trigger is tapping into recent theorising
about the form citizenship might take in truly diverse multicultural
societies that bring together people from very different historical
backgrounds.

Multicultural citizenship

Part III of this book is about the future. It examines how citizenship can
be reconceptualised in the light of surviving indigenous social orders
and demands for recognition of indigenous rights.

Chapter 9, by Peter Read, begins with a litany of contradictory
past practices engaged in by non-Aboriginal officials in attempts to deal
with Aboriginal people. Read suggests that such 'extermination by legislation' indicates that many non-Aboriginal Australians are yet to see
Aboriginality as part of Australia's diversity. He then shifts his focus to the
post-1960s change in the demands made by Aboriginal political activity,
ranging from equal citizenship rights to recognition as indigenous
peoples. This change has caused some unease, Read argues, as non-
indigenous Australians have had to think more deeply about their status
in the country and indigenous Australians have begun to assert that

non-indigenous Australians will never belong in quite the same way as they do. From this, Read argues that further developing citizenship in Australia is a 'two way process'. Neither Aboriginal nor non-Aboriginal people are yet full citizens of Australia, each lacking a different essential ingredient and each having something to offer the other. The question is, can each accept the other as belonging in a legitimate but different way?

Chapter 10, by Richard Mulgan, takes up this issue in the context of the Council for Aboriginal Reconciliation. He endorses the council's 'search for legitimacy and the general enterprise of coming to terms with colonial conquest', but expresses some doubts about the 'optimism of the rhetoric'. He notes the 'delegitimising effects of the history of colonial settlement' and the problems this creates for non-indigenous Australians. While a minority of non-indigenous Australians, 'moralising liberals', may be content to feel shame about this history of settlement and the state that has arisen from it, the majority, he argues, will need to feel more positively. To enable this to happen, we are required to believe that a state can be legitimate though it was founded in injustice. This is not such an unusual requirement, he argues, since many states have such murky origins. As time passes, the legitimacy of states depends less on their origins than on the way their people behave. The test of legitimacy for the present-day Australian state, he argues, is whether it upholds the rights of its present citizens. Mulgan believes that these citizenship rights should include some distinctive rights for indigenous minorities and he argues that the acknowledgement of indigenous rights can become a means of confirming the legitimacy of the state and all its citizens. These indigenous rights need, however, to coexist with the equally legitimate rights of all citizens, so they are limited.

Mulgan argues that, in arriving at this postion of legitimacy, there is a role for acts of public apology or atonement on the part of the non-indigenous majority, the main purpose of which is to express 'moral condemnation' of the past and 'a determination to deal justly in the future'. Such apologies may, in turn, also evoke acceptance of them by indigenous people and in this way lay the ground work for a 'new guilt-free relationship'. However, Mulgan also believes that it is too much to expect indigenous people simply to accept apologies and forget the past. Their ability to 'disturb the conscience of the nation' through reference to the colonial past is one of their few political weapons. So there is 'a deep-seated conflict between Aboriginal and non-Aboriginal attitudes to the colonial past' and hopes of 'true reconciliation' are 'over-optimistic'. Shared citizenship does, he argues, require shared values, but these might be accommodation and compromise, rather than reconciliation and consensus.

In Chapter 11 Garth Nettheim explores the relevance to indigenous Australians of recent developments in international law, particularly the growth of international treaty making. He notes that the Mabo case would not have reached the High Court had Australia not ratified the International Convention on the Elimination of All Forms of Racial Discrimination and implemented its terms in Australian law through the 1975 Racial Discrimination Act. He also notes the way in which the High Court judges, in determining Mabo, made reference to Australia's 'accession' to particular international treaties and drew on this as a 'legitimate and important influence on the development of the common law'. From this Nettheim argues that the international law principle of racial non-discrimination has been of 'immense importance' in recent struggles to have the rights of indigenous Australians recognised. However, he also notes the limits of this equality/non-discrimination principle, with some earlier Aboriginal land rights legislation being interpreted until very recently as offending the principle and being saved only by exceptional 'special measures' provisions. Although this interpretation now appears to be losing acceptance, Nettheim still wants to argue that the racial non-discrimination principle and its exceptional special measures provisions are inadequate mechanisms for dealing with the collective interests of indigenous peoples. He sees the United Nations' Draft Declaration on the Rights of Indigenous Peoples as having some potential in this regard – and so, too, some more established elements of international law, such as Article 1 of both the International Covenant on Civil and Political Rights and the International Covenant on Economic, Social and Cultural Rights. There are, Nettheim argues, possibilities in contemporary international law for advancing the agenda of indigenous Australians towards both equality and the recognition of 'collective differences'.

Chapter 12, by Henry Reynolds, also examines issues in international law, as well as in Australian historiography. Reynolds is primarily concerned with the concept of sovereignty. He recounts, then questions, the 'conventional story': that the British Crown asserted sovereignty over Australia, that indigenous Australians became British subjects who were subsequently excluded from many citizenship rights and that this was remedied in 1967. Those who have tried to question this view have, he argues, come up against two impenetrable barriers: the 'act of state' doctrine and the traditional English view of sovereignty as one 'supreme, irresistible, absolute and uncontrolled authority'. But this conventional story makes sense, Reynolds argues, only if we believe that 'Aborigines were traditionally so primitive as to be almost totally without law, politics or authority'.

If the opposite is accepted, then Aboriginal tribes did exercise 'a form of sovereignty which could have been recognised by the international law of the late eighteenth and early nineteenth centuries'. Mabo undid the conventional story in relation to land, but left it intact in relation to sovereignty. This is a logical nonsense, Reynolds argues. If 'native title was extinguished in a piecemeal fashion over a long period of time, the same clearly happened with sovereignty'. As 'British authority expanded gradually, Aboriginal sovereignty was slowly eroded'. And if some native title still exists today, perhaps some Aboriginal sovereignty does too. This, Reynolds argues, offers a new challenge for Australian federalism. If sovereignty could be divided in one way in 1901, why can't it be cut again 100 years later to create a new level of government which would allow Aboriginal and Islander communities to run their own internal affairs? But the issue, as Reynolds sees it, is not just internal to Australian federalism. Calls for indigenous self-government rights also draw on the international covenants and agreements discussed by Nettheim, and Reynolds sees potential for 'new thinking' at this international level as well. The best way to approach this new thinking about sovereignty, Reynolds argues, is by separating the concepts of state and nation. Aboriginal people and Torres Strait Islanders are citizens of the Australian state, but that state contains several nations.

These, then, are issues about the reshaping of existing institutional structures and establishing desirable new structures for the second century of our nationhood. Ideas for these new institutional structures could arise from debates about sovereignty, the Constitution and reconciliation stimulated by the celebration of the century of federation. They could also occur through more concrete processes of appeal to international forums by indigenous groups. Whatever the processes, the reshaping is unlikely to be either unproblematic or uncontested, as developments since the 1996 Commonwealth elections make clear. John Howard's Liberal government, in its response to the Wik native title judgement, has taken a less sympathetic approach to the recognition of indigenous rights than perhaps any Commonwealth government in the post-1967 period. And the emergence of Pauline Hanson and the One Nation Party also serves as a reminder that convincing Australians of the merits of recognising any group-specific rights for indigenous people is difficult. The essays here, however, make it clear that this issue will not go away – because it impinges on the moral legitimacy of the state and nation.

Conclusion

We began this book by asking how it is possible for people from different cultural and historical backgrounds to be members of a common society on equal terms. It is clear that at present, even with equal rights, the great majority of indigenous people in Australia are not members on equal terms, by any of the standard social indicators relating to health, education or general welfare. Governments of all political persuasions see it as fair and equitable to allocate increased resources to eliminate this disparity, even if they differ on the particular policies and modes of delivery necessary to achieve such a goal. However, when it comes to reshaping citizenship-related ideas and institutions in order to accommodate the persistence of indigenous social orders, and to doing this by recognising additional indigenous rights, the achievement of any easy consensus evaporates.

Central to the liberal conception of citizenship is the notion of equity, or fairness. Can the recognition of difference be justified in ways that are compatible with these understandings of citizenship, which are widely held in Australian society?

In a recent book Will Kymlicka[61] has attempted to develop a theory of minority cultural rights based on liberal principles of freedom of choice and personal autonomy. He argues that membership of a society is an essential component not only of an individual's moral agency but also of a person's ability to meet members of other cultures on equal terms. Majority culture is protected by the language, holidays and other symbols adopted by the state. The challenge is to have policies, symbols and institutional arrangements that reflect and support a country's minority cultures as well as its majority culture. To this end, minority rights may be a useful and even necessary device to allow the country's members to meet the majority on equal terms. To use Kymlicka's words, 'group-specific rights are needed to accommodate our differences' and the 'accommodation of differences is the essence of true equality'.[62] The recognition of indigenous rights thus becomes the pursuit of equal rights at a more sophisticated level. It is itself a process of giving greater effect to equal rights.

If this provides a liberal philosophical basis for minority rights the question is how extensive such rights should be. This is an enormously complex issue but in the world of politics cost is crucial. How far is the majority culture prepared to go in subsidising the culture of the indigenous minority when the majority are likely to see personal identity and much everyday cultural practice as a private matter? Further supporting indigenous cultures raises other difficult issues. How are indigenous group rights to articulate with principles of non-discrimination enshrined in the Racial Discrimination Act? Can the individualistic emphasis underwriting the law and rights of the majority culture be articulated with the rights of indigenous social orders without subverting the longer term strategic group interests that may be vital to their survival? What is to be done when indigenous practices are costly or need government support to survive?

It is hard, at this moment in time, to see which values and symbols may unite indigenous and non-indigenous Australians. Kymlicka suggests that, for citizens to want to keep a multination state together, they must value not only 'deep diversity'[63] but also the particular ethnic groups and native cultures that share the country.[64] The support for sharing the country is fragile in Australia at present and it may take a long time to negotiate terms that will allow all Australians to accept each other as members of a common society.

Given the enduring nature of indigenous social orders and identities, group-specific rights may be central to accommodating differences. Different people can be recognised as 'belonging' to Australian society in different ways, and can in turn recognise the different belongings of others. But, as Mulgan suggests, this may be more about compromise and accommodation than consensus and reconciliation.

Notes

1 We take this term from Chapter 4, by Tim Rowse, using it in recognition of the fact that, once colonisation began, indigenous societies in Australia came to be increasingly dependent, in differing ways and to differing degrees, on the settler society and state. While typically a society is a large scale, relatively self-sufficient and discrete social group, and many indigenous groups are not, indigenous people do constitute many different social orders. Particularly where there are distinct residential communities, the people live out their everyday existence within distinctive sets of social relations, cultural orientations and practices, even where these communites have been deeply penetrated by aspects of the encapsulating society. Thus they often have distinct languages, forms of social classification, social relations of production, religious beliefs and practices, and an economy based on sharing and reciprocity that set them quite apart from Australian society at large. Despite being relatively small populations, their distinctiveness is often reinforced by racism and geographical location.

2 There have been criticisms of Marshall's work on a number of grounds (for example, see Hindess 1993) but the distinction between the three kinds of rights remains central. The criticisms include being too Anglo-centric, evolutionary and weak on the political conditions for the emergence and maintenance of citizenship.

3 See Barbalet 1988: 20.

4 Turner 1990.

5 Barbalet 1988: 37.

6 With the demographic shift that has begun to take place in first world nations since the 1980s, which is seeing a growing proportion of the population in retirement and a great increase in the cost of the provision of pensions and medical services, the welfare state has started to become too costly, in the eyes of many, and is gradually being wound back world-wide.

7 See Kymlicka 1995 and Pateman 1988.

8 Brook and Kohen 1991: 9.

9   See Woolmington 1988: 5–6.

10 Woolmington 1988: 6.

11 Governor Macquarie Historical Records of Australia (1) 9: 143; Collins 1798–1802 (see 1971: 328).

12 See McCorquodale 1987: 419.

13 Reynolds 1996: 62.

14 Reynolds 1996: 63.

15 Christian doctrine committed Christians to the belief in the unity of human-kind. Aboriginal people's 'degraded' status was the result of devolution after being expelled from the Garden of Eden. Despite this negative view of Aboriginal people Christian doctrine also committed missionaries to the belief that they possessed souls and so could be saved. Of course, as John Harris comments, the views of many of the missionaries were, in practice, little different from those of the other colonists (see Harris 1990: 28–29).

16 Brook and Kohen 1991: 70, 263.

17 Of course this was only practically true within the area directly controlled and occupied by the colony and along a blurred frontier.

18 See McCorquodale 1987: 18, 80, 53 and more generally for a full listing of legislation.

19 It can be confidently assumed that few Aboriginal people exercised these rights or were even aware of them. One exception, however, was at Point McLeay, which had its own 'polling station in 1896 with more than 100 people on the rolls, of whom over 70% voted in the election that year' (Stretton and Finnimore 1991: 2).

20 Chesterman and Galligan 1997.

21 Chesterman and Galligan 1997: 69–71.

22 Chesterman and Galligan 1997: 70–73.

23 See Chesterman and Galligan 1997: 85–6; 88–91.

24 Chesterman and Galligan 1997: 144.

25 Chesterman and Galligan 1997: ch. 5.

26 See Haebich 1988: 125, 127, 386–90.

27 Huggonson 1989: 353.

28 Huggonson 1989: 353–4.

29 Hall 1995: 5.

30 Huggonson 1993.

31 See Horton 1994: 672–3.

32 Huggonson 1989: 355.

33 Horner and Langton 1987: 29. Patten and Ferguson were authors of the important manifesto, 'Aborigines claim citizen rights!', published as a pamphlet (Sydney: The Publicist, 1938)

34 Horner and Langton 1987: 35.

35 Commonwealth Parliamentary Debates, vol. 160, 8–9 June 1939: 1571.

36 See Horner and Langton 1987: 35; also Commonwealth Parliamentary Debates, vol. 158, 29–30 November 1938: 2259.

37 See Hall 1989: 8–10.

38 See Hall 1989: 13–20.

39 Hall 1989: 189–90.

40 Hall 1989: 32–59.

41 Hall 1989: 69 and 70.

42 Hall 1989: 72.

43 See Chapter 3 for details.

44 Chesterman and Galligan 1997: 154.

45 Perhaps it should be noted in passing that, in 1962, it was not thought that voting should be compulsory for Aboriginal people, as it was for other Australians. So some difference in treatment did remain in the Commonwealth electoral legislation until 1984. In the period from 1962 to 1984 voting was compulsory for Aboriginal people if they were enrolled, but enrolment was voluntary.

46 See Rowley 1970: 405–15.

47 See Rowley 1970: 383–403. See Chapter 3, note 63.

48 The Communist Party early on had a strong policy on Aboriginal affairs (for example, see the pamphlet written by T Wright in 1939, *New deal for the Aborigines* (Sydney: The Forward Press), which reflected the party's views) and its members were politically active in a number of ways, especially in the Federal Council for Aboriginal and Torres Strait Islander Advancement. This is not to underestimate the crucial role at this time of Aboriginal activists such as Pearl Gibbs, Herbert Groves, Doug Nicholls and William and Eric Onus but to emphasise that grass roots activism was not well developed.

49 Commonwealth Parliamentary Debates, House of Representatives, vol. 65, 11 September 1969: 1290–99.

50 Statement by the Prime Minister The Rt Hon. William McMahon, CH, MP, 'Australian Aborigines: Commonwealth Policy and Achievements', 26 January 1972, Government Printer, Canberra, pp. 1–15.

51 See Engel 1965, who produced a paper for the Australian Council of Churches entitled 'The Land Rights of Australian Aborigines' and the paper put out by the Federal Council for the Advancement of Aboriginal and Torres Strait Islanders in 1968 entitled 'Aboriginal Land Rights Campaign 1968'. The Aborigines' Advancement League's communication to the United Nations on 18 March 1971 is also phrased in this way (see Stone 1974: 230–31). See also Woodward 1974: 2.

52 Whitlam 1985: 466–70.

53 Whitlam 1985: 466–72.

54 Pittock and Lippman 1974; Lippman 1979.

55 See Altman and Dillon 1985, Libby 1989, Jennett 1990: 254–7, Bennett 1989: 33–7.

56 See Jennett 1990: 270–76, Altman ed. 1991.

57 Commonwealth Parliamentary Debates, House of Representatives, vol. 186, 3 November 1992: 2398.

58 ATSISJC 1995: 33.

59 ATSISJC 1995: 36.

60 ATSISJC 1995: 38–40.

61 See References.

62 Kymlicka 1995: 108. In the latter of these two phrases, Kymlicka is quoting a Canadian Supreme Court judgement.

63 See Kymlicka 1995: 191. Here, Kymlicka quotes Charles Taylor (1991: 75). By this term Kymlicka means not only diversity of cultural groups but diversity of ways in which the members of these groups belong to the larger polity.

64 Kymlicka 1995: 191.

References

Aboriginal and Torres Strait Islander Social Justice Commissioner (ATSISJC). 1995. *Indigenous Social Justice Strategies and Recommendations: Submission to the Parliament of the Commonwealth of Australia on Social Justice Package, vol. 1. April.*

Altman, J. 1983. *Aborigines and Mining Royalties in the Northern Territory*. Canberra: Australian Institute of Aboriginal Studies.

Altman, J. (ed.) 1991. *Aboriginal Employment Equity by the Year 2000*. Canberra: Centre for Aboriginal Economic Policy Research, Australian National University, Research Monograph No. 2.

Altman, J. and Dillon, M. 1985. Land rights: why Hawke's model has no backing. *Australian Society*, June: 26–29.

ATSIC 1995. *Recognition, Rights and Reform: Report to the Government on Native Title Social Justice Measures*. Canberra: Commonwealth of Australia.

Barbalet, J. M. 1988. *Citizenship: Rights, Struggle and Class Inequality*. Minneapolis: University of Minnesota Press.

Barbalet, J. M. 1996. Developments in citizenship theory and issues in Australian citizenship. *Australian Journal of Social Issues* 31 (1): 55–72.

Bennett, S. 1989. *Aborigines and Political Power*. Sydney: Allen and Unwin.

Brook, J. and Kohen, J. 1991. *The Parramatta Native Institution and the Black Town: A History*. Sydney: University of New South Wales Press.

Chesterman, J. and Galligan, B. 1997. *Citizens Without Rights: Aborigines and Australian Citizenship*. Cambridge: Cambridge University Press.

Collins, D. (1798) 1971. *An Account of the English Colony in New South Wales, with Remarks on the Dispositions, Customs, Manners, &c. of the Native Inhabitants of that Country (etc.)*. 2 vols. Adelaide: Libraries Board of South Australia.

Elkin, A. P. 1944. *Citizenship for the Aborigines: A National Aboriginal Policy*. Sydney: Australasian Publishing Co.

Engel, F. 1965. *The Land Rights of Australian Aborigines*. Greenacre, NSW: Australian Council of Churches.

Haebich, A. 1988. *For Their Own Good: Aborigines and Government in the Southwest of Western Australia, 1900–1940*. Perth: University of Western Australia Press.

Hall, R. 1989. *The Black Diggers: Aborigines and Torres Strait Islanders in the Second World War*. Sydney: Allen and Unwin.

Hall, R. 1995. *Fighters from the Fringe: Aborigines and Torres Strait Islanders Recall the Second World War*. Canberra: Aboriginal Studies Press.

Harris, J. 1990. *One Blood: 200 Years of Aboriginal Encounter with Christianity – a Story of Hope*. Sydney: Albatross Books.

Hindess, B. 1993. Citizenship in the modern west. In *Citizenship and Social Theory*, (ed.) B. Turner. London: Sage.

Horner, J. 1974. *Vote Ferguson for Aboriginal Freedom: a Biography*. Sydney: Australian and New Zealand Book Company.

Horner, J. and Langton, M. 1987. The 'Day of Mourning'. In *Australians 1938*, eds B. Gammage and P. Spearritt. Sydney: Fairfax, Syme and Weldon Associates, pp. 29–36.

Horton, D. (ed.) 1994. *Encyclopaedia of Aboriginal Australia in 2 vols*. Canberra: Aboriginal Studies Press.

Huggonson, D. 1989. The dark diggers of the AIF. *Australian Quarterly* 61 (3): 352–7.

Huggonson, D. 1993. Aborigines and the aftermath of the Great War. *Australian Aboriginal Studies* 1: 2–9.

Jennett, C. 1990. Aboriginal affairs policy. In *Hawke and Australian Public Policy: Consensus and Restructuring*, eds C. Jennett and R. Stewart. Melbourne: Macmillan, pp. 245–83.

Kymlicka, W. 1995. *Multicutural Citizenship: A Liberal Theory of Minority Rights*. Oxford: Clarendon Press.

Libby, R. 1989. *Hawke's Law: The Politics of Mining and Aboriginal Land Rights in Australia*. Perth: University of Western Australia Press.

Lippmann, L. 1979. The Aborigines. In *From Whitlam to Fraser: Reform and Reaction in Australian Politics*, eds A. Patience and B. Head. Melbourne: Oxford University Press, pp. 173–88.

McCorquodale, J. 1986. The legal classification of race in Australia. *Aboriginal History* 10 (1): 7–24.

McCorquodale, J. 1987. *Aborigines and the Law: A Digest.* Canberra: Aboriginal Studies Press.

Pateman, C. 1988. *The Sexual Contract.* Cambridge: Polity Press.

Patten, J. and Ferguson, W. 1937. Aborigines claim citizenship rights! A statement of the case for the Aborigines Progressive Association. *The Publicist.* Sydney: The Publicist.

Pittock, B. and Lippmann, L. 1974. Aborigines. In *Public Policy in Australia*, ed. R. Forward. Melbourne: Cheshire, pp. 55–92.

Reynolds, H. 1996. *Aboriginal Sovereignty: Reflections on Race, State and Nation.* Sydney: Allen and Unwin.

Rowley, C. 1970. *Outcasts in White Society: Policy and Practice*, vol. 2. Canberra: Australian National University Press.

Stone, S. (ed.) 1974. *Aborigines in White Australia: A Documentary History of the Attitudes Affecting Official Policy and the Australian Aborigine, 1697–1973.* Melbourne: Heinemann Educational Books.

Stretton, P. and Finnimore, C. 1991. *How South Australian Aborigines Lost the Vote: Some Side Effects of Federation.* Adelaide: History Trust of South Australia.

Taylor, C. 1991. Shared and Divergent Values. In *Options for a New Canada*, eds R. Watts and D. Brown. Toronto: University of Toronto Press, pp. 53–76.

Turner, B. 1990. Outline of a theory of citizenship. *Sociology* 24 (2): 189–214.

Whitlam, G. 1985. *The Whitlam Government: 1972–1975.* Melbourne: Penguin.

Williams, M. 1995. Justice towards groups: political not juridical. *Political Theory* 23 (1): 67–91.

Woodward, A. E. 1974. *Aboriginal Land Rights Commission: Second Report.* Canberra: Australian Government Publishing Service.

Woolmington, J. 1988. *Aborigines in Colonial Society 1788–1850: A Sourcebook.* 2nd edn. Armidale: University of New England.

PART I

Historical Conceptions

CHAPTER 2

Nineteenth Century Bureaucratic Constructions of Indigenous Identities in New South Wales

Marilyn Wood

A surface reading of nineteenth century church records and civil registers in New South Wales indicates the inconsistencies, ambiguities and occasional indifference found in the bureaucratic inscription of Aboriginal identities by the state and its church agencies. Michael Herzfeld, in his book *The Social Production of Indifference*,[1] examines the ways in which bureaucratic processes encode categories of identity that become criteria for inclusion or exclusion in the nation state. He argues that bureaucratic neglect of a class of people who should logically be included in administrative processes may look like official indifference but the exclusion is neither meaningless nor inconsequential. Instead, such an oversight indicates 'a [passive] rejection of those who are different' providing a 'moral alibi for inaction' which can tacitly sanction repressive actions against the excluded group. These may range from petty discriminations to genocidal killings.[2] Bryan Turner, in his article 'Personhood and Citizenship',[3] looks closely at the links between legal identity and civil status. According to Turner the extent to which the identity of an individual person or a category of people is socially recognised and legally constituted is related to their qualification to enjoy full civil rights.[4] In this chapter I will argue that, in the case of New South Wales Aboriginal people, the British and colonial administrations were unable to develop a comprehensive and/or appropriate definition of what constituted Aboriginality and its position with respect to European society. As a result, the position of Aboriginal people in the body politic of colonial society became uncertain and inconstant, reflecting ambivalent attitudes towards their citizenship status and civil rights.

Drawing upon church and civil registration records I will explore some of the ways in which indigenous identities were constituted through those bureaucratic processes. I will also comment on how those processes

related to the legal and social limitations of citizenship status that
resulted from perceptions of racial difference. I will show how an analysis
of bureaucratic inscriptions of identity demonstrates that, during the late
eighteenth and nineteenth centuries, perceptions of difference led to
the emergence of various strategies which were used to define and
delineate the boundaries for inclusion in and exclusion from the body
politic. In doing so, I will focus on three periods: the first decade of
British settlement, when relationships between Aboriginal and British
peoples were relatively fluid and exploratory in nature; the 1820s and
1830s, when perceptions of difference began to create exclusionary
attitudes; and the second half of the nineteenth century, when civil
registration purportedly represented a universally applied system for the
valid recognition of all colonial subjects in New South Wales. I will argue
that, by looking at how Aboriginal identities have been constituted on
the public record, we can gain some insight into the strains that existed
between official policy and contemporaneous social attitudes.

European perceptions of Aboriginal kinship and naming systems

One way of understanding what race relations were like in the first years
of British settlement in New South Wales is to look at the journals of
Watkin Tench. Tench was a captain-lieutenant in the marine corps
which sailed on the First Fleet, and lived in the fledgling colony from
1788 until 1792. This was a period when the Governor, Arthur Phillip,
was under instructions from Britain to '"conciliate" the inhabitants [and]
to avoid "any unnecessary interruption" to their activities'.[5] But effective
execution of these directives was hindered by language barriers and the
settlers' ignorance of local social structures and cultural practices.[6]
However, by the end of 1788, the Governor, weary of the incessant 'petty
warfare' and 'unabated animosity' that characterised the attitude of the
'Indians' towards the encroachers, decided to abduct an adult male so
that more of the indigenous customs and attitudes could be learned.[7]
First Arabanoo, then Colbee and Baneelong, were forcibly brought into
the settlement. Later, orphaned children and adolescents were adopted
by European families.[8]

It was only when closer relationships such as these were established
that some understanding of the local social system was gleaned. Yet many
aspects of the indigenous kinship systems remained incomprehensible to
the early British settlers, and Tench wrote that '[t]heir form of government, and the detail of domestic life, yet remain untold'.[9] Nevertheless
Tench was able to record much about the domestic situations he
encountered. Despite his generally tolerant attitude he was repulsed by
the often violent relationship between men and women, particularly

between husband and wife. According to Tench inter-gender relationships were characterised by such brutality that they were indicative of
the degraded state into which a race could descend if it lacked the
'softening' influence on the individual and society provided by 'religion,
philosophy and legal restriction'.[10] Tench therefore strongly condemned
any liberal notions that a 'state of nature [was] above a state of civilisation' and was to be promoted as either an ideal model for society or
the basis of individual happiness.[11] Instead he concluded his description
of the 'Indians' and their customs with the plea that 'the progress of
reason and the splendour of revelation will in their proper and allotted
season be permitted to illumine and transfuse into these desert regions,
knowledge, virtue and happiness'.[12] Inclusion in the newly founded
society therefore depended on change.

Despite what would seem to the modern reader to be an extremely
Eurocentric view of Aboriginal customs, in his dealings with Aboriginal
people Tench was a sensitive and discerning observer. As Tench's relationship with Baneelong developed he began to understand the complexity of Aboriginal naming systems and the ways in which Aboriginal
society could construct complex social networks through the exchange
of names. This practice of name exchange differed radically from the
European naming system whereby a person's name was fixed at birth
and was a means of identifying an individual in a vertically constructed
patrilineal system. Tench writes:

> Although I call him only Baneelong, he had besides several appellations, and
> for a while he chose to be distinguished by that of Wolarawaree. Again, as a
> mark of affection and respect to the governor, he conferred on him the name
> of Wolarawaree and sometimes called him *Beenena* (father), adopting to
> himself the name of governor. This interchange we found is a constant symbol
> of friendship among them.[13]

Without understanding the implications for reciprocity or putative
kinship relationships, Tench did understand that friendships were often
established in these ways. Moreover, by the time Tench came to leave the
colony he had begun to understand also that names were sometimes
used to denote a person's relationship to an animal or a fish:

> An interchange of names with anyone is also a symbol of friendship. Each
> person has several names, one of which, there is reason to believe, is always
> derived from the first fish or animal which the child, in accompanying its
> father to the chase or a fishing, may chance to kill.[14]

Furthermore, Tench records how words describing a distinguishing
feature of a person or their place of origin could be used either as a

generic or an individual name – for example, *gooroobeera*, a stick of fire; or *bereewolgal*, men come from afar.[15]

The relationship between Aboriginal kinship and naming systems and rights in land

Heather Goodall, in her analysis of the importance and meaning of land in New South Wales Aboriginal politics, elaborates more fully on the relationship between kinship and naming systems and rights in land. In the most general case some language groups – for example, the *Paakantji* – took the words meaning '"belonging to" the river named *paaka* (Darling) to identify themselves as the people from that district'.[16] Goodall claims that, within dialects, naming systems may be 'directly associated with the country where [the group] usually lived and for which that group owned customary rights. So some *Ngiyampaa*-speaking people were identified as *pilaarrkiyalu*, "the belar tree mob" or "the people who lived where the belar trees grow".'[17] Langloh Parker's account of the *Yuwalaraay* people is cited as evidence that an individual's birth site may also be reflected in their name and be carefully selected to complement family land affiliations.[18]

Goodall summarises the relationship between land, kinship and identity thus:

> In Aboriginal societies, people are closely identified with their lands and the animal and plant species on them. Aboriginal philosophies do not have a deep dichotomy between 'man' and 'nature' or 'culture' and 'nature' as European traditions do. Association with land therefore mean [sic] association with other people and with other, non-human, living species. Relations with non-humans may arise from a person's birth site being near a place associated with a particular animal or plant, or it may arise from the inherited 'totem' or 'meat' which defines one's relation to an ancestral figure who was transformed between human and animal form during their mythical journeys which in turn created the landforms. 'Within each clan, human and animal are bound together by common descent, mutual concern and shared destiny.' These associations between human and non-human tie Aboriginal people inextricably within the network of other living species, the ecosystem which is adapted to its particular habitat, its land. The structure of relationships within which an Aboriginal person identifies themselves is not then a solely human-focused one.[19]

However, in debates concerning the status that Aboriginal people should be given in the newly established British settlement, the significant factor is that these relationships to the land and their importance in providing social and political structure for Aboriginal communities were not at first understood.

Despite the acknowledged presence of Aboriginal people, New South Wales was declared *terra nullius* because the relationship between Aboriginal people and the land was not deemed sufficient to constitute either possession or economic usage.[20] Hence, their right to continued occupation of the land was invalidated (according to international law) and their status in their own country made uncertain.[21] Moreover, as Goodall comments, a social system that was constituted through inter-connections between humanity, land, and animal and plant species was conceptually opposed to a social system premised upon the prioritising and conceptual separation of human society and its culture from the rest of nature. Naming systems that imputed spiritual or embodied links between Aboriginal society, other species and the natural environment could only feed into prejudices that Aboriginal people constituted an intermediary species between humanity and the apes. Those who believed this would never accept that Aboriginal people had a possible place as equals in the new society.[22] Those, like Tench, who held that Aboriginal people were fully human still considered that they needed to be educated into those systems of thought that would teach them how to transcend their 'brute natures' and 'savage' state.[23] According to Tench their 'inferiority' was due solely to ignorance and environmental factors, failings that could be overcome through tuition.[24]

At the same time as indigenous civil rights and rights to their own land were being determined in distant places, Aboriginal people began to accommodate the new culture and negotiate change within their own. Through strategies such as name exchanges and 'nicknaming', relation-ships between European and local indigenous people began to be estab-lished and consolidated. The consequent changes were not simply imposed on the Aboriginal people encountered; rather, relationships were characterised by active and reflexive attempts on both sides to understand and incorporate the other into their respective social schemas. In the early days of settlement, when the British were absorbed with issues of famine and imperatives to establish and maintain order over the convict population, the balance of power was not so strongly tilted in the Europeans' favour. However, this period of mutual accom-modation and indigenous autonomy began to deteriorate as the area of settlement grew and the ability of the executive government to control violent exchanges between the races decreased. Indigenous population numbers fell dramatically through disease, malnutrition and armed conflict. By the end of the eighteenth century contact with the British had begun to have a profound impact on the indigenous Aboriginal cultural systems.[25]

The effect of the British invasion on Aboriginal social systems

Initial conservatism and caution on the part of the indigenous people, and their ability to continue an autonomous subsistence lifestyle and to maintain social distance, were therefore replaced, by the first decades of the nineteenth century, with an increasing dependency on European commodities for survival. Robert Hughes claims that, with traditional territories for hunting and gathering appropriated by the British invaders, most Aboriginal people in the vicinity of the new settlements on the Cumberland Plain became dependent on Europeans for food, alcohol and tobacco. In the early years of the nineteenth century the complex relationship between Aboriginal people and their land was still not generally understood and so the apparently degenerate social changes that Aboriginal people suffered after losing access to their traditional lands were ignorantly condemned. With spiritual practices linked to particular tracts of land and sacred features in that landscape, loss of land meant loss of social and sacred history as well as the means by which personal and group identities could be continuously constructed and reaffirmed.[26]

It cannot be said, however, that Aboriginal society simply 'collapsed' upon contact with the Europeans. Instead something as particular and apparently insignificant as naming patterns may reveal how, by the 1820s, changes that had begun with the arrival of the First Fleet in 1788 continued to be negotiated through strategies of accommodation, resistance, incorporation and cultural synthesis. These strategies can be seen in the baptism records of the colony, which were the primary form of official individual biographical record until 1856. The census and muster surveys collected during that period provided a more generalised documentation of the colonial population.[27] The baptism records partially record indigenous responses to the pressures of disease, malnutrition, violence and dispossession that collectively eroded Aboriginal people's ability to reproduce their social and kinship systems in the traditional ways.[28] Relationships between Aboriginal women and white men become visible on the record, with children of these unions occupying an intermediate position between two cultures. The adoption of European names by both men and women reflects Aboriginal people's need to accommodate the new culture by partially incorporating it into their own.

Changing Aboriginal naming practices

A perusal of indexed records indicates that many Aboriginal people were known in European society by a single Aboriginal or European name, a practice that continued from Tench's time in the colony. This probably reflected a British inability to grasp the nuances of Aboriginal kinship and naming systems. Sometimes a death record shows only a single name, without parents' names to place the deceased in a context of extended family relationships. Jacky, Toby, Wandelina and Dundally appear as marginal people, apparently not part of any extended social network.

This use of a single name also served to imply illegitimacy, either because a white man had fathered the child of an Aboriginal woman whom he would not acknowledge or because relationships between Aboriginal men and women did not conform to the legal or moral standards for legitimacy imposed by the white society. Far from indicating that these people had a marginal status in their own indigenous societies, the records show not only the widespread inability of European bureaucratic procedures to conceptualise or recognise the place such people occupied in an increasingly complex colonial society but also an unwillingness to accept the idea that the colonial community itself must move towards being more heterogeneous and inclusive.

The way in which 'nicknames' became the primary means of identifying some Aboriginal people is also evidence of the marginality and instability of many Aboriginal identities, as viewed from a British perspective. The names Frying Pan, Bimmito Boy, Black Stephen, Rifle and Tiger still conjure up an image of their bearers more than a century after their death. Tench had recognised the use of such descriptive terms as a naming device and church records reveal a continuation of the custom. However, in a settler society in which status was clearly designated and regulated by formal means of address, it could be assumed that the more informal the name given, the lower the social standing of the person to which it was assigned. Therefore what was apt or amusing in Aboriginal society would be dismissed as puerile by the gatekeepers of European society and a reflection of subordinate social status. People like Rifle and Tiger apparently stood out from others in their indigenous community because of some feature that attracted distinction or notoriety. Yet their names undoubtedly worked to diminish their human status in European eyes by reducing them to caricatures of a semi-savage, semi-domesticated race.

The role of the church as an agent of change

To overcome the perceived 'degradation' and 'savagery' of the indigenous population, governing and philanthropic parties increasingly saw conversion to Christianity as the essential precondition for inclusion in 'civilised' colonial society. Yet little sustained effort was made to work with Aboriginal people until the Roman Catholic priest, Father John

Joseph Therry, arrived in Sydney in 1820. During the first thirty years of settlement the Established Church had enjoyed little success in convincing the indigenous population that conversion to Christianity offered any significant advantages.[29] Of the forty-three Aboriginal baptisms that took place from 1820 until the end of 1827, five were conducted by the Church of England and one by the Wesleyan Methodists. The remaining thirty-seven baptisms were held in the Roman Catholic parish of St Mary's, Sydney, after the arrival of Archpriest John Joseph Therry.[30]

It appears that Father Therry alone amongst the early nineteenth century clergy was willing to baptise Aboriginal children regardless of the extent to which their parents could be described as Christian. Bishop William Ullathorne realised, however, that Father Therry's preparedness to baptise indigenous people was a consequence not of their conversions but of Therry's compassionate nature. Therefore, in the eyes of his superiors, Therry's readiness to baptise was deemed inappropriate in the absence of either imminent death or an observable conversion to the Christian faith.[31] Moreover it cannot be claimed that the work of John Joseph Therry significantly altered the status of Aboriginal people in the wider community. Association with the Catholic Church, and therefore with Irish Catholics, was not considered by the dominant Protestant elites to be evidence of a civilising process. Quite the reverse. For the first thirty years Catholics in the population had conspicuously abstained from having their children baptised or, whenever possible, from attending any Church of England services. This collective act of defiance, from a group made up largely of Irish convicts and ex-convicts, was interpreted by established church and state alike as an indication of an insurrectionary link between the Catholic faith and potential rebels, and it made Catholicism an object of suspicion.[32] Therefore even the loose association of indigenous people with Irish Catholics was regarded as a sign of the further degradation of both populations and cause for contempt and despair.[33]

Baptism as a rite of inclusion

In those early years of settlement the great majority of Aboriginal children were never baptised, nor were their parents married, under white law. In the first three decades of settlement de facto or casual relationships outnumbered legalised marriages amongst the general population. However, most white babies were baptised despite their parents' marital status. For Europeans, before the introduction of civil registration, the rite of baptism was treated as validation of an infant's membership of a particular family and their inclusion in the general community. This view was encouraged by the secular authorities who used the clergy's return books to compile demographic statistics concerning the settlement for the purposes of social and economic planning.[34] Even without marriage, baptism was a symbolic gesture acknowledging at least a nominal conformity to social convention amongst a population largely opposed to establishment values.

For the British, marriage was constituted as a contract between an individual man and a woman designed primarily to regulate society by providing for the support of women and children dependent upon individual men. For the middle and upper classes it also facilitated the accumulation of private property within the family unit and upon death its proper distribution to legitimate heirs of the family's estate.[35] However, Tench's journals clearly demonstrate that Aboriginal naming patterns were connected to a marriage and kinship system that was alien to the British. The European naming system evolved to distinguish the individual from all other members of human society, the division between nature and human society a fundamental premise. Its narrowly focused integrative function was to incorporate the individual into a vertically constructed patrilineal line in which the legal importance of relationships decreased dramatically the further away one was from the biological *pater*, even if voluntary emotional bonds were more widely drawn.

By contrast with the British system, as we have seen, Aboriginal naming systems were designed to integrate the individual not only into human society but into a world view that envisaged community as encompassing significant fauna and the physical environment itself. Relationships were communally structured rather than individualistic and produced complex systems of rights and responsibilities created through named and interlinked associations with people, place and environment. The vast gulf between British and Aboriginal people, in appearance, social customs and beliefs, meant, however, that differences would only be negotiated slowly and painfully. The words 'native', and later 'aboriginal', marked the official records of those who were identifiably different, either by appearance or cultural practice, from the Anglo-Saxon majority. Those words placed their subjects on the boundaries of society, designating them as vulnerable to exclusionary practices.

Aboriginal baptisms

One of the first Aboriginal children to be baptised by Therry was Mary, daughter of Corumba and Milbona. When Therry baptised Mary she was living at Windsor and her parents were noted to be 'natives'. Mary's parents did not have conventional European names, despite what had probably been lifelong contact with white settlers. In this they were typical of many of their generation whose names – such as Morghey, Cucumdum, Mercanna, Cooman, Simebuna, Murragurra and Ghindell – appear on the early church registers. However, by the 1820s, European names such as Mary, Sally, Nelly, Jacky, Biddy and Polly had also been acquired by many Aboriginal people. Others had hybrid names such as Nancy Yoiwyn, Nelly Oolonga, Curring Biddy and Jacky Gogy, juxtaposing Aboriginal names with British. Some records reveal how, consistent with Tench's earlier observations, European and Aboriginal names such as Kitty and Wyemba could be interchanged, presumably in accordance with different social circumstances. Therefore the variations in the naming patterns of this generation are evidence of the continuing complexity of cultural change that Aboriginal people were negotiating thirty or so years after white invasion.

European first and last names were given when an apparently orphaned Aboriginal child with parents 'unknown' was baptised. European names were also given to children by parents who continued the practice of using names to cement relationships between social groups and individuals. Hence, Bennelong (Baneelong), who had exchanged names with the governor, chose to name his son Thomas Walker Coke. Similarly, Mary Keane, Thomas Walton, Frank Hall and Sophia Cochrane emerge from the record.[36] In other cases the single names of Aboriginal fathers or even mothers were adapted to conform to British naming patterns. Thus the identities of Ann Morphey, Caroline Bone, George Charles Namut, Patrick Bundong and Gertrude Tamara stand out on the record, demonstrating a transformation of the Aboriginal naming patterns as well as a synthesis of two cultural systems.

A few adult Aboriginal women were incorporated into the British familial system through their legal marriage to white men, their children then automatically becoming heirs to that system. Miscegenation therefore began breaking down the barriers between Aboriginal and European populations ahead of both public and administrative acceptance. Hence, naming patterns began to reflect situations in which last names were provided by white fathers and grandfathers, so that the heritage of the children of Aboriginal mothers began to be subsumed under the mantle of the dominant kinship system. One son of an unnamed Aboriginal woman was named Charles Quin after his father; likewise, Thomas, Barraby's son, was surnamed Murphy after his father, William Murphy, and Samuel Coleby was given the first and last name of his father.

Towards a policy of exclusion

In 1834 William Ullathorne described the Aboriginal population 'in the neighbourhood' of the Sydney parish as 'so grossly corrupted by their communications with the convicts, that we can hope nothing from them'.[37] While English policy makers still favoured policies aimed at integrating Aboriginal people into colonial society, on the basis that they were now subjects of the British Crown, local opinion increasingly favoured the segregation of indigenous Australians as the only method by which they could be both 'protected' and 'civilised'.[38] Caught between competing interests and opposing philosophies, governments, both local and distant, embarked on policies of equivocation which sought to reconcile irreconcilable interests. A G L Shaw writes that, during the first half of the nineteenth century, ' "westernisation" became the basis of Imperial policy. Rather than accepting the idea that the Aborigines had any right to keep the land, official spokesmen argued only that they should be protected from physical violence and encouraged to assimilate with the new westernised society'.[39]

On the local front, however, this policy was almost impossible to implement due to the determination of the squatters to secure their holdings at any cost to the indigenous owners. Also, even the most compassionate of the Europeans living in settled areas were anxious to have Aboriginal people removed to missions where they could be 'civilised' away from the corrupting influences of the convict population.[40] But, as Rowley points out:

> ... protective legislation is inevitably discriminatory in effect ... [as] the categories of protected persons are often most easily defined in racial terms. The very attempt to protect the 'native' British subject in such rights as are to be left to him involves a separate status in law, which places him at the discretion and the mercy of the protecting agencies. Traditionally, emphasis has been on control and tuition as the prelude to eventual full citizenship. Thus while the goal of 'assimilation' expressed the best intentions, the special laws introduced to bring it about through tuition and control inevitably set the 'native' apart in a special category of wardship: the greater the effort towards assimilation, the more rigidly defined the differences in status became.[41]

The marginal, ambiguous and vulnerable position of Aboriginal people was therefore, if anything, intensified during this period. While the church and the state refused to recognise Aboriginal rites of passage based on traditional law or adapted practices, they also demarcated Aboriginal people from inclusive administrative processes recognising their life events. By doing so, state and church implicitly excluded

Aboriginal people symbolically from the societies of which they had demonstrably become a part. Before 1856 this may be viewed simply as an exclusion that automatically resulted from 'heathen' Aboriginal people rejecting the 'salvation' offered by Christian rites. However, given the often bemoaned 'ungodliness' of the convict population and the willingness of the established church to baptise, marry and bury *that* population, it would appear that different and higher standards were imposed on Aboriginal people. As Harris points out, there was a constant conflation of Christianity with European civilisation so that most members of the clergy considered that a 'savage' could never be presumed to be Christian despite their avowed faith, unless their lives demonstrated a total abandonment of all Aboriginal cultural practices.[42]

Administrative reactions to difference

By the mid-nineteenth century the colony of New South Wales was largely governed by its own legislative parliament and administered by its own civil service. This movement away from imperial rule towards local autonomy had been accompanied by a split between church and state which should, in theory, have led to a more value-neutral administration of population policies. With the change from a system based on the recording of baptisms, Christian marriages and funerals to one based on the secular system of registering births, deaths and marriages (whether civil or Christian), religious affiliation was no longer the prerequisite for inclusion on public records.

Why, then, was this law not applied uniformly to all people in New South Wales? A search of the register reveals that some Aboriginal people were included on the record without any distinguishing comment, that others were included but were labelled as different from the rest of the population on the basis of race, and that possibly the largest group did not have their existence officially recognised at all. Inclusion or exclusion therefore apparently depended on the extent to which the subject 'passed' as European.

It is certainly the case that Aboriginality became increasingly difficult for bureaucrats either to define or to identify. While appearance and cultural practices would have immediately distinguished Aboriginal people from the British at the time of first British settlement, miscegenation and cultural integration would have begun to have an effect by the mid-nineteenth century.[43] The question might therefore be asked: why were informal bureaucratic practices perpetuated that distinguished between peoples in this way? Rowley puts forward the following explanation:

The common administrative practice of using skin colour and facial features to determine who is an Aboriginal is not, to be fair, merely a reflection of the popular prejudice. It is in part a consequence of that prejudice [...] It has happened over the whole course of interaction between Aborigines and other Australians that those of light skin coloration have had special opportunities, not available to their darker brothers and sisters, to resign or escape from Aboriginal society and to 'pass' into the general community.[44]

Following Herzfeld's hypothesis that informal exclusionary and discriminatory practices reflect social attitudes towards the subject group I would argue that the continuity in the ambiguous and inconsistent treatment of Aboriginal people reflected the wider social perception that people who were observably Aboriginal were not acceptable as members of the wider community. Particularly as social Darwinianism took hold on public discourse, there was a conflation of 'colour' with racial 'blood' concepts as well as theories that conflated intelligence with cultural practices. The secularisation of society, of which the change from church records to secular registration systems was but one example, did not therefore automatically improve the status of Aboriginal people in the way in which the transition to supposedly universal forms of administration could have been assumed to do. Religious biases based on the moral condemnation attached to 'savagery' and 'degeneration' gave ground to scientific biases based on comparative physiological and psychological attributes, although the two forms of discrimination always overlapped.[45] There was not, therefore, a sharp break in actual bureaucratic practices between the two eras of clerical and secular recording, but rather a continuity of underlying criteria for social inclusion/ exclusion carrying over into the supposedly more rational secular bureaucratic processes.

Clerks continued the practice of marking the records of very dark or socially marginal people 'native', 'half-caste' and later 'aboriginal', on the basis of subjective judgements regarding appearance at the time of registration. This practice actually went against the surface intention of registration procedures, which was to determine a person's civil status purely on the basis of whether they were born in the colony. These discriminatory practices, however, were consistent with Herzfeld's analysis of bureaucratic procedures which encode in supposedly rational administrative processes symbolic terms that mark the boundaries between inclusion and exclusion of the dominant group. Herzfeld claims that, far from being expunged by the rationalisation of government, these deeply emotive signifiers are carried over from one form of government to another because they are capable of encoding a multiplicity of ambiguous messages which transcend the boundaries between social and political spheres.[46]

Some effects of discriminatory bureaucratic practices

After 1856 the colonial administration made no discernible effort to accommodate the ambivalence of Aboriginal people's relationships with the dominant culture. Although the remoteness and nomadism of many Aboriginal communities were often cited as reasons for not systematically including them in statistical and demographic data collections, by the second half of the nineteenth century the majority of Aboriginal people in New South Wales lived in relatively close contact with white settlements or on pastoral properties and were therefore not more remote from the newly established administrative centres than Europeans were in outlying regions. According to law everyone in New South Wales was subject to the same legislation governing the regulation and notification of these events. In practice no attempt was made to enforce the relevant provisions with respect to the vital events of 'full blood', 'mission' or 'fringe dwelling' Aboriginal people. The prevailing attitude, judged by the paucity of records concerning Aboriginal life events, was a blatant disregard for their inclusion, even when it must have been common knowledge that an Aboriginal person had died or given birth in the district.

In the first half of the nineteenth century the state's failure to include those Aboriginal people living on the frontiers of settlement in their secular registration system undoubtedly meant that the impact of frontier violence, the appropriation of women and the begetting of 'half-caste' children was obfuscated.[47] Drawing on grosser statistical information, such as that provided by census and muster counts, it was possible to portray in official documents the disappearance of 'full-blood' Aboriginal people in urban, pastoral and farming areas as the natural replacement of an inferior race by a superior one, an argument that relied on the scientific discourse of natural selection and romanticised views of the noble but doomed savage.[48]

In the early 1880s Jinnie (or Jenny) Griffin died at Parker's Paddock on the outskirts of Coonabarabran. She was given an Aboriginal funeral, and her body and belongings were cremated, no trace of her existence remaining except for an axe head which was 'souvenired' afterwards by a white boy. Jinnie was a 'full-blood' Aboriginal woman who was well liked in her community for her ability to tell lively stories about the 'old' days when Aboriginal people in the district still lived by traditional customs. She married a white man, Samuel Griffin, but after his death went back to live with her people, becoming the partner of King Cuttabush.[49] Jinnie

Griffin, King Cuttabush, King Togy and several other senior people were notable figures in the district. There was, however, no official record of their deaths. While in one sense they were part of the local community because they lived within its bounds, like thousands of others throughout New South Wales there was no official recognition of their existence. Living together in small camps on the outskirts of towns such as Coonabarabran, they were marginal people whose viability as an autonomous cultural group had been crippled by the loss of their land to the graziers and the loss of women and children to white men.[50]

The effects of their absence on the record was twofold. Not only did it support the proposition that they were a 'disappearing' race but it also served to break their descendants' links with an Aboriginal heritage. This lack of official documentation has had ramifications for many Aboriginal people seeking to establish their continuous links with place or people. With the validity of one's legal identity increasingly dependent on the production of official documentation, the traditional or historical link with particular locations and extensive kinship networks that many contemporary Aboriginal people would have been able to authenticate had been broken.[51] Thus not only have the oral historical traditions of their ancestral heritage been lost but in many cases the very existence of their families is 'missing' from official records.

The qualified inclusion of some Aboriginal people

This is not meant to imply that a widespread conspiracy operated at political and administrative levels. Herzfeld claimed that bureaucratic practices are always negotiated within the space between official policy and informal social practice. That is, there is a two-way power flow between state and society, with compromise sometimes reached at the level of actual administrative practice.[52] In the nineteenth century both church and state recordings of a child's birth were the result of face-to-face encounters between family, clergy or clerk. People with lighter skins were often 'passed' as Europeans, particularly if they had adopted British family names and marriage customs. The local clerk would be sure to know the extent to which they had cut off ties with marginal Aboriginal kinfolk and had 'come in' to the local white settlement.

Some four years before the death of Jinnie Griffin, the birth of 'Annie' was registered in a mundane manner at Coonabarabran's local court house. Her parents were George and Mary Jane Cain, her grandmother was Jinnie Griffin. Annie's descendants today identify as Aboriginal but, because her parents were 'half-castes', born of Aboriginal mothers and white fathers, nothing distinguished the registration of her birth from that of white children in that north-western district. Annie's mother had been born on a local property, baptised by a Catholic priest and married according to law, and both her parents had worked in the district.[53] We can see the extent to which Tench's prerequisites for acceptance as a 'civilised' person were visible in Annie Cain's family.

The example of the Cain family reveals how, by the late 1870s, some Aboriginal people were afforded a certain degree of social acceptance in communities where they were known and played an active social and economic role. Goodall records that many Aboriginal people in New South Wales filled an important place in rural economies as labourers, shearers, fencers and general hands.[54] While the 'full bloods' such as Jinnie Griffin were diminishing in numbers, Aboriginal people of mixed descent were, by the turn of the century, beginning to increase once again the total Aboriginal population. But government policies of the time revealed the deep ambivalence towards the 'problem' of the 'half-caste'. The Griffin–Cain family was, like thousands more, deeply affected by the social and political discrimination arising from this ambivalence. The two strategies that emerged – assimilation and segregation – operated under the guise of 'protection' policies. While segregation was demanded by many rural folk who deeply resented the continued presence of Aboriginal people squatting in fringe camps around country towns, others believed that dispersion and assimilation were the answer. From the second half of the nineteenth century to the mid-twentieth, both policies would be implemented in inconsistent and arbitrary ways. The civil rights of Aboriginal people were correspondingly subject to arbitrary definitions of these people's identity and shifts in government policies.[55]

The 'cult of forgetfulness'

Bureaucratic indifference thus shielded the state from both account-ability and the responsibility to do more than react half-heartedly, in a patronising and ad-hoc way, to a situation imbued with elements of racial and cultural genocide. In a general sense this neglect was indicative of the collective exclusion of indigenous people, on racial and cultural grounds, from the colonial community and the resulting con-sequential socio-political location outside its boundaries of a great many individuals identifiable as Aboriginal. However, it also facilitated the inclusion of many Aboriginal people within the boundaries of the body politic, but their inclusion was conditional upon the erasure of their difference. This erasure then lent weight to the myth that Aboriginal people were 'dying out' and no longer occupied the contested land that had been appropriated by the British.[56]

While civil registration, like the franchise, theoretically applied equally to all citizens of New South Wales, irrespective of race, colour or cultural background, practices evolved or were carried over from church record days that employed the category 'aborigine', or its equivalent for exclusionary purposes. These practices operated either to deny official recognition of a person's existence or to mark the records of a category of people as different and thereby to limit the quality and extent of their inclusion in the colonial state.[57] These exclusions and limitations reflected ambivalent social attitudes on the extent to which Aboriginal people should enjoy full civil rights and citizenship status in society. Such practices served to divide Aboriginal communities through the ways in which they enforced separations between those who were classified as Aboriginal and subject to segregationist policies and those who were not. At the same time the inclusion of Aboriginal people in the records with no distinguishing notation was, in assimilationist eras, indicative of the general perception that Aboriginal people as a distinctive racial and cultural group had been subsumed into Anglo-Celtic society. While such inclusive practices appear anti-discriminatory on the surface, they were not necessarily indicative of an acceptance of difference. Rather, they probably reflected a desire to erase recognition of such difference from the public sphere.

Conclusion

I have used personal stories here to demonstrate how, throughout the late eighteenth and nineteenth centuries, the bureaucratic imputation of racial categories reflected the uncertain and ambiguous citizenship status of all who identified as being, or were imputed to be, Aboriginal people in New South Wales. In most cases identity and social location were negotiated at a local level. These ambiguities and inconsistencies may have operated to the advantage of some individuals who 'passed' as Anglo–Celtic and welcomed the opportunity to identify as such. At the collective level, though, where the subjective treatment of those whose civil rights were contingent upon shifting categorisations of their identity, it was sadly indicative of the power of racially discriminatory practices to influence supposedly universal government policies and objective administrative practices.

Moreover, as the nineteenth century unfolded the discrepancy between the formal equality of administrative practices and the discriminatory nature of social relationships between the races exposed the growing chasm between policy and local intolerance. By the end of the nineteenth century this intolerance was formally enshrined in 'protective' legislation which effectively restricted the inclusion of people identified as Aboriginal within the body politic of New South Wales and severely curtailed their civil rights. The alternative strategy was for the bureaucracy to erase difference on the record where there was sufficient conformity to the mores of the hegemonic culture to justify inclusion. While this entitled some people in difficult times to a measure of equality, such equality often came at a cost – the loss of identification with an Aboriginal heritage.

Notes

1 See References.
2 Herzfeld 1992: 33.
3 Turner 1986.
4 Turner 1986: 8.
5 Shaw 1992: 266.
6 At the time of early British settlement presumptions about indigenous social structure and cultural practices were based on the conjectural evidence of people such as Joseph Banks who had made a cursory study of Aboriginal people encountered on exploratory expeditions. Banks believed that 'the indigenous inhabitants of New South Wales were peoples who had "neither religious beliefs nor any trace of social or political organisation, who did not want to buy or sell anything and had no idea of private property"' (Quoted in Shaw 1992: 266.)
7 Tench 1996: 93–5.
8 Tench 1996: 105–6, 117.
9 Tench 1996: 257.
10 Tench 1996: 263–4.
11 Tench 1996: 264–5.
12 Tench 1996: 267–8.
13 Tench 1996: 119.
14 Tench 1996: 266.
15 Tench 1996: 266.
16 Goodall 1996: 15.
17 Goodall 1996: 15.
18 Goodall 1996: 15.
19 Goodall 1996: 6–7.
20 Shaw 1992: 266–7.
21 Shaw 1992: 267.
22 Reynolds 1974: 45.
23 Reynolds 1974: 46.
24 'Let those who have been born in more favoured lands and who have profited by more enlightened systems, compassionate, [sic] but not despise their destitute and obscure situation. Children of the same omniscient paternal care, let them recollect that by the fortuitous advantage of birth alone they possess superiority: that untaught, unaccommodated man is the same in Pall Mall as in the wilderness of New South Wales.' (Tench 1996: 267–8.)
25 Goodall 1996: 23–8.
26 Hughes 1987: 273–4.
27 Camm (1984) reviews the general muster and census counts from first British settlement until federation. Musters, whether general musters or those directed at specific categories of people, were for the purposes of

determining the needs of the European population only. The census system was introduced in 1828, and between 1828 and 1856 (inclusive) seven census surveys were held. The Census Acts of 1833 and 1836 explicitly excluded the Aboriginal population of New South Wales. In other census surveys they were largely ignored (Camm 1984: 9).

28 Authors such as Goodall (1996: 23–33) and Harris (1990: 36–42) have examined the effects of disease and violent encounters on Aboriginal peoples after the British invasion. Tench provided a graphic first-hand account of the effects of disease and malnutrition (Tench 1996: 102–7).

29 Harris 1990: 77–82.

30 Campion 1987: 17; O'Farrell 1977: 1, 24.

31 O'Farrell 1969: 34; Harris 1990: 48.

32 Campion 1987: 8, 11–12.

33 O'Farrell 1969: 34.

34 Grocott 1980.

35 Currey 1955: 97–9.

36 Harris 1990: 53.

37 O'Farrell 1969: 47.

38 Reynolds 1974: 52–3.

39 Shaw 1992: 268.

40 Shaw 1992: 268–78.

41 Rowley 1970: 20.

42 Harris 1990: 77–82.

43 Rowley, 1970: 138–9.

44 Rowley 1970: 343.

45 Harris 1990: 24–35.

46 Herzfeld 1992.

47 Millis 1992; cf Herzfeld 1992: 29–33; Rowley 1970: 18–23.

48 Hughes 1987: 7; Rowley 1970: 25.

49 Somerville et al. 1994: 53–4.

50 Rowley 1970: 32–3.

51 For example, Somerville et al. 1994: 54–5.

52 Herzfeld 1992: 21, 49.

53 Somerville et al. 1994: 51–2, 60–8; Pickette and Campbell 1983: 54, 96, 122.

54 Goodall 1996: 57–66.

55 Goodall 1996: 109–48.

56 Goodall examines this general social amnesia to the continued existence of Aboriginal people which typified later nineteenth century British culture – the 'cult of forgetfulness' (Goodall 1996: 104–9).

57 Herzfeld 1992: 22–8.

References

Camm, J. C. R. 1984. *Past Populations of Australia: A Review of the Historical Development of Australian Colonial Censuses, 1828–1901*. Newcastle, NSW: Department of Geography, University of Newcastle, Research Papers in Geography, No. 28.

Campion, E. 1987. *Australian Catholics: the Contribution of Catholics to the Development of Australian Society*. Ringwood, Victoria: Viking.

Currey, C. H. 1955. The law of marriage. *Royal Australian Historical Society, Journal and Proceedings* 41 (3): 97–114.

Goodall, H. 1996. *Invasion to Embassy: Land in Aboriginal Politics in New South Wales, 1770–1972*. Sydney: Allen & Unwin.

Grocott, A. M. 1980. *1788–1851 Convicts, Clergymen and Churches: Attitudes of Convicts and Ex-convicts Towards the Churches and Clergy in NSW from 1788*. Sydney: Sydney University Press.

Harris, J. 1990. *One Blood: 200 Years of Aboriginal Encounter with Christianity: A Story of Hope*. Sydney: Albatross Books.

Herzfeld, M. 1992. *The Social Production of Indifference: Exploring the Symbolic Roots of Western Bureaucracy*. Chicago and London: The University of Chicago Press.

Hughes, R. 1987. *The Fatal Shore: A History of the Transportation of Convicts to Australia, 1787–1868*. London: Collins Harvill.

Millis, R. 1992. *Waterloo Creek: The Australia Day Massacre of 1838, George Gipps and the British Conquest of New South Wales*. Sydney: University of New South Wales Press.

O'Farrell, P. 1969. *Documents in Australian Catholic History 1788–1884, volume 1*. London: G. Chapman.

Pickette, J. and Campbell, M. 1983. *Coonabarabran: As it Was in the Beginning*. Dubbo: Macquarie Publications.

Reynolds, H. 1974. Racial thought in early colonial Australia. *Australian Journal of Politics and History* 20: 45–53.

Rowley, C. D. 1970. *The Destruction of Aboriginal Society: Aboriginal Policy and Practice – volume 1*. Canberra: Australian National University Press.

Shaw, A. G. L. 1992. British policy towards the Australian Aborigines, 1830–1850. *Australian Historical Studies* 25 (99): 265–85.

Somerville, M., Dundas, M., Mead, M., Robinson, J. and Sulter, M. 1994. *The Sun Dancin': People and Place in Coonabarabran*. Canberra: Aboriginal Studies Press.

Tench, W. 1996. *1788: Comprising a Narrative of the Expedition to Botany Bay and a Complete Account of the Settlement at Port Jackson*, ed. T. Flannery. Melbourne: Text.

Turner, B. 1986. Personhood and citizenship. *Theory, Culture and Society* 3 (1): 1–16.

CHAPTER 3

From Nomadism to Citizenship: A P Elkin and Aboriginal Advancement

Geoffrey Gray

The 1938 Day of Mourning,[1] held in Sydney on 26 January, was (to the knowledge of many white Australians) the first public demonstration on the issue of citizenship rights by Aboriginal people. It was a demand for full citizen status and equality. The following resolution was unanimously passed:

> We, representing the Aborigines of Australia, assembled in conference at the Australian Hall, Sydney, on the 26th day of January, 1938, this being the 150th Anniversary of the whiteman's seizure of our country, hereby make protest against the callous treatment of our people by the whiteman during the past 150 years, and we appeal to the Australian nation of today to make new laws for the education and care of Aborigines, and we ask for a new policy which will raise our people to full citizen status and equality within the community.[2]

Fourteen days earlier Jack Patten, president of the Aborigines' Progressive Association, and Bill Ferguson, organising secretary, had sent their manifesto, 'Aborigines Claim Citizen Rights', to the press, national libraries and selected people. Jack Horner rightly described it as 'very brash' and its plain style 'somewhat offensive'. To have spoken politely to a white audience would have seemed to Patten and Ferguson to be doing what Europeans expected of them.[3] Supplication was not their purpose. What they sought was 'justice, decency and fair play'. 'Is this too much to ask?' they wrote. 'Surely your minds and hearts are not so callous that you will refuse to consider your policy of degrading and humiliating and exterminating Old Australia's Aborigines'. Their call was for a national policy of acceptance and equal status: 'we ask to be accorded full citizen rights and to be accepted into the Australian community on a basis of equal opportunity.'[4] The response from the Australian press ranged from bewilderment and faint hostility (*Sydney Morning Herald*) to a recognition that it contained a good deal of truth but was hopelessly idealistic (*Argus*).[5]

Twelve months later, but not in response to the manifesto of the Aborigines' Progressive Association or demands from other Aboriginal organisations,[6] John McEwen, Minister for the Interior, announced a 'New Deal' for Aboriginal people. The Commonwealth was intent on:

> raising of their status so as to entitle them by right, and by qualification to the ordinary rights of citizenship, and enable them and help them to share with us the opportunities that are available in their own native land.[7]

Its purpose was to 'convert [Aboriginal people] from their traditional nomadic inclinations to a settled life.' Aboriginal people had to be shown that 'in any settled life there must be laws and property rights and penalties for those who break them. They should be shown that there are rewards for those who, by training, adapt themselves to a settled life.'[8] Unlike the demand of Patten and Ferguson, McEwen's offer was conditional; citizenship was to be learnt by undergoing training and education in an institutional setting and given to those who satisfied the criterion of adopting a white Australian lifestyle.

Adolphus Peter Elkin, professor of anthropology in the University of Sydney, with J A Carrodus, secretary of the Department of the Interior, and McEwen, had formulated the 'New Deal'.[9] Elkin, an ordained Anglican priest, was professor of anthropology from 1934[10] to 1956, president of the Association for the Protection of Native Races (APNR), a council member and advisor on indigenous affairs of the Australian Board of Missions (ABM) and the Australian National Missionary Council (NMC),[11] chair of the Australian National Research Council's (ANRC's) committee for anthropological research, editor of the journal *Oceania* and from 1942 vice-chairman of the New South Wales Aborigines Welfare Board (AWB),[12] a position he held until it disbanded in 1969. In 1938 he published *The Australian Aborigines: how to understand them*, which became the leading text on Aboriginal people's life and culture.[13]

Elkin saw the 'New Deal' as a landmark and he made frequent reference to his role in its formulation.[14] He had argued from the early 1930s that Aboriginal people were a national responsibility,[15] and, because Australia's treatment of them was of international concern, the Commonwealth should take a national role. If the Commonwealth was, by virtue of the Constitution, unable to take control of Aboriginal policy and administration it was possible to have what Elkin called 'parallelism' (and from the early 1940s 'convergence of policies'), which meant that the Commonwealth would pay a substantial proportion of the cost, and the States' policies would converge with the Commonwealth policy towards a national goal.[16] This, he hoped, might be brought about by McEwen's 'New Deal'.

The fourteen point referendum held in August 1944, to transfer powers from the States to the Commonwealth for five years on an all-or-nothing basis, had as its final point the proposal to provide the Commonwealth with the 'power to make laws [...] with respect to [...] the people of the aboriginal race.'[17] Elkin was hopeful that, from this, a national policy for Aboriginal people would develop. The referendum failed. Elkin observed, however, that there was 'little doubt that had the welfare of Aborigines been a separate clause [...] it would have carried.'[18] The defeat of the referendum has since been seen as a watershed in the movement of social reform between 1944 and 1949 and ensured that subsequent reform would be piecemeal and protracted.

McEwen's 'New Deal' was directed towards changing Commonwealth policy in the Northern Territory. Although not stated, McEwen's aims were premised on the adoption of assimilation, which was in contrast to a previous policy of indifference, segregation and protection. Two years earlier, in 1937, at the Initial Conference of the Commonwealth and State Aboriginal Authorities held in Canberra, it was stated 'that the destiny of the natives of aboriginal origin, but not of the full blood, lies in their ultimate absorption by the people of the Commonwealth and it therefore recommends that all efforts be directed to that end.'[19] This was a call for biological absorption rather than solely a social and cultural absorption of people of Aboriginal descent. The 'New Deal' shifted the emphasis to social, economic and cultural concerns but it did not preclude the continuance of calls regarding biological absorption;[20] however, World War II intervened and the implementation of social (cultural) assimilation as Commonwealth government policy was delayed.[21]

This chapter is primarily concerned with explicating Elkin's role in advocating 'full citizenship'[22] for Aboriginal people. The granting of full citizenship was a way of distinguishing between, on the one hand, the fact that Aboriginal people were citizens by birth and, on the other, their social exclusion as citizens. Elkin developed his concept of full citizenship over a period from the late 1930s, culminating in his *Citizenship for the Aborigines: a national Aboriginal policy* which was published in September 1944. This and subsequent writings[23] were strongly influenced by the Atlantic Charter's Fourteen Points and particularly the ANZAC Pact in which Australia had declared that the main purpose of the trusteeship was the welfare of the native peoples and their special economic and political development. I argue that Elkin saw limited opportunities for Aborigines in the context of white Australian society and that caste (colour and blood) determined the degree of acceptance of Aboriginal people into the white society and their perceived ability to make the necessary adjustments to live within it. Elkin's discourse on citizenship was premised on a social evolutionary model of society, and Aboriginal people had to move or be moved along the scale of civilisation. Thus, while the aim, from the late 1930s, was full citizenship, Elkin was ambiguous and ambivalent about who could be granted it, and when.

Initially Elkin was concerned with endeavouring to ensure the future of Aboriginal people 'as a people'[24] through 'uplift' and 'advance',[25] these being the conceptual terms which dominated the discourses of the late 1920s and 1930s.[26] It was necessary, he stated, to envisage a 'place in a plan which might eventually be filled by the natives'; that is to say Aboriginal people had to be included in the future development of Australia and to make their contribution 'in their own way' to the progress of Australia; although, as we will see, Elkin did not state clearly how that would be achieved. The task, he wrote, 'of civilizing agents is to so preserve and modify or supplant the aboriginal view of life and the rites and practices arising from it, that primitive man may still feel at home in the universe, a sharer of that common life which animates all that therein is – including ourselves.'[27] Missionaries had an important role in guiding Aboriginal people 'through the difficult transition stages, and to do so in such a way that eventually this people will be still themselves, though transformed and Christianized, and may be also adepts with some of the more useful arts and crafts of civilization'.[28] Nevertheless, despite training and preparation as well as exposure to the wider white society, Aboriginal people found it hard to leave their past: 'there are many quite civilized Aborigines whose attitude to sickness and death is that of the uncivilized [Aboriginal person].'[29]

Elkin did not engage with Aboriginal groups, such as Ferguson's and Patten's, who sought citizenship as a birthright, nor did he refer to them when elucidating the case for citizenship. Rather, he was often critical of the role they played and the positions they adopted. Part of Elkin's difficulty lay in his inability to recognise that people such as Patten and Ferguson ('half-castes', to use his term) were Aboriginal and that Aboriginal people could play an active role in demanding citizenship rights.[30] As the only professor of anthropology in Australia, Elkin placed himself, especially in the eyes of government and mission bodies, as an expert on Aboriginal people and argued that anthropology was crucial in developing an 'understanding of Aborigines' (one of Elkin's key phrases), and assisting in, if not overseeing, the necessary changes and modifications to Aboriginal life.[31]

From the early 1920s, and particularly with the establishing of the chair of anthropology in 1925, anthropology had, in Australia, become an agent for understanding and helping governments control and develop indigenous people. The Australian territory of Papua and the

League of Nations mandated territory of New Guinea both appointed government anthropologists, in 1916 and 1924 respectively.[32] J H P Murray, Lieutenant Governor of Papua, hoped anthropology might help bridge the 'gap between the Stone Age and the Twentieth Century.'[33] There were attempts, especially by A R Radcliffe-Brown, foundation professor of anthropology at the University of Sydney, to have a government anthropologist appointed in the Northern Territory. Like Elkin after him, he was unsuccessful in this appeal. The view taken by State governments and the Commonwealth was that the future of Aboriginal people as a people was under threat and it was confidently predicted that 'full-blood Aborigines' would 'pass away'.[34] There was therefore no need for anthropology to provide a means of understanding Aboriginal people so that they might become members of the wider white society.

However, Elkin was successful, from the late 1920s, and especially after his appointment as professor of anthropology, in convincing the Commonwealth Government that anthropology could provide the knowledge required to understand Aboriginal social and cultural life:

> [anthropology] can render invaluable service by ascertaining the principles of social cohesion and of social change. The knowledge thus gained is then available for the guidance of the conscientious administrator in controlling and effecting modifications in native life. [Anthropologists] like all good members of a 'higher' and trustee race, are concerned with the task of raising primitive races in the cultural scale.[35]

Government agencies appreciated such an understanding of anthropology. For government and its administrators, Elkin's greatest value was, in the words of Carrodus, that he was 'not a purely academic anthropologist but [was] very realistic in his outlook'.[36] Elkin's essay 'Anthropology and the Future of the Australian Aborigines', published in 1934, reads like a guide for government administrators and missionaries in changing the beliefs of Aboriginal people so that these people could participate in the development of, and be of benefit to, white Australia. Thus anthropological knowledge would enable Aboriginal people to be raised on the 'scale of civilization'; while missionaries would inculcate their 'higher [Christian] views of life.'[37] Elkin explained to the superintendent of the Mount Margaret Mission (Western Australia) that anthropologists sent out by the ANRC 'aim at helping both the missionaries and the government in working for the advance of the aborigines'.[38]

Elkin practised an anthropology that was useful in helping the colonial administration to control and develop indigenous people with the aim of civilising them. For Elkin, Aboriginal people who were 'civilised' were those who had in 'varying degrees forsaken their native view of life and

[had], also in varying degrees, become involved in our economic system and in a few cases [...] to some extent adopted our view of life.'[39] Aboriginal life had to be modified in the face of changed circumstances – namely, civilisation. This was the primary task of a 'practical' anthropology. Elkin thus carved out a unique role for anthropology in Australia, which was characterised by the closeness of its relationship with government and the major mission bodies and was premised on the notion of anthropology being a helping discipline.[40]

Aboriginal advancement

Elkin first questioned the belief that Aboriginal people were destined to extinction (they 'need not die out') in 1927, although he was uncertain whether they 'could adapt themselves to such altered conditions as European civilization of the Twentieth century presented to them'. The 'blacks might not reach our stage of development [but] we can help them to advance.' He saw the task of 'ethnology' as doing more than treating 'the Australian aboriginal or any other primitive race as a mere interesting living fossil. It must help the higher races to give the lower [races] those elements of culture which would enable them to rise in the scale [of civilisation].'[41] Governments, protection societies and missions, he stated, were 'almost wholly concerned with protecting Aborigines from injustice, cruelty and immorality, and apart from a passing reference to welfare in the objective of some Government Acts, there was no suggestion in the 1920s of any future for the Aborigines'.[42] Elkin recognised that Aboriginal policy and practice needed to undergo a change in direction and purpose to replace the existing approach, which he characterised as 'merely protective measures [...] not aimed at advancing the race.'[43] What was needed, he argued, was a 'positive policy'.[44]

Elkin first publicly formulated a 'positive policy' for Aborigines when he addressed the Association for the Protection of Native Races in October 1933, although he had articulated something similar when he published 'A Policy for the Aborigines' in the *Morpeth Review*.[45] A positive policy, Elkin argued, included education as well as 'law, order, harmony and pacification'. Education was not to be confined to the three Rs and 'useful geography', but should include training in various technical and industrial pursuits, especially carpentry, stockwork and farming. He wrote that, 'with regard to the last', Aboriginal people were 'showing on some of the missions, and also on the Government station[s ...] much more aptitude than we have been disposed to place to their credit.' Religious education should be included as a co-operative venture between government and mission.[46]

Elkin's view was in keeping with the humanitarians' notions of making Aboriginal people useful members of society. He encouraged humanitarian groups such as the APNR, the most active group within mainstream politics concerned with Aboriginal issues,[47] and the major mission bodies not only to support but to promulgate a positive policy in contrast to the usual policy of humanitarian groups, which was to react to specific injustices done to Aborigines. Under Elkin's guidance, in the mid-1930s the NMC issued a pamphlet, 'A National Policy for the Protection, Education, Health and Better Government for the Aborigines', which argued for a positive policy and among other things advocated Commonwealth 'oversight and control' of Aboriginal people, stating that in any scheme for their uplifting, provision had to be made to train them to be capable, industrious and self-reliant people.[48] Humanitarian groups called for the recognition of Aboriginal people as human beings with an 'unquestionable birthright of citizenship with its freedom'.[49] But some supporters of citizenship rights for Aboriginal people believed that some humanitarian groups were not doing as much as they could. One critic argued that the APNR 'does not and has not supported these Aborigines who are striving for citizenship status. [...] I pay willing tribute to what the APNR has tried to do for the backward full-bloods, but I am surprised when I think how little we try to help those mixed-bloods who are asking to become citizens.'[50] The division between 'backward full-bloods' and 'mixed-bloods' striving for citizen rights was compounded by the problem of who was Aboriginal. 'Half-castes', 'mixed-bloods', 'part-Aborigines' were, because of blood, colour and place, usually considered closer to obtaining citizenship than 'full-bloods'.[51] Humanitarian groups were usually more interested in the welfare of Aboriginal people living outside of settled south-eastern Australia.

By the end of the 1930s full citizenship had become the clearly stated aim of both Aboriginal political and welfare movements and white humanitarian organisations. 'Advance' and 'uplift' were intertwined with calls for 'full citizenship'. Such calls for citizenship for Aboriginal people were premised on a series of exclusions and on classifications of readiness to accept the responsibilities entailed in citizenship. Various Aboriginal political movements of the 1930s and 1940s embraced these categories of readiness to exercise citizenship rights as a way of entering the white dominated discourse. The Australian Aborigines' League constitution, for example, categorised Aboriginal people as three types – those living in a 'primitive state', 'semi-civilised and de-tribalised Natives' and 'civilised Natives'. For the latter they demanded 'full political, social and economic rights [...] including the Franchise and eligibility for maternity bonus'.[52] McEwen, in his 1939 statement, divided Aboriginal people into four classes: 'the fully detribalised; the semi-tribalised; the

Myalls or aboriginals in their native state; [and] half-castes.' Within these classes there were further divisions, so that the 'fully detribalised' fell into two groups, 'those living around the pastoral stations and those in the neighbourhood of the principal towns'. The 'Myalls and semi-tribalised' were in need of training, education, medical attention and general care. Such people were to be left to 'their ancient tribal life' so that 'gradual contact [was made] with civilization'. In addition there were two sub-classes of 'half-caste' – 'those born in wedlock of half-caste parents, and those born of an aboriginal mother and a non-aboriginal father'. It was the latter who were the responsibility of the government, as they could be trained in 'useful occupations' but the 'near white children were to be trained apart from the general half-caste.'53 Here we see the privilege of colour as a means of acceptance into white Australian society and thus citizenship.

Elkin was part of this discourse of race, colour and privilege. In response to a query on his definition of 'half-blood' and 'quadroon'54 in *Citizenship for Aborigines*, Elkin replied:

> You are quite right about the definitions on p. 91. Though the definitions of half-blood and quadroon are not identical they do overlap; the trouble arises with the person who is three-eights [sic] aboriginal, that is, has three great-grandparents aboriginal. Is such a person to be called quadroon or half-caste? Or are we to invent a new term? [...] You will notice that I suggest that in the case of the quadroon, 'such a person would normally have two great-grant-parents [sic] who were full-blood aborigines', and in any case such a person would be less than fifty per cent aboriginal. [...] Obviously if ever the Act were altered and we wanted precision, we might well include in the definition of quadroon persons who are three-eights aboriginal. Even then that is not mathematically correct. It would, of course, be ideal but impractical to decide each case on its merits, so that a light three-eights might be classed as a quadroon, and a dark one as a half-blood. [...] As the years [go] by the mathematics will become even more difficult. We will be dealing with sixteenths, but probably by that time we will only be concerned with full-bloods including three-quarter castes, and with half-castes perhaps including three-eights to be regarded as white.55

In the same year Elkin stated that Aboriginal people would have to move through transition stages from 'Aboriginal to European culture, from nomadism to citizenship'. While undergoing these stages Aboriginal people needed 'security'; that is, they needed protection, which would be afforded by the provision of 'inviolable and controlled reserves and settlements' where they might 'return between periods of employment and in times of [emotional] depression', provided that they observed the rules and endeavoured to play a part in its community life. Reserves and settlements would be able to control the rate of contact and change and provide the means for Aboriginal people to be educated for the 'inevitable change'. Thus reserves would be places of training and preparation 'from which Aborigines will go forth equipped to meet civilization and [be] able to accommodate themselves successfully to modern conditions'.[56] Elkin argued that Aboriginal people needed their cultural heritage as a 'source of moral strength and courage' that enabled them to be on firm ground as they advanced to assimilation.[57]

Citizenship for Aboriginal people

Calls for citizenship were frequently associated with the demand for the Commonwealth franchise, entitlement to social welfare benefits and a right to drink alcohol. For Aborigines the latter was symbolic in attaining all the rights and privileges of citizenship.[58] Without going into a detailed discussion about citizenship, I want to underline a point made by Jeremy Beckett that the formation of a new state entailed the definition of citizenship, which is to say participation, and who was to enjoy it. Citizenship was a privilege of the settlers and extended only to the indigenous people under special circumstances.[59] Despite their status as British subjects and de facto Australian citizens,[60] for Aboriginal people citizenship was constrained by legislation and regulation and differed from that of other Australian citizens. Citizenship was available to certain categories of Aboriginal people who were often not recognised by the state as being Aboriginal. Whereas other citizens were able to exercise their rights of citizenship, this was denied to Aboriginal people.

Aboriginal people were barred from the federal franchise.[61] The *Commonwealth Franchise Act 1902* was amended in 1925 but only to include a 'native of British India [and a] person issued with a (current) certificate of naturalisation'. It was further amended in 1949 so that an 'Aboriginal native of Australia who is entitled under the laws of the State in which he resides to vote for the more numerous House of Parliament, or who is or has been a member of the Defence Force' was entitled to have their name placed on the electoral roll.[62] In 1962 it was amended again so that all Aboriginal people were entitled to have their name placed on the electoral roll (although it was not compulsory for them to vote, as it was for other voters). In the States the franchise was capricious and changing. Aboriginal people in Queensland, Western Australia and the Northern Territory were not entitled to vote except under special entitlement. Those living in Victoria, Tasmania,[63] South Australia[64] and New South Wales did have the franchise, although many were unaware of their entitlement. But the opportunity to exercise the franchise did not necessarily confer full citizenship. Except for those living in cities, Aboriginal people were subjected to a range of protective measures that controlled their movements and restricted them from exercising their entitlement.

Elkin expressed the opinion that, while government 'might require' that an Aboriginal person, in order to be qualified to vote, should not be totally dependent on an institution, he disagreed that the government should demand more than the ability to speak and understand English. Yet he wanted to include an understanding of the:

> significance of the numbers one to twenty. After all, Aborigines are British subjects, and all we require from non-British immigrants seeking naturalization is evidence that they have a satisfactory knowledge of English.[65]

Although social welfare benefits were an entitlement of citizenship, Aboriginal people were, until the 1940s, denied access to them; the social welfare legislation enacted in the early years of the century contained specific exclusions relating to 'aboriginal natives'. From 1941 child endowment did become available for Aboriginal people who were not 'nomadic' or whose child was not 'wholly or mainly dependent upon the Commonwealth or State for support'.[66] From 1942 maternity allowance and age and invalid pensions also became available to Aboriginal people who were 'exempt' from the laws of their State or Territory relating to Aboriginal people or, where no such provisions for exemption existed, were judged by the Director General of Social Services to be of sufficient 'character, standard of intelligence and development'.[67] From 1944 this last phrase was also used, theoretically at least, to allow some Aboriginal qualification for unemployment and sickness benefits.[68] However, the general rule was still exclusion and the numbers of Aboriginal people being paid under these exceptional provisions during the 1940s was extremely small. Child endowment appears to have been the payment that was becoming slightly more widespread, being seen as a way of enabling missions and pastoral stations to provide services for Aboriginal women and children.[69]

Elkin played a significant role in the initial gains for welfare payments for Aboriginal people. He argued in 1944 that the provision of social service benefits should be extended beyond those of 'half- and lesser caste' exempted from State and Territory Aboriginal legislation and not living on reserves. Some Aboriginal people living on reserves should, he argued, be permitted to receive pensions and other conditions for exemption be relaxed.[70] In 1979 Elkin observed that the extension of child endowment and maternity allowance indicated 'defacto Commonwealth recognition of their citizenship rights.'[71] William DeMaria, on the other hand, argues that factors such as the 'increased use-value of

Aborigines once they were detribalised', and the use of welfare as a 'form of social reward for a lifestyle that reflected the dominant and prevailing values',[72] furthered the aims of assimilation.

The consumption of alcohol was looked upon by Aboriginal people as one of the main entitlements of citizenship (a position which Elkin supported in the 1950s); exemption provided the opportunity to consume alcohol. The problem was that the exemption certificate declared that the person was no longer Aboriginal and that he or she was not to provide alcohol to relatives who were not exempted. Elkin pointed out to Paul Hasluck, Minister for Territories, that Aboriginal people would 'object more and more to having to produce Exemption Certificates (passports, like foreigners have, is the way they put it), whenever they want social services, the vote or a drink. There is a good deal of resentment already on the part of mixed-bloods, and it will spread further.'[73] Ten years later he observed that citizenship for Aboriginal people had become correlated not so much with the franchise as with the freedom to buy and consume alcoholic liquor.[74] The right to drink represented the last bastion in the quest for citizenship for Aboriginal people and an emblem of successful assimilation.

Assimilation, the linchpin to McEwen's 1939 'New Deal', was introduced as policy in the States from the early 1940s, and was keenly advocated by Elkin.[75] For Elkin it meant 'that the Aborigines will be similar to us, not necessarily in looks, but with regard to all the privileges and responsibilities of citizenship. That is in life's various situations – economic, political, religious, recreational and social, fitness alone is to count, without any reference to skin colour or to ancestry.'[76] He was keen to point out, in 1958, that assimilation did not mean miscegenation, 'that is being lost in the community', although it was, nonetheless, 'a matter of individual decision' as Aboriginal people should, if they desired, be able to live 'in a way similar to ourselves and take part in the general life of the community.'[77] Fourteen years earlier he had been more explicit: 'with regard to mixed-blood children, mostly quarter caste and octoroons, in the closely settled regions of the states, it is essential that as much as possible of their education should be given in the general state schools along with white children. These mixed blood people, especially the children will be assimilated into the general community. [...] Let us face the fact and prepare both the mixed bloods and ourselves for it, and see that as they become full citizens they will be at least as useful and worthy as our average [sic]. Assimilation will be smooth in the future if both the white and the mixed blood children learn to play together at school – later they may work together without comment.'[78] The ambivalence and contradictions of Elkin's sense of assimilation had not substantially altered between 1944 and 1960.[79]

Elkin and citizenship for Aboriginal people

Elkin was driven by a sense of justice (juridical equity) and fair play. He believed that Aboriginal people who were living after the manner of white Australians should be granted the same rights, privileges and entitlements as any other Australian citizen. He saw it as a moral task to assist in the advancement, uplift and civilising of 'full-blood' Aboriginal people or those with a preponderance of Aboriginal blood. He was also conscious of the international gaze upon and judgement of Australia. If the Commonwealth were to be criticised for the poor treatment and conditions of Aboriginal people in any of the States then it should take national responsibility. He put moral pressure on white Australia, including government and humanitarian groups, by providing a critique of white prejudice against Aboriginal people.

Nevertheless, what Elkin understood by citizenship remained ambiguous and ambivalent. Elkin was aware of the contradiction between citizenship (that is, citizenship as a birthright) and full citizenship (meaning the full use of all citizenship rights), but nevertheless he advocated a gradual granting of citizenship rights to Aboriginal people. Settler discourse saw Aboriginal people lacking in the qualities that bestowed civilisation upon the settlers (and later immigrants). Elkin's discourse on citizenship recognised this same lack. In order to overcome their shortcoming Aboriginal people had to be removed from reserves to townships, with the aim that they would live in the community like other Australians. The two impediments to this were prejudice from the white community and Aboriginal people's inability or reluctance to advance and be like white Australians: 'The Aborigines must desire, understand and fit themselves for citizenship, whether they want to realize it dispersed in the general community or living in their own separate communities.'[80] The mention of separate communities should not be misunderstood. Elkin was uncomfortable with the idea of Aboriginal people being a group apart. This was an impediment to citizenship. The fact that they would live apart as a group, 'for some considerable time especially in the North and the Centre',[81] was a reality that had to be acknowledged as part of the transition process only.

Elkin was ambiguous about the categories of Aboriginality,[82] and uncertain about the preparedness and ability of Aboriginal people to accept the rights and responsibilities of citizenship which contrasted with his advocacy for legal entitlements. This ambiguity is explained in part by Elkin's notions of blood and the effect degrees of blood had on the way people looked and behaved as well as their cultural beliefs. Elkin's categories were racially based – that is, he imbued people with social and cultural characteristics on the basis of blood (race). He conflated blood and culture to explain individual behaviour and potentiality. Elkin distinguished between 'full-blood' Aboriginal people and 'part-Aborigines', sometimes making finer distinctions within the category of 'part-Aborigines'. He also recognised that the position and cultural status of the 'full-bloods' differed from that of the 'part-Aborigines', adding that they were Aboriginal in 'more than skin-colour, while the latter are near-whites in more than skin-colour.'[83] By the late 1960s he noted that the 'present trend [was] for all who identify themselves as Aborigines even though they be almost white and have no heritage of Aboriginal culture, to be regarded and treated as such'. He doubted the 'logic and wisdom' of such practice, 'remembering [...] the amount of miscegenation which is going on, and whether the goal is really integration or separation'. He questioned the motives of this identification, 'or pseudo identification'.[84]

These differences were further reflected in Elkin's assessment of when Aboriginal people could attain citizenship, who was entitled, who was able, and the conditions of achieving citizenship. In Elkin's scheme of things, 'full-blood' Aborigines were unlikely to be ready for citizenship for two or three generations (and he even raised the possibility that there might not be any 'full-blood Aborigines' in two or three generations); they needed to be protected from the worst excesses of white civilisation, so missions and government reserves would act as a buffer and train them for eventual citizenship and entry into the white community. In effect they would, Elkin anticipated, be Christian citizens within the larger Australian polity although mainly confined to the northern and central parts of Australia, working for (white) Australia.[85]

Elkin's concept of citizenship was a moral and social one. Citizenship was lifestyle and it incorporated attitudes towards work, property (including furniture), housing and rent, family (eating together), saving money, and the acceptance of white legal structures; it encouraged individuality and individual responsibility – the individual was more important than the group and group relationships. It was based on the idea that Aboriginal culture was in opposition to civilisation. Elkin demanded more of Aboriginal people than he did of non-Aboriginal people. They had to demonstrate their fitness for citizenship. White people had only to abandon their colour prejudice but white society did not need to change, while Aboriginal people were enjoined to abandon their Aboriginality before they could be admitted to white society.

Elkin argued that Aboriginal people, other than those who were 'less than half-Aboriginal', were able, in principle, to achieve citizenship but it would take time, because 'as a people they cannot do it in one or two generations' although individuals could achieve it earlier.[86] Thus not all Aborigines would benefit from an immediate granting of citizenship. There was, Elkin suggested, no value in giving exceptional 'full-blood'

Aboriginal people citizenship because they still lived in a manner that impeded living as a citizen.[87] There was the possibility, from Elkin's understanding of Aboriginality, that Aboriginal people could revert to 'savagery' and uncivilised behaviour.[88] Elkin wrote in 1940 that citizenship rights 'would obviously be of no use to some [Aboriginal people]', especially those who were nomadic.[89] Elkin still held the same opinion about the value of granting citizenship rights to 'full-blood Aborigines' in 1960, stating for example:

> It may seem pointless to make the franchise available to nomadic tribesmen whose knowledge of English, let alone politics, is negligible. The number of such Aborigines, however, should be, and is, decreasing early. In any case, their non-use of a legal right will not cause any confusion.[90]

Nevertheless 'citizenship is their right and the franchise should be theirs if they want it.' Combining the uncombinable he argued both for a general and unconditional granting of citizenship rights and the exclusion of 'full-blood Aborigines' from using their rights, by describing the exclusions as a voluntary self-exclusion. The granting of citizenship was thus premised on its non-use: 'even though they had the franchise, thousands of full-bloods would not enrol.'[91] It was not out of humanitarian concern[92] alone that Elkin advocated the granting of citizenship rights to 'full-blood Aborigines'; rather, such an act would be of 'significant value symbolically and in the eyes of the world.'[93]

The 1950s saw a significant change in the way government consulted Elkin,[94] as well as increasing opposition to Aboriginal assimilation. By the start of the 1960s it was becoming increasingly clear that assimilation was under challenge but by then Elkin was convinced that, with few exceptions, the aims first set out in the 1930s had been accomplished. By the late 1930s he and other humanitarians were only turning 'our minds as an act of faith towards' the goal of citizenship; fifteen years later 'we [Aborigines and white people] face the future confidently'. With mutual behaviour more and more based on understanding and goodwill there would be a time, 'not so far ahead, when the Aborigines, full-bloods and mixed-bloods, will share proudly with us all an Australia which they have helped to enrich.'[95]

Unlike Aboriginal groups concerned with the demand for civil rights for Aborigines, citizenship being an unfettered right irrespective of descent, Elkin wanted to make citizenship available to Aborigines who were ready, through training and preparation. Elkin saw citizenship as a process, a preparation for life in the general community, a reward for being like white Australians, and thus the goal of assimilation.

Notes

Research for this chapter was assisted by a grant from the Centre of Citizenship and Human Rights, Deakin University.

1 See Horner 1974: 56–67.
2 Resolution passed at the meeting. Handbill, nd. in author's possession. Only 'Aborigines and Persons of Aboriginal Blood [...] are invited to attend'. But this was not the first call for civil rights by Aboriginal people. See, for example, Goodall 1982a: passim; Markus 1988: especially 1–20.
3 Horner 1974: 57.
4 *Abo Call*, 1938. William Cooper and the Australian Aborigines' League made a similar call in 1936: 'the ultimate object of the League shall be the conservation of special features of Aboriginal culture and the removal of all disabilities, political, social or economic, now or in the future borne by aboriginals and secure their uplift to the full culture of the British race' (Markus 1988: 37, 41; see also Markus 1990: 173–89).
5 Horner 1974: 60.
6 But responsive more to those humanitarian organisations such as the APNR and mission bodies such as the Anglican ABM and the Protestant NMC.
7 McEwen 1939.
8 McEwen 1939.
9 Markus argues that by the end of the decade (1930s) Elkin was at the peak of his influence with government (Markus 1990: 156). My contention is that throughout the decade of the 1940s Elkin's position with respect to Aboriginal Australia was unchallenged but that this was not so with regard to Australia's territories. See Gray 1994.
10 Firth was acting professor of anthropology from A R Radcliffe-Brown's departure in 1931 to his own departure for London at the end of 1932. Elkin was made lecturer in charge (at the behest of Firth) while the future of the department was negotiated. Elkin was informed of his appointment as professor on 22 December 1932 but did not take up the position until January 1934.
11 In 1932 the APNR, the ABM, the United Missionary Council (later the NMC), 'with the concurrence of the Aborigines' Protection Board' set up a committee of inquiry into the 'present conditions and future development of the remaining aborigines in New South Wales.' Elkin was the 'Anthropologist to the Committee', in the 'first instance [...] conducting the inquiry for the Committee' (*ABM Review* 1932, vol. 19 (4): 68).
12 Elkin advocated a number of changes to the *Aborigines Protection Act 1936*, including a change of name for the Aborigines' Protection Board to the Aborigines' Welfare Board, which were incorporated into the *Aborigines Protection Act (Amendment) 1940*.
13 In 1931 Elkin had written *Understanding the Australian Aborigine* (Morpeth). *The Australian Aborigines: how to understand them*, was reprinted in four editions until the late 1970s.
14 Elkin, in his opening address to the Conference of Mission Authorities and the Northern Territory Administration held in Darwin on 25 and 26 August 1948, stated that he had 'been closely associated with the various movements aimed at improving native policy throughout Australia' and that McEwen, Carrodus and he had formulated in a meeting 'the principles of the present policy for aborigines' (Australian Archives (hereafter AA): CRS F 126 22). In 1939 he wrote to the secretary of the Church Missionary Society that he was

'one intimately concerned with the Government policy' (Elkin to Hulme-Moir, 8 March 1939, 65/1/12/105, Elkin Papers, University of Sydney archives (hereafter EP). See also 60/1/12/57, EP).

15 Elkin 1934a: 52–60.

16 Elkin 1964: 370. What was required, as the Commonwealth could not directly legislate for Aborigines, was a 'convergent system of national policy somewhat along the lines I outlined in my book, *Citizenship for the Aborigines*, in 1944'. Elkin to PA McBride (Minister for the Interior), 5 September 1950 (183/4/2/333, EP).

17 In March 1943 Elkin had started preparing for the possible transfer of this power. Late that year he was engaged in two projects. One was preparing a national policy for Aboriginal people and their administration in case powers for this purpose were handed to the Commonwealth either by the States or by referendum. The other was the effect on Aboriginal people of development in the northern parts of Australia. Elkin wrote letters to the chief protectors seeking information on funding and numbers and getting his researchers, especially Marie Reay, Grace Sitlington and Ronald and Catherine Berndt, to provide him with information of fertility, infant death rates, vitality and diet. He also wrote to the army and mission bodies. See 73/1/12/206, EP. For a discussion about 'vitality' ('vitalism') see Michael Roe 1984: 1–21.

18 Elkin c.1946: 16. R G Menzies, the Federal Opposition leader, stated that if this amendment was voted on separately 'we would support it' (*Sydney Morning Herald*, 11 August 1944). However, this was probably a pretence as Menzies was opposed to such federal intervention in general.

19 Jacobs 1986 (2): 15. It was a conference dominated by A O Neville, Chief Protector of Natives in Western Australia, Dr Cecil Cook, Chief Protector of Aboriginals and Chief Medical Officer in the Northern Territory and J W Bleakley, Chief Protector of Aborigines in Queensland.

20 See Neville 1947.

21 E W P Chinnery, appointed the director of the Department of Native Affairs in 1939, attempted to bring about some of the changes outlined by McEwen, but it was not until Paul Hasluck was appointed Minister for Territories in May 1951 that the policy of assimilation received a new impetus. See Thomas 1994: 73–119 for an excellent discussion on Hasluck and assimilation.

22 'Full citizenship' is a term that makes no sense outside a social order based on a social evolutionary discourse.

23 Such as 'Post-war and the Aborigines', *Aborigines' Protector*, 1946, vol. 2 (1); *Post-war and the Aborigines*, National Missionary Council Pamphlet, Sydney, c.1946; 'Recent Developments in Aboriginal Affairs', *Aborigines' Protector*, 1948, vol. 2 (4).

24 Elkin 1934b: 18.

25 For Elkin 'advance' meant in 'health, numbers [population], conditions of living and work, and education' (Elkin c.1946: 4).

26 Throughout his life Elkin advocated the need for white Australians (settlers) to understand Aboriginal people and to realise that interfering with their social organisation, for example, required consideration of how it worked; ignorance had caused the problems of the past. 'Aborigines do possess a social, economic, legal, political and religious organisation by which they are able to adapt themselves to their own geographical and social environment. This fact should be proclaimed from the house-tops, respected by all, and taken into consideration in our endeavours to do them justice and to frame

and put into operation a policy designed to raise them in the scale of civilization' (Elkin 1934b: 15). Compare Kenelm Burridge, who argues that the anthropological impulse has much in common with Christian missionary experience.

27 Elkin 1935: 119, 145.

28 Elkin 1933: 9.

29 Elkin 1935: 131. In 1954 he commented on the 'pull' of their background as a hindrance to their advance (see 1954: 337).

30 See Goodall 1982b: passim; also Elkin's dismissive comments, 1966: 377ff.

31 *The Australian Aborigines: how to understand them*, was dedicated to the development of an understanding of Aborigines 'which should inspire our attitude to, our treatment of and work for, the Aborigines' (Elkin 1938: x).

32 J H P Murray, Lieutenant Governor of Papua, appointed the Chief Medical Officer, W M Strong, as government anthropologist in 1916; F E Williams was appointed assistant anthropologist in 1922; E W P Chinnery was appointed in the Territory of New Guinea.

33 West 1968: 11.

34 See McGregor 1993: 14–22.

35 Elkin 1934b: 2–3.

36 Carrodus to Driver, 15 July 1946, AA: CRS F1 1946/767.

37 Elkin 1934b: 14–15.

38 Elkin to Schenk, 21 March 1934, 64/1/12/86, EP. He reiterated this view to a mission critic of anthropology, J H Sexton, President of the Aborigines' Friends Association (SA), stating that anthropologists were 'concerned with the study of primitive peoples and civilised peoples – not to chronicle them for historical purposes, but to understand their lives from the point of view of Sociology. This understanding includes the whole process of change and the contact of cultures and peoples. I am glad to say that most Governments and Missionaries agree that Anthropology is worthwhile'. Elkin to Sexton, c.1947, 67/1/12/127, EP. Social anthropology is frequently presented as a hand-maiden of the colonial enterprise, and in the sense that anthropology was interested in helping the colonial administration to civilise indigenous people there is little dispute; the success or otherwise of the anthropological enterprise is problematic.

39 Elkin 1935: 117.

40 See Cowlishaw 1990; Gray 1996; also Markus 1990: 173–89.

41 Interview, *West Australian*, 29 October 1927; copy in 8/1/1/92, EP.

42 Elkin 1944: 11.

43 *Sydney Morning Herald*, 16 June 1933. AA: A1, 36/6595.

44 On his return from his initial field work in northwest Western Australia, Elkin formulated a mission policy for the ABM. While in the Kimberley, Elkin wrote a critical report for the ABM on E R Gribble, superintendent of the Forrest River mission. The ABM committee was pleased with his discretion and suggestions for the future of the mission. As a consequence he was asked to develop policy for the ABM, which he did in 1929 (see MSS 4503 (ABM Papers) Mitchell Library). This placed Elkin in a position of considerable authority on indigenous people in mission circles. He did not publish his mission policy until 1933 (Elkin 1933: 31–45).

45 'A Policy for the Aborigines', *Morpeth Review*, 1931; he states a similar policy in 'Anthropology and the Future of the Australian Aborigines' (1934b; see also 1934a).

46 Elkin to editor, *ABM Review*, 10 November 1933. 68/1/12/146, EP.

47 Markus 1990: 161.
48 Quoted in Elkin 1944: 15.
49 Editorial, 'Federal Government Policy. Use of Natives in Industry', *The Aborigines Protector*, 1935, vol. 1 (1): 15.
50 Sawtell to President of APNR (Elkin), 19 February 1940. 68/1/12/144, EP.
51 See Cowlishaw 1986: 2–11.
52 See Markus 1988: 42.
53 McEwen 1939.
54 Carrodus to Elkin, 17 November 1944. 177/4/2/213, EP.
55 Elkin to Carrodus, 7 December 1944. 177/4/2/213, EP. See *Understanding Aborigines*, 1954: 330–35 for further descriptions of Elkin's racial categories. See also later editions.
56 Elkin 1944: 38.
57 Elkin 1954: 336.
58 Merlan 1996.
59 Beckett 1988: 4.
60 Snedden (A-G) to Menzies (PM), 20 August 1964. AA: A432/1, 1967/3321, Part 1.
61 '[F]ull-blood aboriginals (or those in whom the aboriginal blood predominates) are disqualified from Commonwealth enrolment (except in very rare cases where entitled under Section 41 of the Constitution – see Note) and in the States of Queensland and Western Australia are also disqualified from State enrolment. They are however not so disqualified from State enrolment in NSW, Victoria, South Australia and Tasmania. (Note: To be qualified for Commonwealth enrolment under Section 41 of the Constitution an aboriginal must have obtained a State enrolment prior to the passing of the Commonwealth Franchise Act 1902 and to have retained that enrolment continuously since)' (Chief Electoral officer to Elkin, 22 October 1945. 177/4/2/214, EP).
62 Carrodus noted that 'In Western Australia aboriginal natives are in the main disqualified from enrolment and from voting at State elections but the "Natives (Citizenship Rights) Act 1944" permits any adult native to make application for a certificate of citizenship to a Resident Magistrate or Stipendiary Magistrate, and if the Magistrate is satisfied as to the suitability of the applicant, a certificate of citizenship is issued whereupon the holder is deemed to be no longer an aboriginal but to have all the rights, privileges and immunities and to be subject to the duties and liabilities of a natural born or naturalised subject of His Majesty. The suggested amendment of the Commonwealth law should entitle any aboriginal native resident in Western Australia who secured a certificate of citizenship under the Natives (Citizens Rights) Act to be enrolled on the Commonwealth roll and to vote at Commonwealth elections' (Carrodus to Elkin, 23 September 1948. 177/4/2/213, EP).
63 Rowley 1970: 384 stated that 214 Aboriginal people were counted in the 1947 state census.
64 Graham Jenkin, author of *Conquest of the Ngarrindjeri*, stated in a letter to the *Australian* (6 May 1996) that 'Aborigines have never been excluded from the franchise in South Australia. When South Australian adult males were given the right to vote in 1856 this applied to non-Aboriginal and Aboriginal men. [...] At Federation South Australian Aboriginal men and women were guaranteed commonwealth voting rights under section 41 of the constitution. [although] during the interwar period commonwealth suffrage was a matter for dispute.'

65 Elkin to Carrodus, 23 October 1948 (177/4/2/213, EP).
66 Act No. 8 of 1941.
67 Acts Nos 3 and 19 of 1942.
68 Act No. 10 of 1944.
69 Elkin observed that in 'some parts, Missions simply regard Child Endow-
    ment as an extra source of income for the general running of the Missions'
    (Elkin to Moy, 18 February 1948, 177/4/2/218, EP). See also De Maria
    1986.
70 Elkin 1944: 89. He added that care be taken 'lest "social benefit" allowances
    be an inducement for [Aboriginal people] to leave the reasonably good
    conditions of a Settlement to makeshift in undesirable conditions off a
    Settlement' (Ibid).
71 Elkin 1979: 309. Elkin pointed out to Paul Hasluck that 'we have agreed to
    ignore the Constitution and give child endowment for full-blood children
    gathered in what we deem to be institutions. I am glad we do this' (Elkin to
    Hasluck, 29 June 1951. 183/4/2/329, EP).
72 DeMaria 1986: 35, 27.
73 Elkin to Hasluck, 29 June 1951 (183/4/2/329, EP).
74 Elkin 1960: 14.
75 As noted above, McEwen did not actually use the term 'assimilation' in his
    1939 statement. The first traceable public use of the term on record is in
    Elkin 1944, p. 88. However, the New South Wales *Aborigines Protection
    (Amendment) Act 1940*, at section 7, specified the 'duties' of the newly
    reconstituted and renamed Aborigines Welfare Board as including 'assisting
    aborigines to become assimilated into the general life of the community'.
    Also in 1940, Elkin's private notes from a meeting with Anderson, Chairman
    of the New South Wales Aborigines Welfare Board, quote Anderson as saying:
    'One of the main concerns of my Board is the preparation of the aborigines
    for their ultimate assimilation into the general community as self respecting
    citizens, independent of Government aid' (59/1/12/44, EP).
76 Elkin 1960: 9.
77 Elkin to Marian Alderdice, 25 June 1958 (67/1/12/123, EP).
78 Elkin c.1946: 11–12.
79 Thomas argues that Elkin's anthropologically based respect for difference,
    and a desire to preserve a distinctive people whose continued existence he
    believed to be threatened, informed what was closer to an integrationist's
    vision than to an assimilationist's one (Thomas 1994: 1). That is to say that
    Elkin's policy foresaw Aboriginal culture granting precedence to the
    European, a position that allowed for continuity in Aboriginal cultural forms
    within an adaptive response to the dominant European order. This position
    is inconsistent with one which Thomas states is generally accepted by
    scholars, that Elkin articulated a policy that aimed to eradicate Aboriginal
    heritage and reconstitute Aboriginal people as Europeans in all but skin
    colour (Thomas 1994: 51). I think there is some substance in her argument
    but that it elides the ambiguity and ambivalence in Elkin's racial and cultural
    categorisations of Aboriginal people and their anticipated different futures.
    Elkin's position is often contradictory and, in general terms, there is a
    tension between what he desires for 'mixed-blood Aborigines' and 'full-blood
    Aborigines' and the futures he envisages for them. In addition Thomas
    downplays the racial discourse based on blood informing culture. Social
    evolutionary theory underscores Elkin's discourse.
80 Elkin 1960: 18.
81 Elkin to Marian Alderdice, 25 June 1958 (67/1/12/123, EP).

82 See Cowlishaw 1987 for a discussion about confusion and collapsing of the categories.
83 Elkin, typescript, c.1967, 109/1/17/156, EP.
84 Elkin, typescript, c.1967, 109/1/17/156, EP.
85 He wrote that the ABM, instead of involving itself in the politics of the Guided Projectiles Project 'should get on with its positive task of helping the Aborigines to become Christian citizens' (Elkin to Cranswick, 17 July 1947, ABM Papers, Mitchell Library Mss 4503 Add on 1822 ML 1961/71, Box 25).
86 Elkin 1960: 18. He wrote to Marian Alderdice of the Aboriginal–Australian Fellowship that 'as for full-bloods – I simply use the word "citizenship" for in the northern parts of Australia, while they should become citizens, it would be an even longer time before they become part of the general community in the way in which the aborigines of New South Wales and Victoria will become' (Elkin to Alderdice, 25 June 1958. 67/1/12/123, EP).
87 This has resonance with the way in which some missionaries would not accept an individual convert but would rather use the individual to help convert the group (village), which was the aim of the mission. I would like to thank Christine Winter for pointing this out.
88 See Stepan 1982: 111–39.
89 Elkin to R Swann, honorary secretary, Association for the Protection of Native Races. 24 September 1940 (68/1/12/144, EP).
90 Elkin 1960. This article was written for an Aboriginal audience; *Dawn* was the official organ of the New South Wales AWB.
91 Elkin 1960: 14.
92 Elkin wrote that, when he first went into the field, he had 'no humanitarian motive' (Elkin 1962: 212).
93 He is quoted in Wise 1985: 231: 'Those of us working for a change in the attitudes and policies of in the Northern Territory and the North generally were not thinking of assimilation, but to prevent the extinction of full-bloods [...] we thought of them as a distinct group or series of groups with no thought of miscegenation or absorption as a policy goal.' See also Elkin 1960: 14.
94 See Gray 1994: passim.
95 Elkin 1954.

References

Beckett, J. 1988. Aboriginality, citizenship and nation state. In Aborigines and the state in Australia, ed. J. Beckett. *Social Analysis* 24: 3–18.
Burridge, K. 1973. *Encountering Aborigines: A Case Study. Anthropology of the Australian Aboriginal.* New York: Pergamon Press.
Cowlishaw, G. 1986. Aborigines and anthropologists. *Australian Aboriginal Studies* 1: 2–12
Cowlishaw, G. 1987. Colour, culture and the Aborigines. *Man* (NS) 22: 221–37.
Cowlishaw, G. 1990. Helping anthropologists: cultural continuity in the constructions of Aboriginalists. *Canberra Anthropology* 13 (2): 1–28.
DeMaria, W. 1986. White welfare: black entitlement: the social security access controversy, 1939–1959. *Aboriginal History* 10 (1): 25–39.

Elkin, A. P. 1931. *Understanding the Australian Aborigine.* The Morpeth Booklets No. 2.

Elkin, A. P. 1933. Missionary policy for primitive peoples. *Morpeth Review* 3 (27): 1–15.

Elkin, A. P. 1934a. The Aborigines, our national responsibility. *The Australian Quarterly* 6 (21): 52–60.

Elkin, A.P. 1934b. Anthropology and the future of the Australian Aborigines. *Oceania* 5 (1): 1–18.

Elkin, A. P. 1935. Civilised Aborigines and native culture. *Oceania* 6 (2): 117–46.

Elkin, A. P. 1938, 1954, 1964, 1966. *The Australian Aborigines: How to Understand Them.* Sydney: Angus & Robertson.

Elkin, A. P. 1944. *Citizenship for the Aborigines: A National Aboriginal Policy.* Sydney: Australasian Publishing Company.

Elkin, A. P. c.1946. *Post-war and the Aborigines.* Sydney: National Missionary Council.

Elkin, A. P. 1960. Aborigines and Citizenship. *Dawn* 9 (5).

Elkin, A. P. 1962. Australian Aboriginal and white relations: a personal record. *Journal of the Royal Historical Society* 48 (3): 208–30.

Elkin, A. P. 1979. Aboriginal–European relations in Western Australia: an historical and personal record. In *Aborigines of the West, Their Past and Present,* eds R. M. Berndt and C. H. Berndt. Nedlands: University of Western Australia Press, pp. 285–323.

Goodall, H. 1982a. A History of Aboriginal Communities in NSW, 1909–1939. PhD thesis, University of Sydney.

Goodall, H. 1982b. An intelligent parasite: A P Elkin and white perceptions of the history of Aboriginal people in New South Wales. Unpublished paper presented to the Oral History Association conference, 1982.

Gray, G. 1994. 'I was not consulted': A. P. Elkin, Papua New Guinea and the politics of anthropology. *The Australian Journal of Politics and History* 40 (2): 195–213.

Gray, G. 1996. 'The natives are happy': A. P. Elkin, A. O. Neville and anthropological research in northwest Western Australia. Journal of Australian Studies 50/51: 106–117.

Horner, J. 1974. *Vote Ferguson for Aboriginal Freedom.* Sydney: Australian and New Zealand Book Company.

Jacobs, P. 1986. Science and veiled assumptions: miscegenation in Western Australia 1930–1937. *Australian Aboriginal Studies* 2: 15–23.

Markus, A. 1988. *Blood from a Stone: William Cooper and the Australian Aborigines League.* Sydney: Allen & Unwin.

Markus, A. 1990. *Governing Savages.* Sydney: Allen & Unwin.

McCorquodale, J. 1987. *Aborigines and the Law: A Digest.* Canberra: Aboriginal Studies Press.

McEwen, J. 1939. *Commonwealth Government's Policy with Respect to Aborigines.* Canberra: Commonwealth Government Printer, pp. 1–6.

McGregor, R. 1993. The doomed race: a scientific axiom of the late nineteenth century. *The Australian Journal of Politics and History* 39 (1): 14–22.

Merlan, F. 1996. Aboriginal identity and the academy. A paper presented to Australian Institute of Aboriginal and Torres Strait Islander Studies seminar series.

Neville, A. O. 1947. *Australia's Coloured Minority: Its Place in the Community.* Sydney: Currawong Publishing Co. Pty Ltd.

Roe, M. 1984. *Nine Australian Progressivists: Vitalism in Bourgeois Social Thought 1890–1960*. Brisbane: University of Queensland Press.

Rowley. 1970. *The Destruction of Aboriginal Society*. Canberra: Australian National University Press.

Stepan, N. 1982. *The Idea of Race in Science 1800–1960*. London: Macmillan.

Thomas, C. K. 1994. From 'Australian Aborigines' to 'White Australians': Elkin, Hasluck and the Origins of Assimilation. MA thesis. Melbourne: Monash University.

West, F. 1968. *Hubert Murray: The Australian Pro-Consul*. Melbourne: Melbourne University Press.

Wise, T. 1985. *The Self-made Anthropologist: A Life of A. P. Elkin*. Sydney: Allen & Unwin.

PART II

Contemporary Conceptions

CHAPTER 4

Indigenous Citizenship and Self-determination: The Problem of Shared Responsibilities

Tim Rowse

In their recent review of academic studies of citizenship, Will Kymlicka and Wayne Norman argue that although citizenship is a status to which not only entitlements but also responsibilities attach, entitlements have been of disproportionate interest to theorists of citizenship. In particular, 'the left has not yet found a language of responsibility that it is comfortable with, or a set of concrete policies to promote these responsibilities'.[1]

In Australia it seems gratuitous to spell out the responsibilities of indigenous Australians as citizens. Perhaps those responsibilities are no more and no less than the responsibilities of all Australian citizens. Or perhaps there are distinct indigenous responsibilities, just as many people would argue that there are distinct indigenous entitlements, such as native title. Perhaps there are ways in which indigenous Australians, as the original and colonised people, have fewer responsibilities as citizens. Whichever way you begin to look at the matter, it is easier to criticise a residual colonialism for failing to actualise indigenous citizenship entitlements than to write of the responsibilities of indigenous Australian citizens.

Yet our understanding of the contemporary forms of Australian citizenship is impoverished if we do not ask what responsibilities are implied in indigenous citizenship. The notion of indigenous self-determination entails a proposition about distinct indigenous citizenship responsibilities: indigenous people are responsible (though not exclusively) for the reproduction of their indigenous social order. This contribution to social reproduction seems to be what Kymlicka and Norman meant by 'responsibility' – the 'civic virtue and public spiritedness' presupposed in the social policies of contemporary liberal democracies. They invite us to 'consider the many ways' in which 'public policy relies on responsible personal life style decisions':

the state will be unable to provide adequate health care if citizens do not act responsibly with respect to their own health, in terms of healthy diet, exercise, and the consumption of liquor and tobacco; the state will be unable to meet the needs of children, the elderly, or the disabled if citizens do not agree to share this responsibility by providing some care for their relatives; the state cannot protect the environment if citizens are unwilling to reduce, reuse, and recycle in their own homes.[2]

In the case of indigenous Australians, we might add: how can the state promote collective forms of indigenous self-determination if indigenous people do not strive to reproduce their social forms and identity as a more or less officially recognised enclave within the Australian nation?

The opportunity and (according to my inference) responsibility to do this arrived when Australian governments, in the 1970s, gave up trying to assimilate indigenous Australians and began to recognise the legitimacy of their continued difference. In progressing from assimilation to self-determination, it was necessary to give the indigenous social order a future as well as a past. Notoriously, advocates of assimilation held that Aboriginal society had crumbled, or was now crumbling, into fragments.[3] The future of these fragments, it was confidently projected, lay in their absorption into the wider Australian society. Indigenous people now tell us that they experienced the policies based on this scenario as a series of demands for them to give up their culture, including their land. Yet from the point of view of many advocates of assimilation, it was a humane crusade against the many inherited exclusions and tyrannies of 'protection' policy.

Can we write history from both of these perspectives? That is, can we honour the emancipatory intentions and effects of assimilation, while registering fully the cultural arrogance that looms large in indigenous memory? I believe not only that we can but that we should. Nothing less than that commitment will do justice to the complexity of assimilation.

Assimilation, I will argue in this chapter, was an effort to undermine two powerful structures: the stubbornly surviving bases of Aboriginal solidarity and identity *and* the colonial mechanisms of tutelary domination, or protection. In the part of Australia which I have studied most, Central Australia, these two structures had become intertwined.

That intertwining requires some elaboration. The material practice that bound the two structures together was the region's most enduring practice of colonial government – rationing. Assimilation's greatest triumph was to put an end to rationing, by shifting the basis of Aboriginal subsistence from rations to cash (wages and welfare payments), a transition which could be given a date range: 1960 to 1980. To convey the magnitude of this transformation, I will sketch the social features of Central Australian rationing regimes.

Rationing: the roots of welfare

The institutional practices of 'assimilation' were built on the colonial institutional heritage of rationing. After a period of intense violence in the 1880s, non-Aboriginal people of various kinds and motives began to find that they could manage relationships with Aboriginal people by issuing food, clothes, blankets and other necessities (and luxuries such as tobacco). This was what missionaries, pastoralists and miners did – not just to keep Aboriginal people from starving, but also because the issue of rations implied the forging of a more or less predictable relationship – permitting evangelism and use of labour – across a cultural gulf so wide that it jeopardised the mutual intelligibility of donor and receiver. As a means to social order, rationing can be understood as an informal instrument of colonial government.

Yet rationing was also subject to one of the fundamental ethics of European philanthropy: the imperative to distinguish between the deserving and the undeserving, in order not to corrupt morally (that is, pauperise) recipients. Although sacred to philanthropic tradition, the distinction between deserving and undeserving was difficult to maintain on the frontier, for three reasons. One, indigenous customs of distribution and redistribution persistently violated it. Two, at some times and in some places, people would have perished if not rationed, and this was ethically and politically unacceptable. Three, some liberality on the part of the donors made local Aboriginal people friendly and more amenable to non-Aboriginal people's requests for their labour, for their respect for livestock and other property, and for their attention to Christian instruction.

This contradiction – between the tendency to ration without distinction of desert and the desire to avoid pauperising undeserving Aboriginal people – has never ceased to haunt the apparatus of Aboriginal welfare in Central Australia (and no doubt in other regions). The contradiction could be eased, to a great extent, by widening the criterion of desert, in two ways. One was to broaden the definition of work, so that if 'deserving' has usually meant 'working or available for work', then more, rather than fewer, people would be 'deserving' of rations. A second way to widen the criterion of desert was to regard recipients of rations as being 'in training' – as Christians, mothers or citizens. In short, rationing – an indispensable instrument of colonial governance – was rationalised as an exchange for broadly defined services and/or as a reward for submission to some program of tuition.

Rationing was different from paying people money, in that the donor of rations preserved considerable powers over the recipients' consumption. The donor determined the quantity and quality of goods consumed by Aboriginal recipients of rations. The necessity to relax the deserving/undeserving distinction may have militated against donor control over work output, but the fact that sustenance was paid in kind recouped considerable donor authority. Compared with wage relationships, the authority of the rationing relationship focused less on the productivity of Aboriginal labour power and more on the appropriateness or inappropriateness of Aboriginal consumption. Rationing regimes were regimes of managed consumption. This capacity to manage consumption was the material basis of colonial paternalism in Central Australia, however varied the motives and rhetorics of paternalism may have been.

What could have been understood by the appropriateness or inappropriateness of Aboriginal consumption? It is in the different answers to this question that rationing regimes, in all their diversity, can be understood. Let me give some illustrations.

Three regimes of managed consumption

In the 1930s the Hermannsburg missionaries thought that *where* Aboriginal people consumed introduced commodities was important. They were extremely apprehensive of the fate of Western Desert people (Pitjantjatjara, Ngalia Warlpiri, Pintupi, Kukatja) who might venture so far east as to find themselves in Alice Springs. In that town a number of 'evil' trades (prostitution) and diversions (grog and cinema) would 'demoralise' and even kill them. The Lutherans' solution was to set up an economy of exchanged goods in the western MacDonnell Ranges. That economy was based on the government's bounty for dingo scalps. Aboriginal people could bring scalps to the mission store(s) and exchange them for flour, tea, tobacco and other novel and labour-saving goods which Aboriginal people found highly attractive. The mission would redeem the scalps for cash, when the police called. 'Native curios' (including the first 'Hermannsburg School' paintings) were also sold to the missions' supporters in other States and to the first hardy tourists. Through this mediation, Western Desert people were given access to new goods of which they were becoming desirous, without having to handle money or to go to a town. As well, they 'earned' those goods by exercising their traditional skills; they did not have to acculturate to a foreign labour process.

The Lutherans thus developed a mission program in which the retailing of certain goods was fundamental. After World War II, they continued to advocate the rural store as a moral bulwark. In a paper to the Missions/Administration Conference of 1955, Finke River Mission Superintendent F W Albrecht remarked on the restlessness of Aboriginal people on a number of the region's cattle stations. He urged not only a moderate increase in wages, but also that pastoral lessees build better accommodation and open stores on their properties. Aboriginal people could thus satisfy their growing material aspirations by expenditure based within their own country, and not be lured into town. The Finke River Mission made sure that there were retail services on many Central Australian properties by operating a hawker van in the 1950s and 1960s. For a while F W Albrecht's son, Paul, was the hawker.

Lutheran efforts to establish a regime of managed consumption were paralleled in the work of the Welfare Branch. The Welfare Branch tried to form certain consumption desires, preferences and habits in the Aboriginal people who gathered at their settlements. Branch files attest to the careful consideration that was given, from the mid-1950s to the early 1970s, to a number of issues of managed consumption: the mix of cash and goods with which Aboriginal labour was paid, the opening and stocking of canteens, the opening of savings bank branches, the introduction of communal feeding, the design and allocation of settlement dwellings, and, after social security payments became cash in Aboriginal hands in 1969, the institution of small charges for use of the communal dining room.

The urgency of this program of tuition in consumption increased when it became clear, in the mid-1960s, that Aboriginal stockmen would soon be paid award wages. Mr D L Busbridge, some time Welfare Branch officer at Papunya, expressed the logic of such tuition in 1966, just after the Arbitration Court had ordered that equal wages for pastoral workers be phased in over three years, from 1966 to 1968.

> If people are going to have excess funds when they are moved onto the social wage, then the standard they are living at at present is not up to what is required by society. Therefore with the introduction of the social wage it is important that steps be taken to increase the conditions or the circumstances so that they will want to spend more money to attain this standard. This will bring about an acceptance of responsibility, and an understanding of what is necessary to lead the life that is regarded as necessary in the community.[4]

In the late 1960s and early 1970s, the Welfare Branch experienced a crisis in its ability to manage consumption and to make consumption a matter of tuition in a new form of family life.

The Welfare Branch's venture into regimes of managed consumption included issuing rations in communal dining rooms, and persuading mothers to bring themselves and their children to clinic in order to have the quality and outcomes of their mothering monitored. But communal dining rooms proved to be unacceptable, for different reasons, to the Department of Health's hygiene inspectorate and to many of the

Aboriginal people who were supposed to eat in them. To the extent that settlement residents did use communal dining rooms, Aboriginal women were denied the chance to develop some of the skills appropriate to modern housekeeping: budgeting, shopping, cooking, cleaning up. Nor did the Branch find it easy to train Aboriginal men to be 'good fathers'. As the largest employer of Aboriginal people in the Northern Territory from the early 1960s, the Welfare Branch expected Aboriginal men to become breadwinners – that is, to regard their earnings, increasingly in cash form, as the basic livelihood of their wife and children. If men were slow to accept this responsibility, they were not to be paid much cash. However, the Welfare Branch was under political pressure from other Northern Territory employers to introduce monetary rewards for labour, at first as a cautious supplement to rations and later, by the late 1960s, as a substitute for rations. Advocates of the emancipatory potential of assimilation also called upon the government to make social security benefits available, in cash, to all Aboriginal people.

Such pressures combined with the intrinsic limits of communal feeding to accelerate the transition from rations to cash welfare pay-ments. With cash, people could choose to eat in the communal dining room (where tickets were introduced in 1969) or they could buy from the settlement store. By 1975, every category of cash welfare payment was available to Welfare settlement residents, on the same basis as to other Australians. Restricted access to unemployment benefit was the last defence of managed consumption to fall.

The sudden flow of unprecedented amounts of cash into the settle-ments and missions in the period 1969 to 1975 prompted the Welfare Branch to commission research assessing people's uses of money. They uncovered a crisis of nutrition, a shortage of food in some families and little application of principles of nutrition in many. The nuclear family/household was not to be found in the flows of money and goods between Aboriginal people, nor in the use made of such dwellings as the Welfare Branch had endowed. The Welfare Branch's regime of managed consumption had somehow resulted in what is now called an 'unhealthy lifestyle' – though how much the Branch should be blamed for that is unclear.

A different crisis of managed consumption was emerging on the pastoral leases, where rationing had longest been customary. After World War II, the Northern Territory Administration had undertaken to sub-sidise pastoralists for the rations they gave to Aboriginal people other than employees and their immediate (nuclear) family. Some lessees ran their properties without a resident camp of rationed Aboriginal people; either they made no use of Aboriginal labour, or they drew it as needed from another station or from a nearby mission or settlement. But other lessees accepted large camps (in the range 50 to 150) most of whose residents were rationed under government subsidy. From the point of view of such pastoralists it was important not only to see that workers did their jobs as directed but also to manage the whole camp's consumption. This was so for a variety of reasons: to preserve stock from depredation, to maintain a continuing labour pool, to keep faith with old friends, to escape the strictures of inspecting Welfare Branch officers. When some of those in the camp became eligible for pensions, some of it received as cash in the hand, more pastoralists were inspired to open stores – not only to make money but, more importantly, to maintain a certain localised social order. Above all, it was imperative to keep alcohol off the lease. A pastoralist could indulge his men's taste for alcohol by taking them to town with him and paying them some cash, but having grog on or near the property would disrupt the camp and undermine the quality and availability of labour.

Pastoralists lost control of this regime of managed consumption in the 1960s. We will not understand the changes in the social relationships on pastoral lands at this time if we think of the cattle station only as an enterprise where wages suddenly rose, through the inclusion of male Aboriginal stockworkers in the Cattle Station Industry (Northern Territory) Award, by December 1968. Through changes in the award and corresponding changes in the welfare system, more cash began to come into the hands of Aboriginal people on pastoral properties. The quantity and kind of goods that cattle station residents could acquire was less and less a matter for the pastoralist and his senior Aboriginal lieutenants to determine.

Such pastoralists complained about this to staff of the Office of Aboriginal Affairs, the Canberra-based engine of policy reform which was set up after the 1967 referendum. In the files of that bureau we can find two perspectives on the station owners' disquiet. Some reforming bureaucrats and academics took the view that, with cash in their pockets, Aboriginal people could break free of the many bush fiefdoms over which missionaries, pastoralists and Welfare Branch staff had for too long held sway; they could go into town and take advantage of the health and education services there, and they could try themselves out on the mainstream labour market. The alternative view was that something valuable was being lost as the pastoralists and those whom they had rationed became alienated from one another: attachments to places and to persons were under threat. The pastoralists' traditions of care, though minimal, had been real, and now they were giving way to the impersonal logic of a reformed labour market.[5]

To draw together the threads of this brief social history of rationing, I want to contrast rationing with the wage relationship.

From comprehensive to selective

Under the ration regimes described above there was a tendency for all adults to be rationed. In a reformed social order in which Aboriginal breadwinners were employed and paid award wages in cash, only a select sub-set of the Aboriginal population would receive wages: male bread-winners. Not all Aboriginal adults could earn wages, but they could get cash according to the category of claimant into which they fell – pensioner, widow, mother, unemployed. So the transition from rations to cash was a move from a system that tended to be comprehensive and relatively undiscriminating to one in which people were selectively assigned to specific categories of entitlement.

From consumption to production

In the rationing regimes that I have described, the focus of authority was to some extent on relations of production (supervision of work gangs, stock camps) but considerable effort was also put into training and into regulating the consumption behaviours of Aboriginal people – by spatial segregation, by retailing strategies, by communal dining rooms, and by the deliberated and graduated substitution of cash for goods. In the wage/welfare regime that succeeded rationing, any continuing super-vision of Aboriginal people's consumption was open to criticism as indefensible paternalism. To move from rations to cash was to access the freedom to consume as one wished. Cash had become a marker of citizenship.

Changing modes of authority

Rationing regimes tended to be local regimes of authority with a familiar, identifiable and accessible figure in charge – the missionary, the pastoralist, the public servant. If these figures lasted long in such positions, it was because they learned, through many informal negotiations with free-sprited men and women, the contextual limits of their dominion. Part of the point of the emancipation of Aboriginal people from rations to cash was to eliminate the possibility of such authorities. In the waged/welfare regime, authority assumed the imper-sonal and distant form that other Australians were used to and accepted. These included the limited authority of employers, of public servants administering welfare entitlements, of police stripped of any special powers over Aboriginal people.

In short, the transition from rations to cash can be described in the terms used by Michel Foucault and Jacques Donzelot – as a change in the rationalities of government, from tutelary/pastoral to liberal/ contractual. Was this progress?

Two critiques of assimilation

The triumph of contractual relations over tutelary ones can be told as a noble story of emancipation and inclusion. Yet there are at least two critical alternatives to such a celebratory account.

One critique draws attention to a specific assimilationist practice – that of taking Aboriginal children from their families of origin and raising them in non-Aboriginal families and institutions. It has been argued (and who could dissent?) that such intervention into the links between generations (often against the express wishes of parents) was far too high a price to pay for whatever benefits the individual then enjoyed. We have begun to hear, and we are likely to hear for some time, of the psychological damage this process of 'emancipation' inflicted. The attempt to repair these severed links is one of the indigenous resistance stories of our times.

However, the story of the 'stolen generations', though emotionally powerful, provides only a limited contradiction of the history of assimilation as emancipation. Limited, because not all who were subject to assimilation were victims of child theft. Many Aboriginal people were under pressure to reform their family life, not give up their kin. The reformation of the family was the dominant mode of assimilation in rural Central Australia. On missions and settlements (but not so much on pastoral properties) Aboriginal adults were not asked to give up their children but to take new kinds of responsibility for them and to share these new responsibilities with teachers, spiritual advisors, nurses and sports coaches.

The second known critique of the emancipation history of assimilation invokes in a more comprehensive way the compromised ideal of Aboriginal solidarity. In this critique some of the relationships that flourished under regimes of managed consumption, relationships condemned as paternalistic and tutelary in the emancipist account, are recalled with nostalgia; their eclipse is regretted. Those local figures of authority who dispensed rations for years are sometimes very well remembered; the bonds between donor and receiver of rations are not necessarily recalled as exploitation. Taking the critical force of such nostalgia seriously makes it possible, indeed necessary, to contrast the narrative of emancipation with another possible narrative of the Central Australian transition from rations to cash: a tale of the crisis and disruption of long-standing and valued associations.

The plausibility of this second critique of assimilation rivals the plausibility of the narrative of emancipation. The plausibility of both narratives points to an ethical ambiguity in the supervision of Central Australian Aboriginal people's lives in the era of assimilation. That is, the regimes of managed consumption can be recalled as situations in which authority, shared informally between rationers and receivers of rations, secured the continuation of an encapsulated Aboriginal social order. With the dissolution of these regimes of managed consumption, who was to succeed to the responsibility of making sure that children grew up with some sense of kin and country? Would Aboriginal adults now have to do this by themselves? In the new, emancipated world of contractual relations, what was the place of traditional Aboriginal authority?

Assimilation policy had postulated that, in the long run, there would be no distinct Aboriginal social order to maintain. That is, according to the social change scenarios that underpinned the convictions of many adherents of 'assimilation' policy, the indigenous social order was in ruins and the fragments were to be eased into the wider society – where, as Australian citizens, they belonged. However, in the midst of the accelerated transition from rations to cash, there emerged critics who queried the speed with which contractual relations were being promoted. Some doubted that Aboriginal people could be conceived as an ensemble of autonomous individuals; the strength of their 'group life' was a well established ethnographic fact. The essential case made by these critics was that the state had a continuing duty to Aboriginal people not only as a series of more or less coping individuals, but also as a series of groups. Aboriginal people were not just individual people in need of 'welfare'; they were a surviving social order.[6]

Alcohol and 'the social'

The policy issue that has most inspired these appeals to the notion of a surviving Aboriginal social order was the regulation of Aboriginal people's access to alcohol. Alcohol became central to both the emancipation and the crisis scenarios, as they were put forward in the midst of the transition from rations to cash.

A number of writers, including Maggie Brady and Basil Sansom, have noted that Aboriginal people have sometimes made an association between citizenship and the right to consume liquor under the same regulations as non-Aboriginal people. I do not doubt that alcohol became the exemplary instance of the rights and wrongs of continued discriminatory laws and regulations, a metonym for 'citizenship'. The argument of emancipation, as some non-Aboriginal people advanced it, also sometimes made this link. In a 1962 booklet published by the Council for Aboriginal Rights, Barry Christophers critically reviewed the legislative restrictions on Northern Territory 'wards'. He dwelt on their low wage minima and on the Director's powers over Aboriginal association and property; he also mentioned the poor standard of their housing and the denial of their languages in education. Christophers introduced the term citizenship only towards the end of this rehearsal of tyranny and discrimination. He related citizenship to the prohibitions on wards' access to alcohol, in the following way:

> Excessive drinking by Aborigines is a symptom of their complaint. The disease itself is lack of citizenship, low wages and colour prejudice. The Aborigine is pauperised and degraded to such an extent that many seek solace in alcohol [...] Morphia is administered to cancer sufferers to kill pain, but no one would blame morphia for the patient's poor health. The cancer in the case of the Aborigine is lack of citizenship, low wages and colour prejudice.[7]

In contrast with this vision of emancipation, in which alcoholism was a symptom of the denial of the attributes of citizenship, Paul Albrecht, practitioner of managed consumption, warned of the perils that had begun to befall Aboriginal people who had attained one of those attributes – full award wages.

> Without a doubt, the most serious of the detrimental consequences of higher wages is that most of the extra money is going into drink – and *not* into better living standards and conditions, and *not* to the families of the men concerned [...] The number of alcoholics is increasing, and by alcoholics is meant anyone whose drinking seriously interferes with his economic, social and family life. The family unit is being weakened. Many women who initially opposed their husband's excessive drinking are themselves becoming excessive drinkers. Immorality and loose living are increasing. These are matters which are undermining the very social fabric of these people.[8]

Albrecht was at pains to deny that he advocated 'keeping Aborigines on the lowest possible wage because of the detrimental effects of higher wages.' Instead he urged governments to give 'back to the Aborigine the authority to deal with his own problems' and to 'rebuild the authority structure among Aboriginal people'.

In this plea, Albrecht anticipated much of what is now advocated by Aboriginal organisations as a proper policy of 'self-determination'. Twenty-five years after Albrecht's paper, Tangentyere Council used the same language (though their consulting anthropologist, Paul Memmott, did not acknowledge Albrecht) in submissions for funding for their 'Social Behaviour Project', an attempt to rebuild Aboriginal authority over the town camps and riverbeds of Alice Springs, sites of alcohol-inspired mayhem.

At the May 1966 symposium in which Paul Albrecht stated his fears, two responses are noteworthy. The first was from Kath Walker (Oodgeroo Noonuccal), at that time Secretary of the Queensland State Council for Advancement of Aborigines and Torres Strait Islanders. She told the conference what had happened when Stradbroke Island people who had been paid less than award wages 'under the Act' began to receive award wages:

> Aborigines did waste their money. It was the equivalent of giving a child of five a 10 pound note and saying: 'right, you can go and do what you like with it.' That child is going to go mad on it too. It is the same thing, at first, but after a while they levelled off. There are some who will never ever make the grade, but the average are not any different from any other society or any other race. You all have your rejects. We are no different. We too are quite well aware of the fact that some of our people will not make the grade and we are not as naive as to think that all of us can be rescued. Some of us will be left behind, as you yourselves have left some of your own people behind.[9]

The second noteworthy comment was made by Mr A T Duncan, an adult educator from the New South Wales Workers' Educational Association. He could not see the relevance of 'Pastor Albrecht's worries' about drinking.

> Although it is a worry it is a social question. In Sydney, where we have one-armed bandits and plenty of grog, there is a big social question there with regard to drinking and gambling but nobody suggests this has any relevance to wage tribunals.[10]

Duncan's confidence that 'social questions' had nothing to do with rights to a fair wage throws into stark relief Albrecht's and Walker's concerns for the social texture of Aboriginal life. Walker's disagreement with Albrecht amounted to saying that, after a period of disorder following the grant of higher wages, only a few people would be badly affected by grog, and a few 'rejects' were an inevitable and tolerable feature of any society. Albrecht's position was that Aboriginal society in the Centre could not afford the number of 'rejects' (we might now say 'dysfunctional individuals and families') that the change in income was likely to throw up.

Both Walker and Albrecht wanted a consideration of Aboriginal people's income rights to take 'the social' into account. For Walker, however, the social fabric was resilient (and the grounds for compassion, perhaps, limited); for Albrecht the social fabric was vulnerable (and his sense of governmental responsibility and compassion unqualified).

In the light of these comparisons in the weighting of 'the social', the difference between the two narratives – emancipation and crisis – can now be stated in different terms.

On the one hand, the theme of emancipation, which drove assimilation policy as a program of legislative and administrative reform, tended to focus on the state's responsibility for guaranteeing the legal and administrative equality of individual Australian citizens. This perspective could class as irrelevant, or portray in optimistic terms, the ways in which the emancipated individuals fitted into their Aboriginal social context. Their formal entitlement was primary, and if there were any social context for the exercise of their rights it was unproblematic; it was only Australian society as a whole.

On the other hand, the theme of crisis treats the indigenous social context as highly problematic and as central to any debate about the state's responsibilities towards Aboriginal people. In this perspective, it was irresponsible to confer rights on Aboriginal people if the manner in which they enjoyed those rights weakened their social fabric. In 1972, Paul Albrecht lamented the perverse synergy between non-Aboriginal and Aboriginal notions of entitlement.

> Our legal system, by guaranteeing to the individual these freedoms which are an integral part of our social system, has made it possible for the Aborigine to flout the rules of his own group, while continuing to live as a part of his group and demanding from it his traditional rights.[11]

Albrecht's argument postulates the continuing co-existence of two social orders, one of which is detrimentally affected by the normal conduct of the other. In this, again, he anticipated the arguments of such exponents of self-determination as Tangentyere Council and its consultants. In 1991, when Paul Memmott made a case in favour of licensing Tyeweretye Social Club, he evoked the two social orders by contrasting their distinct cultures of drinking when alcohol consumption was deregulated:

> The discriminatory aspect of the equal-drinking-rights principle is that the existing norms of Anglo-Celtic drinking [...] are neither culturally suitable nor sufficiently accessible to be put into practice by most Central Australian Aborigines. What was required, in hindsight, was a more cross-culturally sensitive approach to the introduction of drinking to Aboriginal people in order to obtain a less stressful and a closer fit between drinking behaviour and other Aboriginal social norms and values. What was needed was not equal drinking rights but equal rights in choosing a culture of alcohol consumption.[12]

This line of descent between Albrecht and Tangentyere (Memmott) is intriguing. On the one hand, the name Albrecht is easily (if glibly) associated with the 'paternalism' of the Lutheran missionaries from the 1920s to the 1960s; on the other hand, Tangentyere (including its consultants, shaped by the ideals of the Whitlam years) is exemplary of Aboriginal agency bursting the fetters of paternalism. There are individual Aboriginal people whose lives make a link between these two eras/organisations/persons. (I am thinking of Eli Rubuntja, Lutheran protégé and leading member of Tangentyere Council's Liquor Committee.) But even if there were no biographical links such as these, the line of intellectual filiation between Albrecht and Memmott would be clear, for both the Albrecht passage and the Memmott passage are about the same thing: they both strive to evoke an Aboriginal social order which, while continuing to manifest specific, beneficial dynamics, chafes subtly and fundamentally against the enfolding social order of liberal, contractual individualism.

Self-determination and 'the social'

Liberal ideologies of government allow considerable variation in the degree to which 'the social' is understood as problematic. In highlighting the phrase 'the social', I am deliberately invoking the work of writers in the Foucauldian tradition, such as Jacques Donzelot. In *The Policing of Families* Donzelot reviewed two centuries of French theory and practice of government to show the ways in which certain relationships among the population of France became matters for government to investigate and to intervene in. In other words, his book charts the emergence of 'the social' as an object of government. The salience of 'the social' is historically contingent, and different governmental regimes highlight as problematic different sets of relationships among the governed populace. Governmental regimes also differ in their blendings of tutelary and contractual rationalities of government. My outline of the transition from rations to cash, and of some policy intellectuals' accounts of the problems of this transition, is intended to show the emergence of 'Aboriginal society' as an object of governments' sympathetic reflection and optimistic action. The new policy of self-determination announced in the early 1970s committed governments to the intellectual production of accounts of that social order, its authorities and reproductive strategies.

At this point, it is possible to return to the theme of responsibility. I suggested in my introduction that when Australian governments attribute to indigenous Australians a capacity for self-determination they assume that the indigenous Australian citizen is in some way engaged in the collective task of reproducing the remnant indigenous social order. This assumption is not usually articulated, but I have no doubt that it is implicit in any genuine commitment by governments to indigenous self-determination. Such a commitment by government includes trying to frame public policies so that government action enhances, rather than vitiates, the indigenous capacity for collective self-determination. However, it remains unclear how governments and indigenous people 'share' (that may not be the right word) the responsibilities of reproducing that capacity.

In the remainder of this chapter, I give two vignettes of the difficulties of working out a mutually satisfactory and effective articulation of government and indigenous efforts towards indigenous self-determination.

A home for old *Anangu*

Do Aboriginal people of the Western Desert have the resources to look after their old people properly? The Ngaanyatjarra, Pitjantjatjara and Yankunytjara (NPY) Women's Council has been dubious that they have, but unsure about the kind of help to ask for. The Women's Council commissioned research.

Anthropologist Susan Woenne Green and her collaborators (Mantatjara Wilson, Sandra Lewis, Tjikalyi Colin, Jorna Newberry, and Valeri Foster) first tried to document what it means to *Anangu* ('Pitjantjatjara people') to look after old people 'properly'. This led them to formulate a criterion for classifying old people as 'at risk'.

> 'At risk' refers not only to the possibility of dying but also to the possibility that the person might soon be in circumstances which will force a temporary or permanent *removal* from community, family and country to a nursing home, quite possibly without their agreement or against their wishes.[13]

They documented old people's distress at being away from their homelands and country in the final period of their lives. They found that 'properly' refers not only to place but also to the involvement of those family whom the old person deems to have a duty of care. 'Properly' refers also to *waru* (fire and firewood). *Waru* is metonymic: it stands for a complex of things of which it is but one part, the social relationships and activities of a hearth.

Place, family and *waru* – these are the ingredients of an old age lived within nurturant tradition. Yet Green and co. were determined to discourage any sentimental assumptions about the contemporary adequacy of 'Aboriginal traditional way'. Too many old people, they argued, have endured neglect because of a misplaced confidence among social planners and indigenous leaders that traditions of nurturance are strong enough to meet old people's needs. The NPY report makes a case for new, community based institutions to buttress the traditions of care. From the point of view of my argument in this chapter, it is important that Green and co. not only define and advocate old people's needs, but that they also imply the emerging salience of 'community' as a category of both administrative discourse and Aboriginal governance.

The NPY researchers had a chance to observe an experiment in institutionalising new forms of care for old people. At Docker River a cluster of serviced pensioner houses began to provide a new home for several old folk in April 1993. ATSIC funding for the four staff soon ran out, but from this brief experience there flowed a discussion about whether such care was 'culturally appropriate'. Those who thought it inappropriate worried that the cluster of twelve units looked like a town based residential facility. They protested that the residents should not be lumped in together: they should be 'at home', in nearby camps, being looked after by their 'family'. Green and co. were not persuaded by this critique. In their view, the Docker River facility's appearance was irrelevant; the important thing was that it enabled families to *limit* their involvement in caring for old people. Each caring family could thus develop a caring regime that it could sustain. That way, the old people ceased to be 'at risk' (of being sent to town).

Reporting discussion among *Anangu*, the authors revealed a prescriptive culture. That is, people referred to older ways as better than now, and they put forward a duty of care, by young for old, which was continuous with the duty of care by which older people had 'grown up' the young. Inter-generational responsibilities are extolled and exhorted, even if they are not always acted upon. One respect in which older ways were said to be better was that contemporary housing tends to nucleate families, making it less likely that older folk will camp together. People also compared store food unfavourably with 'bush' food. These norms and evaluative contrasts are the cultural basis for contemporary *Anangu* standards of care, but such standards, argued the NPY report, were not being met in sustainable programs: housing, nutrition, transport (for people and for goods such as *waru*), laundry facilities, accessible toilet/shower/laundry, cheque-cashing and money management. This is a failure of policy, the authors insisted, thus invoking a seamless blend of responsibilities among politicians, government officials and *Anangu*.

This lapse in joint responsibilities has had some interesting ideological bases common to government officials and politically articulate Aboriginal people. The NPY report was implicitly a challenge to some versions of the arguments of the Healthy Aboriginal Life Team (HALT) whose interventions into petrol sniffing in this region in the late 1980s extolled the nurturant capacities of *walytja* (kin) and viewed with scepticism the building up of externally funded systems of social support. The popularity of the HALT view in government had much to do with its fiscal implications. Its potency drew also on the widely felt and legitimate need, among both Aboriginal and non-Aboriginal people, to affirm the capacities of Aboriginal people for self-determination and to question any residual assimilationism implicit in programs of social support.

More explicitly, the NPY report dealt with ideological problems among *Anangu* themselves. Old *Anangu* are not a powerful constituency, partly because they view their circumstances as personal misfortune, and also because of the persistence of the assumption (among *Anangu* and others) that relieving such misfortune is the responsibility of family rather than community. Old people are also victims of their own nurturant outlook. For example, they have been easily induced to place their own need for housing behind that of younger folk for whom they have a duty of care. The Docker River initiative began to lift old people out of this political trough. Staff of the facility became advocates of the poorly mobilised pensioner constituency. Yet these new advocates did not necessarily usurp a political capacity that belonged to others, as a 'zero-sum' view of power (all too common in accounts of colonialism) might have it. The facility, a publicly subsidised communal effort, made it easier for families to exercise their responsibilities, to keep their old people with them; it therefore reinforced the normative fiction that it is towards family that old people properly turn for help. It also freed, for more concentrated political effort, those 'family' who were most practically concerned with the needs of the old folk.

The NPY report vividly forces our attention to be focused on a possibility that is in danger of being overlooked: a communal facility may complement and enhance 'family', not detract from it. It has become a cliché of political critique to question the cultural appropriateness of remote indigenous communities, to characterise them as the unwanted residue of the era of assimilation, an administrative imposition on the indigenous order of country based kinship. The NPY report tries to subvert such easy antinomies between old and new, imposed and authentic, institutions. It makes a case for the development of externally funded community facilities, not in a spirit of capitulation to the attrition of tradition, but out of a researched conviction that communal facilities are now essential to *livable* traditions. The report therefore addresses directly the central issue of self-determination that I have been highlighting in this chapter: the appropriate articulation of the responsibility of indigenous people to reproduce their social order with the responsibility of governments to assist them.

The rights of 'communities'

The Commonwealth Race Discrimination Commissioner's 1995 *Alcohol Report* has contributed to our understanding of the issue of indigenous responsibility by reminding us that indigenous citizenship is, in some circumstances, a corporate citizenship.[14]

The Race Discrimination Commissioner was asked in 1990 to look into the licensing of liquor outlets in Central Australia. The Pitjantjatjara

Council was critical of what they saw as the Northern Territory Liquor Commission's indulgent treatment of the Curtin Springs licensee. Unlike the licensees of Erldunda and Mt Ebenezer roadhouses, the Curtin Springs licensee had resisted Pitjantjatjara Council proposals that he regulate himself by limiting his sales to *Anangu*, the Aboriginal people living at Imanpa, Mutitjulu and other places within a car ride of Curtin Springs.

According to the Race Discrimination Commissioner, Zita Antonios, the framework of Commonwealth laws against discrimination was providing the Northern Territory Government and resistant licensees with an excuse to reject such self-regulation: limiting supplies to local Aboriginal people and writing such limitations into licence conditions would arguably breach the Commonwealth's Racial Discrimination Act (RDA). Zita Antonios devoted much of her report to evaluating this reason for caution. She admitted that the RDA could be clearer about what is meant by 'discrimination'. She criticised the Act for being insufficiently open to Aboriginal people's collective demands for 'discriminatory' treatment which they think will be good for them. She wrote that she was prepared to certify some grog trading agreements as 'nondiscriminatory', but she could not guarantee that a court would agree with her opinion. The Commissioner therefore undertook to urge amendments to the RDA to give more scope for discriminatory actions sought by groups of Aboriginal people.

In short, the Race Discrimination Commissioner showed herself to be a firm advocate of the recognition of indigenous Australians' 'group rights'. Though High Court judges have on occasions supported notions of 'group rights', statute lags behind them. The RDA is framed to protect the individual from discrimination. Apart from allowing that there can be temporary special measures to enable Aboriginal people to 'catch up' with non-Aboriginal people, the RDA offers little to Aboriginal people as a series of collectivities (for example, the Pitjantjatjara or the Mutitjulu community) who seek to be dealt with distinctively. In this respect, the RDA is a legacy of assimilation times, ill-suited to Aboriginal self-determination, argued the Race Discrimination Commissioner.

Zita Antonios's report is a thoughtful attempt to spell out the implications of the right of collective indigenous self-determination in a matter of public policy and law that is of fundamental importance to governing the people of Central Australia: the regulation of access to alcohol. It is clear from her approach that, if group rights are to be taken seriously in the law, there must be political means to represent groups. 'The wishes of a community may be difficult to determine', she concedes. However, the Commissioner's practice in this report was to accept the Pitjantjatjara Council's representations of the wishes of *Anangu* living along the Lasseter Highway. That is, she was persuaded by the Council that the inadequate regulation of liquor trading detracts substantially from *Anangu* enjoyment of their human rights. Her critique of the adverse circumstances facing *Anangu* rested on her acceptance of the Pitjantjatjara Council's representations of its clients as a group.

The notion of group rights complicates the governmental rationality that resulted from the transition from rations to cash – a contractual rationality. In the assimilationist conception of the emergent contractual relations, the individual was the sovereign party. The liberalism of assimilation gave pride of place to the right of the individual, without asking which community and tradition that individual belonged to. The Race Discrimination Commissioner's foreshadowed changes to the RDA (which are not assured of political acceptance) would seek to renovate that contractualism by reconciling it with the right of collective indigenous self-determination – creating the statutory possibility of a degree of group sovereignty. Groups could demand differential treatment in which all their members were implicated.

However, group rights have only as much integrity as the political organisations that represent group interests. If there is no representation of the Pitjantjatjara interest, then there is little or no political effect in the notion of their group right. In this sense, the Race Commissioner's report was a political triumph for the Pitjantjatjara Council. By the same token, the existence of the Pitjantjatjara Council (and bodies like it in other regions) would seem to be an essential condition of the Race Discrimination Commissioner's continuing ability to refer to the rights and needs of groups.

If indigenous citizenship is, in some circumstances, corporate, 'responsibility' becomes a more complex notion. On the one hand indigenous corporations have a responsibility to give a defensible account of the views and interests of their constituents; at the same time, those constituents may or may not agree that, as individuals, they have obligations to the corporation that speaks for them. Indigenous collectivity is a political scene with its own internal dynamics and tensions, its own philosophical issues of liberty and obligation.

Conclusion

Much of this chapter has been an historical narrative, or rather contrasting narratives of the transition from rations to cash, from the paternalism of managed consumption to the opportunities and tasks of self-determination. The point of this history has been to question whether it is really so easy to define 'self-determination' by contrasting it with paternalism. In some parts of Australia, such as Central Australia, the effort to preserve an indigenous social order – as an enclave within the wider Australian nation – began with government policies of protection in the first years of the twentieth century. As rationing became more systematic, protection gave way to a more tutelary policy of assimilation, a policy goal enunciated around 1950. The practice of colonial rule, in both these eras of government policy, centred on rationing regimes – social forms in which the authorities and responsibilities of the state and indigenous leaders co-existed and even, in some ways, were intertwined. Assimilation envisaged a future in which the forms of indigenous authority would continue their irreversible decline. But the instruments of assimilation were relatively weak and internally contradictory. The practice of assimilation conferred rights more easily than it engineered new social forms. The renunciation of assimilation in the 1970s and the enunciation of a new policy, self-determination, gave new vigour and unprecedented sanction to the traditional and revised forms of indigenous collective action.

The outcomes of this sequence of policies are undoubtedly progressive. Indigenous citizenship entitlements have been redefined (land rights) and extended (full access to welfare benefits), and indigenous individuals may assert their sovereignty vis à vis the state and other citizens in ways that were once denied them. The rights of indigenous people as a people are to some extent actualised in institutions – corporations, associations and statutory representative bodies – that are subsidised by governments. These institutions substantiate the supra-individual sovereignties solicited under the policy of self-determination. Through such mechanisms the reproduction of an indigenous social order is politically, legally and financially supported. Contemporary formations of indigenous authority are thus articulated with the processes of the state. The terms of this articulation are various, and the negotiation of these terms is the focus of much political effort, including political disputes among indigenous people themselves.[15] Indigenous citizenship is an interplay of their entitlement to state support with the mingled responsibilities of indigenous people and government to reproduce the collective forms of indigenous life.

Notes

1 Kymlicka and Norman 1994: 361.
2 Kymlicka and Norman 1994: 360.
3 See P Hasluck's restatement of this fundamental (to him) thesis (1988).
4 Busbridge (comment during discussion) 1966: 193.
5 See the ambivalent view of H C Coombs (1978: 10): 'While the record of the white–black relationship in the cattle industry was rich in examples of exploitation, brutality and crime, of which Aboriginal people were

overwhelmingly the victims, there was also evidence that at its best the pastoralist–Aboriginal relationship came close to being one of mutually understood obligations and interdependence. It was therefore comprehensible and often acceptable to many Aboriginal groups involved in it. Furthermore its claims on those groups were intermittent and flexible, allowing generally the continuance of much of the content of their traditional life. The "equal wage" decision had had the effect therefore of replacing an ill defined (but usually understood) obligation on the pastoralist to provide modest support for a whole Aboriginal group in return for the labour of a few, with a precise and larger, but limited, obligation towards the individuals actually employed.'

6 I have described the confrontation between Sir Paul Hasluck's individualist liberalism and the Durkheimian liberalism of AP Elkin, Ronald and Catherine Berndt, and T G H Strehlow in Rowse 1997.

7 Christophers 1962: 36.

8 Albrecht 1966: 182.

9 Walker (in discussion) 1966: 186.

10 Duncan 1966: 188.

11 Albrecht 1974: 37.

12 P Memmott 'Proof of Evidence'. Unpublished paper, Tyeweretye Social Club and Tangentyere Council Liquor Committee, May 1991: 7–9.

13 Woenne-Green (and others) 1995: 35.

14 Race Discrimination Commissioner 1995.

15 This chapter has not addressed the issue of the difficulties that Aboriginal people themselves now face in reproducing what they consider to be the essential features of their social order. This is a subject too big to be accommodated in an aside from my argument. Ian Keen conveys a sense of social reproduction as endogenous political struggle in his essay 'On Aboriginal governance' (Keen 1989).

References

Albrecht, P. G. E. 1966. The effects of raising Aboriginal wages on Aborigines. In *Aborigines in the Economy*, eds I. Sharp and C. M. Tatz. Brisbane: Jacaranda Press, pp. 180–93.

Albrecht, P. G. E. 1974. The social and psychological reasons for the alcohol problem among Aborigines. In *Better Health for Aborigines?* eds B. Hetzel et al. St Lucia: University of Queensland Press, pp. 36–41.

Busbridge, D. L. 1966. In *Aborigines in the Economy*, eds. I. Sharp and C. M. Tatz. Brisbane: Jacaranda Press, pp. 192–3.

Coombs, H. C. 1978. *Kulinma*. Canberra: Australian National University Press.

Christophers, B. 1962. The Northern Territory. In *The Struggle for Dignity*, ed. W. M. Murray. Melbourne: Council for Aboriginal Rights, pp. 27–37.

Duncan, A. T. 1966. Discussion. In *Aborigines in the Economy*, eds I. Sharp and C. M. Tatz. Brisbane: Jacaranda Press, p. 188.

Hasluck, P. 1988. *Shades of Darkness*. Melbourne: Melbourne University Press.

Keen, I. 1989. On Aboriginal governance. In *Emergent Inequalities in Aboriginal Australia*, ed. J. C. Altman. Sydney: University of Sydney, Oceania Monographs No. 38, pp. 17–42.

Kymlicka, W. and Norman, W. 1994. Return of the citizen: a survey of recent work on citizenship theory. *Ethics* 104 (2): 352–81.

Race Discrimination Commissioner. 1995. *Alcohol Report.* Canberra: Australian Government Publishing Service.

Rowse, T. 1977. The modesty of the state: Hasluck and the anthropological critics of assimilation. In *Paul Hasluck in Australian History,* eds C. Stannage, K. Saunders and R. Nile. Brisbane: University of Queensland Press.

Walker, K. 1966. Discussion. In *Aborigines in the Economy,* eds I. Sharp and C. M. Tatz. Brisbane: Jacaranda Press, pp. 184–87.

Woenne-Green, S. (et al.) 1995. *'They Might Have to Drag Me Like a Bullock': the Tjilpi Pampa Tjutaku Project.* Alice Springs: Ngaanyatjarra Pitjantjatjara Yankunytjatjara Women's Council Aboriginal Corporation.

CHAPTER 5

Welfare Colonialism and Citizenship: Politics, Economics and Agency

Nicolas Peterson

Although the social rights of citizenship lie at the heart of the state's relationship with most Aboriginal people, nowhere are they more important than in the Aboriginal communities of remote Australia. Yet despite full citizenship, the expenditure of much money and effort and twenty-five years of benign government policies, these entitlements and policies have had disproportionately little effect on the material circumstances of the people in such communities. Their life circumstances are a shock to anyone seeing them for the first time; and for those familiar with them, the problems can seem intractable. They raise the question as to why the granting of citizenship has had so little effect.

One concept that both addresses this problem directly and proposes an explanation is that of welfare colonialism. The central proposition of welfare colonialism is that the granting of the social rights of citizenship to indigenous people in first world nation–states is, unintentionally, as debilitating as it is beneficial because of the social and political dependencies it creates.

I want to argue that this view is only a first step in developing an understanding of the problems of social policy in relation to remote Aboriginal citizens and that, if the analysis is to be taken further, it has to incorporate a more situated and complex account of the conjunction, compatibilities and consequences of the two ways of life for each other. In particular, those using a welfare colonialism framework tend to privilege the political to the neglect of the economic and cultural.[1] Obvious and long-standing social injustice, discrimination and inequality create fertile and productive grounds for analyses founded in political economy but such analyses tend to ignore other more difficult issues. They glide over some of the important dilemmas and paradoxes of the situation and often ignore the subtlety of relations of dependency, paralleling the tendency in much welfare state thinking to overlook the explanations for problematic phenomena.[2]

Viewing the situation of remote communities through the lens of citizenship helps sharpen the focus on the issue of wellbeing because it brings theoretical and policy issues into the same frame. Concentrating on a purely theoretical analysis makes it easier either to avoid practical issues or to take an unhelpfully utopian stance in which the analyst occupies the moral high ground, placing more pragmatic analysts in a compromised position that is difficult to defend. On the other hand, if an analyst concentrates on the policy issues alone, they can become overly constrained by existing structures and assumptions and can be seen to be selling people short. Analysts who are not indigenous are quickly charged with being neo-colonialist, paternalistic or assimilationist. And while the utopian analysts frequently overshoot the mark of the possible in their policy prescriptions, the policy oriented often undershoot.

I will begin with a consideration of welfare colonialism and a more situated account of the impact of social entitlements in remote areas. Through this I will argue that many Aboriginal people in these communities retained a relative independence from the state at a local level until they started to receive the full suite of social entitlements. The achievement of full social rights at the end of the 1970s marked a substantive threat to the sources of their relative autonomy, bringing to the fore certain key dilemmas related to citizenship. A policy perspective on these dilemmas makes it necessary to recognise the way in which certain central matters are banished from most analyses although they lie at the heart of many of the difficulties people face in achieving the wellbeing that Australian citizens have the right to expect.

Welfare colonialism

Robert Paine coined the term 'welfare colonialism' in 1977 to describe the situation in the Canadian north as it was during the research for a project on 'Identity and Modernity in the East Arctic (1968–1972)'. This term has been taken up by several Australian authors, notably Jeremy Beckett, who has used it to illuminate his discussion of the contemporary situation in the Torres Strait and Australia more generally.[3]

Beckett explicates the concept:

> Juxtaposing terms which connote citizenship (welfare) and its denial (colonialism), [. . . Paine] suggests a policy that is contradictory and unstable. Historically continuous with classic colonialism, it is 'solicitous rather than exploitative, and liberal rather than repressive' ([Paine] 1977: 3); yet it is still 'the colonizers who make the decisions that control the future of the

colonized' and 'the decisions are made (ambiguously) on behalf of the colonized, and yet in the name of the colonizers' culture (and of their political, administrative and economic priorities)' (1977: 43) [While . . .] it is the colonizers who finally make the decisions, they can no longer impose them arbitrarily. Yet another contradictory feature of welfare colonialism is its need to secure the assent of its subjects as evidence of their political enfranchisement.[4]

The term 'welfare colonialism' appeals in part because it suggests a contradiction between reaping the benefits of being a citizen and being disempowered by those benefits, and in part because it appears to account for the lack of policy effectiveness and the slow improvement in well-being in many remote areas. While these are useful insights they leave some issues unresolved: whether it is still the colonisers who make the decisions; what are the economic aspects of the relationship; and where indigenous agency fits in.

Is welfare colonialism really colonial?

The issue here is whether it is appropriate, for analytical purposes, to describe as colonial the relationship between Aboriginal people and the State in parts of remote Australia since the post-World War II development of the welfare state, or whether to do so is simply a rhetorical and political trope.[5]

In the context of his own usage Beckett defines colonialism in political terms to refer to that aspect of 'Western expansion whereby new peoples are incorporated into a conquering state'.[6] The problem is, in his view, that in attempting to extend citizenship to indigenous people the liberal democratic welfare state falls foul of not only the dependencies and social relations created by the colonial state but also its own efforts, giving rise to welfare colonialism. The contradiction is that the state is so inextricably bound up with trying to improve Aboriginal well-being that it cannot easily disengage, so 'that the state becomes an integral part of the problem it is supposed to be solving'.[7]

Welfare colonialism thus draws together notions of welfare dependency, neo-colonialism, citizenship and self-determination. The un-doubted intellectual mileage that Beckett and others have obtained from this concept has come from the recognition it gives to the importance of understanding the role of the state in the lives of indigenous people. This recognition, which was late in coming to anthropology generally, was a crucial step forward in the analysis and theorisation of the situation of Aboriginal and Torres Strait Island people in contemporary Australia.[8] It is marked in Beckett's own work by a switch away from the more economically oriented model of internal colonialism which did not enable him to make adequate sense of the level of government intervention in the lives of the Islanders.[9]

However, while drawing attention to the state was and is a crucial step forward, welfare colonialism does not provide an adequate analysis of why the state should want to create or perpetuate welfare dependency, nor does it account for active indigenous participation in creating or perpetuating that welfare dependency.

Charles Rowley's original application of the term 'colonial Australia' for the north was stimulating and productive at the time.[10] However, the term was used only in a low level descriptive way to refer to a number of similarities in the social relations between the indigenous and settler populations there and those of earlier phases of European settlement in places like Papua New Guinea.[11] It is significant that he placed colonial in inverted commas, implying some qualification of the usage and that he speaks of the Torres Strait as being an enclave with the ability to delineate the special features of colonial impacts on foragers.[12]

He thus seems to recognise that the purely negative economic connotations usually associated with raw colonial intentions do not apply equally or in any straightforward way across Australia.[13] Presumably it is in recognition of this that Beckett chose a political definition of colonialism that emphasised the asymmetries of power and the loss of rights.

Generally speaking the core motivations for colonisation have been to secure resources, land, labour, and (later) markets, to fuel metropolitan economies. Achieving these goals usually entailed military action and the imposition of governmental regimes. It has long been evident that colonial motivations and capitalist practice did not penetrate the colonised regions evenly and that in some places people remained relatively isolated and left to their own devices to a greater or lesser degree. In Australia such areas would include Arnhem Land, Central Australia, the Kimberley, Cape York and the Torres Strait. In parts of these regions land, labour and resources were not systematically appropriated or commoditised until after World War II and the main agents of the colonial culture were missionaries and pastoralists. The manifestation of the state and its motivations for being in these areas was thus rather different from the normal economically extractive one.

Of course equating colonialism only with the immediately extractive and economic aspect of European activity underplays political and other motivations. The Australian colonial state could have been concerned with a threat to its existence from the indigenous people; however, this has never been a major issue in these regions, nor (for most of them) can an argument about a reserve army of labour be sustained.[14]

A motivation that does receive some support is that the state involved itself with these enclaves to avoid international criticism. While this is certainly a feature of the Australian situation which can be traced back at least to the League of Nations mandate in Papua New Guinea, it was of limited impact until after World War II.[15] Yet the involvement with many Aboriginal people in remote Australia began before the war, with a more philanthropic motivation. Such benign motivations have received little recognition because of what is perceived to be the morally problematic nature of missionary and colonial activity and the focus on 'self-interest' that became entrenched with the materialist turn in the social sciences and the prominence of liberal market theorists. International interest in the Aboriginal situation in recent times has usually been focused on legal and social rights, rather than on political.[16]

Welfare colonialism does, however, encompass more philanthropic or benign motivations for involvement with remote indigenous people, describing them as solicitous rather than exploitative and liberal rather than repressive. But by doing so it largely vitiates the use of the term 'colonial' and tends to overlook the significance of the economic in people's everyday lives, possibly because the economic analysis it provides is seen as fairly transparent.[17]

At best, of course, the situation of indigenous people in Australia today is only an internal decolonisation:[18] even where there are no overt asymmetries of power, mental structures and individual habits may reproduce asymmetrical relations in a more subtle and insidious way. The problem being addressed here, then, is whether these residual aspects of colonialism account for the people's life situation day to day.

The 'welfare' in 'welfare colonialism'

Beckett indicates that welfare in the context of colonialism connotes the social rights of citizenship. As he defines it, welfare colonialism, as manifested in Australian government policy, is where the government supports remote indigenous communities without considering their long-term economic viability, although the ultimate intention is to secure their integration into Australian society.[19] In this process he sees a movement from relations of underdevelopment to the incorporation of indigenous people into the class system. Following T H Marshall he sees citizenship rights as ameliorating class competition:

> While citizenship initially arises as an ideological response to class divisions, it can subsequently spread into colonial enclaves for which it is not intended. Under certain conditions, the extension of citizenship rights to indigenous minorities becomes a moral and political issue for the society at large and even internationally. Welfare colonialism is as much a matter of politics and ideology as of economics.[20]

While this is useful, the term 'welfare colonialism' tends to identify welfare with the welfare state, ignoring the history of philanthropic ministering to Aboriginal people before the appearance of such a state and the different moral economies. It neglects the distinction between welfare provided to prepare people for citizenship and that derived from a theory of citizenship, and makes the questionable assumption that welfare dependency, a seemingly unproblematic and undifferentiated condition, necessarily describes the status of all Aboriginal citizens. Also, because of the political economy orientation of welfare colonialism, the focus is on the delivery of entitlements rather than on their reception and use. Finally, welfare colonialism has never really benefited from the extensive theoretical writings on welfare and the clarity they could bring to some of the issues involved.

A brief history of welfare in remote communities

To illustrate how the historical conjuncture of a variety of factors, including Aboriginal agency, prevented a full-blown welfare dependency until the late 1970s in some remote communities, despite fifty years of mostly indirect involvement with the state, I take the example of the Arnhem Land Trust area. This history will expose the principal weaknesses of the welfare colonial analysis and help locate some of the central factors affecting well-being.

Although the region has a complex history, the portion to the east of Oenpelli remained an almost pre-colonial Aboriginal domain until World War II. There were of course pre-colonial relations with the Macassans, two short and unsuccessful attempts to establish a pastoral station on the west side of the Arafura Swamp, at least a couple of prospecting expeditions (one of which killed a number of people), and two missions, one established in 1916 and the other in 1923 on near-shore islands.

Arnhem Land was created as an Aboriginal reserve in 1931 as a result of a complex of pressures, none of which included the core colonial motivations. It grew directly out of the Coniston massacres in Central Australia in 1928, concerns over the growth of the population of Aboriginal people of mixed descent, the negative impact that contact with Europeans was perceived to have on Aboriginal people who were leading an independent life and the move to establish a black state.[21] All but authorised persons, mainly missionaries, were excluded. Up until the end of World War II a third or so of the population continued a largely self-supporting life in the bush, although almost all of them had had contact with outsiders in one form or another, particularly along the coast.

At 95,828 square kilometres the reserve was three times the size of Belgium and larger than Scotland and Northern Ireland together but had a population of only 3000 or so Aboriginal people at the time of its establishment (it has less than 10,000 now).[22]

The purpose at the beginning was explicitly not to draw the people away unnecessarily from their independent life, but to build relations with them and to relieve sickness and distress while keeping exploitative non-Aboriginal people out of the area.[23] Missionaries were supported in the role of mediating between Aboriginal people and the outside world because the communities they established could be run more cheaply than by government, and missionaries were seen as better equipped to run charitable institutions.[24] Aboriginal people were free to move between what was in effect the status of full citizens of an Aboriginal society by remaining in the bush and the status of wards in Australian society. Many chose to move to the missions, attracted by a less arduous life, commodities, services and protection from feuding.[25]

The two different social and moral regimes under which the people of Arnhem Land could live were closer to each other in the early period than they were to be during the assimilation period (c1951 to c1971). There was some loss of autonomy for Aboriginal people in the missions. People other than the young, elderly and others in need of assistance had to work for any supplies received from the missions: this support was in kind. The limited and more personal moral universe of the bush, where allegiance was primarily to a network of close kin, was replaced with a broader universe in which, ideally, there was commitment to the values of an impersonal collectivity.

Several features of mission life were important. There was a huge social gap (domain separation) between the Aboriginal and non-Aboriginal people. They lived apart, they spoke different languages and they interacted in formal settings only.[26] Further, the missions were isolated from the rest of Australia and were run on a shoe string. This insulated the Aboriginal people of Arnhem Land, like those at Hermannsburg (see Chapter 4), from a substantial consumer dependency and any extensive involvement in the cash economy.[27] Despite this clear separation, the moral, if not the legal and political, constitution of the model persona of the dominant society must have been evident through the sermons, the disciplines of work and school and the punishments meted out by the missionaries.

Although the welfare state emerged with the end of the war, the Aboriginal communities of remote Australia remained isolated from the rest of the community until around 1968. In that year the decision was taken that Aboriginal people in these communities would receive social security directly in cash rather than such monies being paid to the mission and government superintendents of the communities on their behalf. This did not instantly turn Aboriginal people in remote Australia into welfare dependants. Within the general framework of the mission regime, which provided a daily structure of work, there remained ample room for an Aboriginal domain in which indigenous cultural agendas could be pursued largely without interference or today's distractions. An active religious life, considerable supplementary hunting and gathering, the continued existence of strong institutional structures, the regulation of relations with outsiders and no television or easy access to alcohol supported the continued existence of a strongly separate Aboriginal domain.[28] Secondly, access to consumer goods remained constrained, and frugal living conditions continued to prevail.[29]

With the election of the Labor Government in 1972 it became a matter of policy that Aboriginal people would receive the full array of social entitlements of an Australian citizen even though these were tied to a quite different social, economic and political structure. The effect in aggregate was that incomes rose overall in real terms during the 1970s as people gained access first to award wages and then to unemployment benefit from 1977 onwards.[30] It was in *aggregate* because the effect of award wages in the communities was to put two-thirds of the people out of work, just as the introduction of award wages in the pastoral industry did in the mid-1960s.[31] With the payment of unemployment benefit, tellingly referred to by Aboriginal people as 'sit-down money', the levels of income in remote communities were raised dramatically. Because of the economic isolation of remote communities, the levels of income provided as social welfare to unemployed non-Aboriginal Australians, which kept them in impoverished circumstances, were quite reasonable for people who were outside the labour market and urban areas.[32]

The strong communitarian theme that has underwritten and continues to underwrite Aboriginal social policy formation in recognition of the social, economic and political differences between the two ways of life came to the fore in this period.[33] Access to unemployment funds was widely accepted as placing too much money in Aboriginal hands in the sense that it was thought that it would aggravate social problems and be disruptive.[34] As a result the CDEP scheme was developed whereby people would work for the dole, a situation that could be justified in many remote communities because people could not meet the usual tests associated with gaining access to unemployment payments (see Chapter 7).

The history of changing Aboriginal consumption patterns has not been well documented but within a year or two of these higher incomes certain changes were obvious as people's requirements rose to absorb the new wealth. Involvement with cars and alcohol increased dramatically, standards of dress changed and the percentage of income spent on food almost certainly dropped.[35]

Another feature of these changes, brought in as a consequence of Labor's policies, was the rapid secularisation of the remote mission communities. Over the space of a few years the missionaries withdrew from their role of staffing and managing the institutional communities in remote Australia to a small pastoral care role.[36]

In what was seen as a major step in internal decolonisation, super-intendents of the remote communities were abolished to be replaced by community advisors whose role was to advise the Aboriginal councils that took on the responsibility and authority for running the communities. While these new structures can easily be construed as neo-colonial because their role and structure was largely defined to serve the state's purposes, it is unhelpful to do so. As the assimilation, main-streaming and self-determination policies all make clear in their diverse ways, the government was keen to extract itself from any special relationship with the indigenous people. While assimilation and main-streaming in particular are seen as negative and are therefore easily labelled with the generalised pejorative of 'neo-colonial' or its contemporary substitutes, such as 'racist' or 'genocidal', such descriptions do not accurately reflect the intentions of these policies.

The radical change in the nature of life in remote communities that took place between 1968 and 1977 has not been adequately regis-tered or examined. During this period the Aboriginal communities of remote Australia went from closed institutionalised and largely mission run communities to self-governing secular towns. At the same time a process of rapid integration into a cash economy took place, with marked increases in discretionary incomes. The result was a dramatic shift in the nature, structure and moral economy of these Aboriginal com-munities. The Christian ethos that had pervaded most of them and provided a clear rationale for the introduced way of life and general conduct within it weakened dramatically, to be replaced by an un-articulated secular humanism; the structure given to daily life by em-ployment for all those who wanted it disappeared for the great majority; attendance at school declined to well under half in most places; access to alcohol greatly increased and with it came a noticeable rise in social turbulence; domestic violence, child abuse, petrol sniffing and delinquency all became major problems for the first time;[37] and the imposed nature and origins of many communities caused small groups of kin to take up the opportunity to establish outstations away from the main townships while still depending on them as a service centre. In short the changes provoked a transformation with which indigenous and non-indigenous Australians are still coming to terms.

The dilemmas of double citizenship

This history has one clear implication for the theory of welfare colonialism: subsuming economy under politics by concentrating on inequality and powerlessness obliterates the immediate daily reality of Aboriginal people's lives and fails to acknowledge the difficulties and dilemmas created in the articulation of two divergent cultural systems.

Aboriginal people are faced with a 'double citizenship' rather than a dual citizenship or being citizens-plus.[38] Double citizenship differs from dual citizenship in that the two memberships fall within the same political jurisdiction and so confront indigenous people daily with the dilemmas of this articulation. The theory of welfare colonialism fails to provide adequate theoretical grounds for the understanding and form-ulation of beneficial policies in this kind of complex social environment because it brackets Aboriginal culture. Because it focuses only on structural relations it refuses the possibility that some, or indeed any, aspects of cultural practice may be problematic in the contemporary situation.

A case in point is Tim Rowse's argument that the nomination of a list of 'cultural obstacles' (sic) to policy effectiveness by the bureaucracy, 'performs a certain ideological function within the administrative imagination: it prevents or delays the recognition and validation of Aboriginal people's own purposes and interests and of their loose and temporary forms of collective action – their tendency to dis-aggregation'.[39] From the moral high ground, a utopian vision effortlessly overlooks mundane economic policy practicalities: is there to be no limit to the subvention of Aboriginal desires? Of course, subsuming economics within politics is partly grounded in the realistic political analysis that there are limits to the economic benefits that the standard social rights of citizenship can deliver to Aboriginal people but such an analysis is more appropriate for the political arena than it is for the social analytic. While this difficulty is fairly transparent it is linked to one that is more opaque.

This relates to cultural maintenance and lies closer to the heart of the problems surrounding the achievement of well-being. Cultural main-tenance is unequivocally endorsed by policy and Aboriginal people at large, with considerable resources being allocated to it. The policy goals appear to assume that secular assimilation is possible. That is to say that material circumstances can be substantially improved while leaving cultural heritage unchallenged. An indigenous culture injected with affluence yet remaining unchanged has, however, to be understood in ideological and political terms: it is a touchstone for the culture of resistance, a mind-set that emphasises difference and ignores similarities and changes that reduce that difference. Although beliefs and values cannot be reduced to the product of any simple economistic or social determination they clearly have their basis in social life. If they have autonomy from material circumstances the degree is constrained and the autonomy only relative. Classical sociology has long assumed that secularisation, technological rationality and individualism are among the entailments of capitalism and that cash and commoditisation play a crucial and influential role in introducing these features to, and thus transforming, pre-capitalist societies. There seems no reason to suppose that the enhancement of Aboriginal material well-being, however it takes place, does not have transformative entailments, yet government policies do not recognise this.

A political response to this point might be that, of course, no culture is unchanging and that the issue is Aboriginal autonomy: the real objective is acquiring funds for people to pursue their own ends. Again, a discourse that is appropriate to the political arena spills over into the academic.

Well-being within the existing economic system entails a particular economic persona for the model Australian citizen. This emerges quite clearly from the now defunct Acts and Ordinances that list the grounds on which an Aboriginal ward could apply for the revocation of the status of ward. In the Northern Territory Welfare Ordinance 1953 the grounds for appeal are:

> 32(2.) The grounds for an appeal under this section shall be that, having regard to his manner of living, his ability, without assistance, adequately to manage his own affairs, his standard of social habit and behaviour and his personal associations, he does not stand in need of the special care and assistance provided under this Ordinance.

and even more explicitly in the Western Australia Native (Citizens Rights) Act of 1944:

> to obtain 'the rights [...] of a natural born or naturalised subject of His Majesty' an Aborigine had to demonstrate to a magistrate he or she: had, 'dissolved tribal and native association except with respect to lineal descendants or native relations of the first degree'; had 'adopted the manner and habits of civilised life'; could 'speak and understand the English language'; and was 'of industrious habits and of good behaviour and reputation'.[40]

That is to say that to become an Australian citizen an Aboriginal person had to be economically self-sufficient, selling his or her labour to support an independent household composed only of a spouse, children and possibly elderly parents and siblings. This could be elaborated on but the essential features are of an economic responsibility to a nuclear family built around individualistic striving, capital accumulation and a generalised moral commitment to an impersonal collectivity ruled on the basis of a democratic electoral process.

While the pre-colonial Aboriginal citizen would have been an economically active member of a household the impact of social rights has been to make most Aboriginal people increasingly economically passive in securing cash income from the outside world, in the sense of selling their labour. For many Aboriginal people, in remote Australia especially, the only regular sources of income are from social entitlements supplemented in some areas by earnings from art and craft and periodic royalty and rental distributions. Yet, if achieving the common national standard of living in the longer run is a measure of citizenship, the only way Aboriginal people can achieve this is by selling their labour.

Additional subsidies – through project funding, special programs of various sorts and infrastructure grants to remote communities, in particular – entrench the reproduction of situations in which statistical equality can only be achieved at the cost of high levels of dependency. Subsidy has a further down side. Equality of outcome in a social welfare system is achieved by bureaucratic surveillance, which entails some loss of individual autonomy.[41] As the degree of subsidy increases so does the surveillance or, as it is called in Aboriginal affairs, accountability. But this increased accountability is in direct conflict with the emphasis on self-determination, unless Aboriginal people take on the responsibility for their own accountability.

Finally, it might be argued that some Aboriginal citizens, living out a distinct cultural agenda, will accept a different and lower standard of living. But this is not without its problems. It raises the possibility of a moral hazard for the state, given the extent to which ideas of equality and equity underwrite citizenship. If the state has a moral obligation to relieve suffering, people may raise their consumption levels in line with increased incomes on the understanding that the state will make adequate provision for them.[42] A case in point was the frequent theft of funds in the past from the communal stores by the European managers. Little concern was ever shown about this in the community because people were safe in the knowledge that such thefts would have little if any effect on the operation of the store: the government had to keep them functioning because the stores were the only source of food in the communities and without them people would starve.

Conclusion

I have attempted to show that the dependency arising from the provision of the social rights of citizenship in some remote communities is not adequately analysed in terms of 'welfare colonialism'. The main difficulties are that the concept not only tends to obscure the economic and cultural issues with a political analysis of dependency but offers no comprehensible explanation for the state seeking to create or perpetuate such a dependency or for indigenous people actively participating in it. Indeed the efforts of governments of all persuasions to introduce mainstreaming of government services and user-pays systems for Aboriginal citizens suggests the opposite. Further there is no space in the concept for a sophisticated analysis of the various cultures of engagement between the two ways of life beyond the culture of dependency.

The difficulties facing people in remote communities do, of course, require political as well as economic solutions. Self-determination, including the newly introduced concept of regional agreements, is an important and possibly essential, although only partial, way out of the difficulties. Even then the combination of entrenched egalitarianism and a consumption ethic will pose complex moral, economic, political and social problems which will not go away even with the strongest form of self-determination.

In essence the problem is existential: what do people want out of life and what is their place in the world? These are questions that few people are forced to contemplate as directly as the double citizens of Aboriginal Australia.

Notes

I have benefited considerably from conversations with and comments by Jon Altman, Bill Arthur, Julie Finalyson, David Martin, Will Sanders and Diane Smith.

1 While Beckett's analysis of life in the Torres Strait does encompass substantial discussion of the economic circumstances of Islanders, his programmatic statements about welfare colonialism emphasise the political (see 1988: 4).
2 cf Barry 1990: 13.
3 Beckett 1985, 1987, 1988; see also Sackett 1990; Rowse 1992; and Yu 1994. Jeremy Long raised this same question in his review of Beckett's book (1987; see Long 1989). Beckett replied with a letter (see Beckett 1990) which makes the same points as are covered here.
4 Beckett 1988: 14.
5 Easy use is made of the description 'colonial' because of the historical origins of the Australian state and the undeniable subordination of and discrimination against Aboriginal people that originally caused Aboriginal people's problems. However, the use of terms like 'oppression', 'subordination' and 'colonialism' today is usually the language of political activism rather than one appropriate for social analysis. This is not to deny the existence of racism, discrimination and other problems resulting from the original colonisation.
6 Beckett 1988: 4.
7 Beckett 1988: 4.

8 See Smith 1989.
9 See Beckett 1987: 8, footnote 13.
10 Rowley 1971: 1–26.
11 Rowley 1971: 1–2.
12 Rowley 1971: 6–8.
13 There are, of course, many Aboriginal Australias. The one dealt with here involves only around ten per cent of the total Aboriginal population, yet it is one that looms large in the public consciousness of Aboriginal people, such as it is. The impacts of colonialism were far more devastating and destructive for the majority of the population than they have been for this fraction who have been protected to a considerable extent by their geographical location. At the end of World War II there were around 5000 Aboriginal people living an independent life in the bush.
14 The Aboriginal labour force on which the pastoralists mainly drew was the population resident on their station. Most Aboriginal people who lived in the large reserves, such as Arnhem Land, had no experience of stockwork and were not needed. Indeed reserves were seen as places to send the Aboriginal dependants whose labour was not used. Some marxists argue that growth of the state sector, with particular emphasis on social expenditure, is necessary to the maintenance of capitalism (see Bell 1994: 189) but this does not account for welfare colonialism specifically.
15 According to Jessie Street (1957: 1) the treatment of Aboriginal people in Australia was first raised at the United Nations in 1947 in connection with the imprisonment in Western Australia of some of the 'Pindan Mob' who had formed a trade union and planned a strike (see Wilson 1979).
16 eg see Adler et al. 1981.
17 The use of the term does flag, however, that the relationship is valued negatively by those who use the phrase.
18 As Mulgan and Sanders point out (1996), internal decolonisation inevitably creates a state of unfinished business between the indigenous people and the encapsulating society but in terms of the quality of people's daily lives this may have only a marginal significance.
19 Rowse appears to support a slightly different view that identifies welfare colonialism as the treatment of Aboriginal people as just another category of needy citizen (1992: 100).
20 Beckett 1988: 173.
21 Bleakley 1929: 30. Although Bleakley explicitly rejects the idea of a black state as such, the Arnhem Land reserve was established in explicit dialogue with the idea. The concept that was first mooted in the mid-1920s with regard to Central Australia naturally included setting aside large areas of land.
22 Bleakley 1929: 33.
23 Bleakley 1929: 33.
24 Bleakley 1929: 24.
25 Ingrid Slotte, a PhD student in the Department of Archaeology and Anthropology at the Australian National University, has carried out fieldwork in central Arnhem Land and reports an Aboriginal emphasis on the peace brought by the missions.
26 eg Trigger 1986; Martin 1995.
27 Some well known consumer dependencies were established, by far the strongest being the desire for tobacco, closely followed by sugar, tea and flour.

28 The extent of deliberate modification of indigenous cultural practice varied from place to place but in Arnhem Land the Methodist mission was most permissive: mortuary, circumcision and exchange ceremonies are still flourishing today and the main cult banned from the missions but held in the bush, the Kunapipi, is now openly and widely celebrated.

29 This is a cursory summary of a complex and well documented situation (eg see Peterson 1985; 1993; Martin 1995). It is important to stress that this does not mean that Aboriginal people are not interested in consuming but that the nature of social relations (eg domestic mode of production) is such that increasing production and accumulating is difficult (see Sahlins 1972).

30 The history of how Aboriginal people gained access to unemployment benefit is complex but has been well documented by Sanders (1985). Some people in remote communities did obtain it earlier than 1977 but they were few and far between (see Sanders 1985).

31 Sanders 1985, 1988: 34.

32 See Peterson 1985 for the elaboration of this argument.

33 By this I mean that a high value, sometimes explicitly and sometimes implicitly, is placed on trying to ensure that policy reproduces and protects the perceived egalitarian and communitarian aspects of Aboriginal life. The emergence of core features of the encapsulating society, such as class differentiation, are deplored and policy is contrived to reduce their impact.

34 See Sanders 1985: 153.

35 In 1978 I estimated that the expenditure on food at Yuendumu was about 55.5 per cent of income (see Peterson 1982). I have found it difficult to get comparative figures for remote communities for ten years later but the firm impression is that food is a smaller, though still high, proportion of people's budgets than it is for the Australian norm.

36 For WA see Yu 1994: 25. The missions were never total institutions in Goffman's sense (1961) although it is not uncommon to see them referred to in this way. The differences are considerable and include the inmates having a culture quite distinct from that of the people controlling the institution, the inmates living in family groups and having a great deal more autonomy than people in a total institution.

37 For petrol sniffing see Brady (1992: ch. 7); for domestic violence see Bolger (1991).

38 'Citizens-plus' was a description that had currency with respect to indigenous people in Canada during the 1970s and 1980s.

39 1992: 99.

40 Details of the Act quoted in Sackett 1993: 239.

41 Turner 1986.

42 Barry 1990: 116 – the current lump sum–pension problem.

References

Adler, E., Barkat, A., Bena-Silu, Duncan, Q., and Wee, P. 1981. *Justice for Aboriginal Australians: Report of the World Council of Churches Team Visit to the Aborigines June 15 to July 3, 1981*. Sydney: Australian Council of Churches.

Altman, J. C. and Smith, D. 1994. *The Economic Impact of Mining Moneys: the Nabarlek Case, Western Arnhem Land*. Canberra: Centre for Aboriginal Economic Policy Research, Discussion Paper No. 63.

Barbalet, J. 1988. *Citizenship: Rights, Struggle and Class Inequality.* Minneapolis: University of Minnesota Press.

Barry, N. 1990. *Welfare.* Milton Keynes: Open University Press.

Beckett, J. 1985. Colonialism in a welfare state: the case of the Australian Aborigines. In *The Future of Former Foragers: Australia and Southern Africa*, eds C. Schrire and R. Gordon. Cambridge, MA: Cultural Survival, pp. 25–36.

Beckett, J. 1987. *Torres Strait Islanders: Custom and Colonialism.* Cambridge: Cambridge University Press.

Beckett, J. 1988. Aboriginality, citizenship and nation state. In Aborigines and the state in Australia, ed. J. Beckett. Adelaide: *Social Analysis, Special Issue* No. 24, pp. 3–18.

Beckett, J. 1990. Welfare colonialism: a reply to Jeremy Long. *Oceania* 60 (3): 238.

Bell, D. 1994. The revolution of rising entitlements. In *Citizenship: Critical Concepts*, eds B. Turner and P. Hamilton. London: Routledge, pp. 188–225.

Bolger, A. 1991. *Aboriginal Women and Violence.* Darwin: North Australia Research Unit.

Bleakley, J. 1929. *The Aboriginals and Half-Castes of Central Australia and North Australia.* Melbourne: Government Printer for the Parliament of the Commonwealth of Australia.

Brady, M. 1992. *Heavy Metal: The Social Meaning of Petrol Sniffing in Australia.* Canberra: Aboriginal Studies Press.

Goffman, I. 1961. *Asylums.* New York: Anchor Books.

Long, J. P. M. 1989. Review of *Torres Strait Islanders: custom and colonialism.* J. Beckett. *Oceania* 60 (1): 63–5.

Martin, D. 1995. *Money, Business and Culture: Issues for Aboriginal Economic Policy.* Canberra: Centre for Aboriginal Economic Policy Research, Discussion Paper No. 101.

Mulgan, R. and Sanders, W. 1996. Transforming indigenous affairs policy: Labour's [sic] contribution to 'internal decolonisation'. In *The Great Experiment: Labour Parties and Public Policy Transformations in Australia and New Zealand*, eds F. Castles, R. Gerritsen and J. Vowles. Sydney: Allen & Unwin, pp. 129–148.

Myers, F. 1986. *Pintupi Country Pintupi Self: Sentiment, Place, and Politics among Western Desert Aborigines.* Washington: Smithsonian Press.

Paine, R. 1977. The path to welfare colonialism. In *The White Arctic: Anthropological Essays on Tutelage and Ethnicity*, ed. R. Paine. St John: Memorial University of Newfoundland, pp. 3–28.

Peterson, N. 1982. Service delivery and dependency: the economic watershed of the eighties. In *Service Delivery to Remote Communities*, ed. P. Loveday. Darwin: North Australia Research Unit, pp. 56–61.

Peterson, N. 1985. Capitalism, culture and land rights: Aborigines and the state in the Northern Territory. *Social Analysis* 18: 85–101.

Peterson, N. 1991. Cash, commoditisation and authenticity: when do Aboriginal people stop being hunter-gatherers? In *Cash, Commoditisation and Changing Foragers*, eds N. Peterson and T. Matsuyama. Osaka: National Museum of Ethnology, Senri Studies No. 30, pp. 67–90.

Peterson, N. 1993. Demand sharing: reciprocity and the pressure for generosity among foragers. *American Anthropologist* 95 (4): 860–74.

Rowley, C. 1971. *The Remote Aborigines: Aboriginal Policy and Practice, vol. 3.* Canberra: Australian National University Press.

Rowse, T. 1992. *Remote Possibilities: The Aboriginal Domain and the Administrative Imagination.* Darwin: North Australia Research Unit.

Sackett, L. 1990. Welfare colonialism: developing divisions at Wiluna. In *Going it Alone? Prospects for Aboriginal Autonomy*, eds R. Tonkinson and M. Howard. Canberra: Aboriginal Studies Press, pp. 201–17.

Sackett, L. 1993. A post-modern panopticon: the Royal Commission into Aboriginal Deaths in Custody. *Australian Journal of Social Issues* 28 (3): 229–44.

Sahlins, M. 1972. *Stone Age Economics*. Chicago: Aldine.

Sanders, W. 1985. The politics of unemployment benefit for Aborigines: some consequences of economic marginalisation. In *Employment and Unemployment: A Collection of Papers*, eds D. Wade-Marshall and P. Loveday. Darwin: North Australia Research Unit, pp. 137–62.

Sanders, W. 1988. The CDEP scheme: bureaucratic politics, remote community politics and the development of an Aboriginal 'workfare' program in times of rising unemployment. *Politics* 23 (1): 32–47.

Smith, C. 1989. Development and the state: issues for anthropologists. Paper presented at American Anthropological Association meetings 9/9/89.

Street, J. 1957. *Report on Aborigines in Australia*. Roneod report (30 pages).

Trigger, D. 1986. Blackfellas and whitefellas: the concepts of domain and social closure in the analysis of race relations. *Mankind* 16 (2): 99–117.

Turner, B. 1986. *Citizenship and Capitalism: The Debate Over Reformism*. London: Allen & Unwin.

Turner, B. and Hamilton P. (eds). 1994. *Citizenship: Critical Concepts, 2 vols.* London: Routledge.

Yu, P. 1994. The Kimberley: from welfare colonialism to self-determination. *Race and Class* 35 (4): 21–33.

Wilson, J. 1979. The Pilbara Aboriginal social movement: an outline of its background and significance. In *Aborigines of the West: Their Past and Their Present*, eds R. M. and C. H. Berndt. Perth: University of Western Australia Press, pp. 151–68.

CHAPTER 6

Representation Matters: The 1967 Referendum and Citizenship

Bain Attwood and Andrew Markus

The 1967 referendum to alter Australia's Constitution is now seen as an event that marked a major turning point in Aboriginal–European relations in Australia. In this chapter we will examine the referendum from a number of perspectives. First, we explore its constitutional significance: can the argument be made, for example, that it conferred citizenship on the Aboriginal people in a legal sense? Secondly, we consider the much more complex issue of the meanings attached to the referendum, both in the immediate context and in the medium and long term: how was the referendum understood by the government that presented it to the electorate, by the political lobbyists who argued for change, and by those who voted? How have these understandings changed over time, and what explains the divergent meanings attached to the referendum today?

Over the last decade enormous significance has been attributed to what is now called the 1967 Aboriginal Rights Referendum or simply the 1967 Aboriginal Referendum.[1] Meanwhile the nature of the constitutional changes it entailed has been increasingly submerged. Myths about the referendum are promulgated in many forums and have acquired enormous authority over time. It is now commonplace for journalists to characterise the referendum as either a harbinger or a sign of portentous change, and to misrepresent it in one or more of the following ways: the referendum recognised *Aboriginal* rights for Aboriginal people in their own country; it granted them citizenship and so equality under the law, or, more specifically, gave them the vote; it ended discriminatory State laws that had denied Aboriginal people basic human rights; it transferred control over Aboriginal affairs from the States to the Commonwealth.[2]

Politicians, past and present, though somewhat better informed as to the precise terms of the referendum, are also uncertain about the constitutional alterations it approved,[3] while many Aboriginal or black activists see the referendum as a seminal event from which a variety of rights flowed.[4] More generally it seems that many Australians 'know of' the referendum, yet are quite ignorant of its terms; most believe that it resulted in Aboriginal people getting citizenship rights.[5] Many Aboriginal people also speak of the referendum in a way that scarcely has any historical verisimilitude; most apparently 'believe that their right to vote dates from 1967' and are 'surprised to learn that they ever had a right to vote' before this.[6]

More remarkably, perhaps, highly respected novelists and reputable historians and anthropologists in the field of Aboriginal studies are also mistaken about the constitutional amendments proposed by the referendum or misunderstand the changes that can reasonably be said to have resulted from these. Tim Winton's *Cloudstreet*, joint winner of the National Book Council's Banjo Award for Fiction in 1991, perpetuates the myth of the referendum granting the vote to Aboriginal people by imagining this exchange in 1963: 'The bugger laughed when I asked him how he voted. He didn't vote, said Rose, matter of fact. What? Blacks haven't got the vote, she said.'[7] In a popular short history of social justice in Australia by Stuart Macintyre, an entry in the chronological table has the referendum giving Aboriginal people the 'status of citizens' in 1967; a recent prize-winning history of Australia asserts that Aboriginal people were 'excluded from [...] voting for [sic] federal elections until 1968'; Heather Goodall contends in an historical overview of relations between Aboriginal people and Europeans edited by Ann McGrath that the referendum 'won overwhelming support for the proposals [...] to transfer responsibility for Aboriginal Affairs to the Federal Government'; and Richard Broome's widely read general history of Aboriginal–European relations in Australia construes the referendum as an 'overwhelming vote for Aboriginal citizenship and federal control'.[8] Anthropologist Barry Morris also strays into error when he claims that ' "Getting the rights" in 1967 removed many of the discriminatory laws [...] that had limited Aborigines' movements and activities in the wider society'.[9]

Aboriginal people, the Constitution and the 1967 referendum

The Australian Constitution was drawn up at a high point of racism in this country, when there was mounting pressure for the adoption of a White Australia policy that would exclude non-Europeans, including

Aboriginal people, from the new polity, and it was generally believed that Aboriginal people were 'a dying race'.[10]

In this environment, it is hardly surprising that Aboriginal people were paid very little attention by the drafters and indeed there were only two substantive references to them in the Constitution of 1901, both negative in nature and included to limit the scope of measures that would otherwise apply to them.[11]

The first reference related to power granted to the Commonwealth to legislate with regard to racial minorities:

> Section 51. The Parliament shall, subject to this Constitution, have power to make laws for the peace, order, and good government of the Commonwealth with respect to: [...]
> (xxvi) The people of any race, other than the aboriginal race in any State, for whom it is deemed necessary to make special laws.

In drafting this section the primary issue under consideration was the policy to be adopted to deal with Melanesians, known to contemporaries as 'Kanakas', who had been recruited since the mid-1860s to provide field labour for the Queensland sugar industry. Although there was agreement that this power should be granted to the Commonwealth, paralleling the immigration power in order to ensure uniformity of legislation, there was no view that power should also be acquired to legislate over Aboriginal people. As a leading constitutional expert in the first half of the twentieth century, secretary of the Federal Convention's drafting committee and Commonwealth Solicitor General, Sir Robert Garran, explained:

> The real subject-matter of the section was meant to be introduced races, like the kanakas in Queensland, for whom special laws might be necessary. If this provision had not been there, I doubt whether, at the time, any one would have thought of mentioning aboriginals. The federating colonies were very jealous of their powers, and assigned nothing to the Federal Parliament unless they thought it very definitely a matter of federal concern. And, the provision as to special races being inserted, they put in the exception.[12]

The second specific reference to Aboriginal people excluded them from the national census. As we have seen, it provided:

> section 127: In reckoning the numbers of people of the Commonwealth, or of a State or other part of the Commonwealth, aboriginal natives should not be counted.

This clause was little discussed at the conventions that drew up the Constitution and the precise reasons for its inclusion are not clear. On the best evidence available, its main purpose related to the apportionment of funds – to formulas for the distribution of government revenues on the basis of population – and the apportionment of parliamentary seats.[13] It rested on the assumption, unchallenged at the time, that Aboriginal people were inferior – that they were not the equal of European citizens in matters of government expenditure and participation in the political process.

These sections of the Constitution were to remain unchanged for over sixty years (a proposed amendment of section 51(xxvi) was defeated in 1944). When the matter was again put to the electorate in 1967 it was proposed to repeal section 127 and amend section 51(xxvi) by deleting the words 'other than the aboriginal race in any State'. There is no doubt that these changes were immensely significant in symbolic terms. However, they did nothing to alter the legal status of Aboriginal people: repeal of section 127, quite clearly, did not confer citizenship upon Aborigines, and amendment of section 51(xxvi) did not transfer responsibility for Aboriginal affairs to the federal government. Indeed, the power conferred by the new section 51(xxvi) was little utilised by any Commonwealth government until the *Aboriginal and Torres Strait Islander (Queensland Discriminatory Laws) Act 1975*. Contrary to accepted wisdom, much Whitlam government reform proceeded through administrative rather than legislative change, utilising the power to make financial grants under specific terms and conditions (section 96), and other change was based, at least partly, on the external affairs power (section 51(xxix)) and the power of States to transfer functions to the Commonwealth (section 51(xxxvii)). In this regard one should also note that the Commonwealth had already assumed an important role in Aboriginal affairs before 1967, through the extension of social welfare benefits and legislation on voting rights.

Interpreted in this way, the 1967 constitutional changes are, as Scott Bennett has argued, 'humdrum in the extreme',[14] and so the historical importance claimed for the referendum is surprising. The clue to understanding its significance, we will argue, lies less in the textual changes to the Constitution and much more in the other narratives or texts which transformed these into *The Referendum*. In what follows, our task is to *con*textualise these various narratives.

The Coalition Government and constitutional change

In November 1965 the Menzies Government introduced a bill to provide for a referendum to repeal section 127 of the Constitution, a reform that had been demanded by the Federal Council for the Advancement of Aborigines, its successor the Federal Council for the Advancement of

Aborigines and Torres Strait Islanders (FCAATSI) and other pressure groups since the late 1950s, and recommended by a Commonwealth Parliamentary Joint Committee in 1959.[15]

The Cabinet minutes suggest that the Liberal–Country Party Government was largely motivated by considerations that had little if anything to do with a desire to introduce significant change in Aboriginal affairs. Attorney General Billy Snedden argued that 'the inclusion of this proposal would [...] tend to create a favourable atmosphere for the launching of the proposal regarding section 24' (dealing with the number of Senators relative to the number of Members of the House of Representatives, which became known as the nexus issue). In fact, Snedden was of the opinion that 'it would [...] be politically inexpedient, in the present climate of public opinion, to put any proposals for Constitutional amendments to a referendum without including in these proposals the repeal of section 127'. The Menzies Government undoubtedly had international as well as national opinion in mind; Snedden believed that since section 127 'savours of racial discrimination [... its] repeal could remove a possible source of misconstruction in the international field'. The following month, when the Minister for the Territories, Charles Barnes, recommended that the government intervene in the industrial case pressed by the North Australian Workers Union for equal wages for Aboriginal stock workers in the Northern Territory, he too argued that the move 'would reduce the scope for national and international criticism of Australia's treatment of Aborigines'.[16]

In assessing the Coalition Government's approach, it is also noteworthy that, in February and August 1965, Cabinet rejected Snedden's recommendations to amend section 51(xxvi) of the Constitution. Snedden believed that the Commonwealth should play a greater role in formulating policy but did not advocate that it assume an administrative function, reminding Cabinet of the opinion long held by the States' Aboriginal authorities – that 'in view of the widely varying conditions in different States [...] it would not be in the best interests of the Aboriginal people to have uniform Commonwealth legislation or uniform administration' – and pointing out that, were this constitutional change to be approved, 'it would not follow that [the Commonwealth] would exercise its powers and so long as the State – and Territory – laws were operating satisfactorily, the Commonwealth Parliament need not intervene'. In other words, 'the status quo would remain'. It is also apparent that Snedden's main interest in amending section 51(xxvi) actually lay in a perceived need to address public opinion: 'There would be a large area of dissatisfaction if the Commonwealth did nothing [...] I believe the Government would be criticised, albeit mistakenly, for lacking sympathy for the aborigines [...] On the other hand, to delete the words would [...] meet the wishes of those making the representations and would appeal to the broad public conscience'.[17]

In rejecting Snedden's advice and the demands for the amendment of section 51(xxvi), Menzies revealed that an important consideration was the government's unswerving commitment to the program of assimilation, rather than to any major changes in Aboriginal policy. Characterising 'a separate body of [...] laws relating exclusively to Aborigines' as discriminatory and likely to 'have most undesirable results', Menzies was emphatic that:

> What should be aimed at [...] is the integration of the Aboriginal in the general community, not a state of affairs in which he would be treated as a being of a race apart [...] Should not our overall objective be to treat the Aboriginal as on the same footing as all the rest, with similar duties and similar rights? [... The] best protection for Aborigines is to treat them, for all purposes, as Australian citizens.[18]

The following month Barnes reaffirmed 'the objective of assimilation', emphasising the commonly held belief that Aborigines could not 'retain fully their own racial separateness' if they were also to attain 'full membership of the Australian community' since these were 'objectives that are mutually incompatible'.[19]

Although Parliament passed the Constitution Alteration (Repeal of section 127) Bill, in March 1966 the Federal Liberal Government decided to defer the referendum, perhaps because Menzies' successor as prime minister, the more progressive Harold Holt (who, within two months of assuming office, had overhauled Australia's racially discriminatory White Australia policy),[20] was reluctant to proceed with a referendum that did not propose to amend section 51(xxvi). Like Snedden, Holt believed that more was at stake than the narrowly legalistic view, held by Menzies and the former Minister for the Territories Paul Hasluck, that section 51(xxvi) was discriminatory; they recognised that many Australians now held it to be discriminatory and believed that it was important to remove this appearance. Consequently, in February 1967, the government decided to sponsor such a referendum.[21]

Like his predecessor, Attorney General Nigel Bowen had argued in Cabinet the previous month that there would be 'a large area of dissatisfaction' if the Commonwealth failed to include amendment of section 51(xxvi) in any referendum, and that removing 'words alleged to be discriminatory against aboriginal people' would meet the demands of those 'urging action with respect to aborigines' and 'would be welcomed by a very large section of the Australian people'. At least one key member of the Cabinet was opposed to this course of action: Barnes was aware of the increasing national and international pressures but argued that any advantages deriving from the change would be 'outweighed by the practical and political disadvantages of placing the Commonwealth in a position where it [had to] either take responsibility for Aboriginal welfare throughout the Commonwealth – or be subjected to increasing criticism for not doing so'. The Government, however, decided to proceed with the amendment but it only did so on the basis of a Cabinet agreement that administration of Aboriginal affairs would remain in the hands of the States.[22]

For many reasons, this should not be interpreted as a dramatic change of heart by the conservatives. This proposal was, once again, to be presented to the electors with the one to alter section 24.[23] This political manoeuvre did not escape the attention of observers at the time: the *Age* remarked that 'two, entirely separate issues [are] linked in one referendum', and observed that the government was 'hoping that support for an uncontentious proposal' would have 'a carry-over of Yes voters for the less popular one'.[24] The arguments advanced by the government, in both proposing and campaigning for the referendum, indicate, moreover, much the same motives that were evident in 1965. Like Menzies, Holt recognised that section 127 was incompatible with the image of Australia that his government wished to project – that of a modern, egalitarian, non-racial nation; he told Parliament and, later, the electorate: 'The simple truth is that section 127 is completely out of harmony with our national attitudes and modern thinking. It has no place in our Constitution in this age.'[25]

As in 1965, furthermore, the government found it necessary to respond to opinion, whether at home or abroad. In his final appeal to the voters on 26 May, Holt claimed that 'anything but a Yes vote to this question would do injury to our reputation among fair-minded people everywhere'.[26] Government was now more responsive to local opinion articulated by FCAATSI and other campaigners, and, as already suggested, this explains why it had decided to amend section 51(xxvi) instead of just repealing section 127: while it continued to be of the opinion that the former was not discriminatory, the Coalition Government now thought this was nevertheless a 'popular' and 'deeply rooted' impression, and so decided it had to 'remove any ground for the belief' that overt racial discrimination continued to exist.[27]

It was also quite clear, moreover, that the Holt Government had no more intention of playing a greater role in Aboriginal affairs than had its predecessor. As the *Age* wryly observed during the referendum campaign: 'It must be assumed that the Government now wants to act vigorously for [the Aborigines'] advancement. It is a pity that the Prime Minister has not made this clear.'[28] Instead, Holt maintained that it was unable 'to forecast [...] what precise measures we or [the States] may decide upon', and refused even to contemplate what these might be in general terms; nor did he instruct the bureaucracies most directly involved in Aboriginal affairs to make any plans for new directions in policy.[29] Similarly, the Government's lack of commitment to the referendum can be discerned in its lack-lustre campaigning.[30]

One cannot but conclude, then, that the government's belated decision to conduct the referendum was a rather uninterested, even cynical, one that had little if anything to do with any program of change in Aboriginal affairs, and much more to do with maintaining the status quo, shoring up the government's position at home, and bolstering Australia's image abroad. The approach of the Holt Government draws into question, therefore, the widely accepted assumption that amending section 51(xxvi) of the Constitution necessarily translated into the Commonwealth assuming a greater role with respect to Aboriginal people.

Talking up the referendum

Our conclusion that, contrary to conventional wisdom, there is an implied, rather than a necessary, relationship between the amendment of section 51(xxvi) and the Commonwealth assuming a role in Aboriginal affairs, provides a very important clue to the complex of meanings that the referendum assumed in 1967. Many of the principal proponents of the referendum – the national leftist pressure group FCAATSI, and its allies in the churches and trade unions, the Australian Parliamentary Labor Party, and much of the metropolitan press – recognised that, in and of itself, approval of the plebiscite would mean little. 'The [...] changes it envisages are necessary but they are no guarantee of action [...] the significance of the change would be the removal of a statutory discrimination rather than the beginning of a sweeping new deal', one newspaper editor noted; what was required, another asserted, was an 'undertaking to use the power [... provided] in the repeal [sic] of section 51'.[31] FCAATSI, or at least its more astute leaders, recognised, then, that the referendum was ultimately a matter of representation,[32] and that their task was to persuade the electors that it was a 'matter [...] of the greatest importance'[33] in order to create a climate of opinion that would compel the government not only to hold the referendum but also to use the powers granted by the constitutional change to improve significantly the position of Aboriginal people.

Following in the footsteps of earlier campaigners for equal rights for Aborigines and their 'uplift', such as the APNR founded in 1911,[34] FCAATSI and its allies saw a greater Commonwealth role as *the* pre-requisite for realising change. As the national government representing all Australians and possessing 'great resources', the Commonwealth was held to be the means of achieving equality and ending racial discrimination and the 'enormous economic and social gulf' between Aborigines and other Australians.[35] Consequently, the campaigners for the referendum adopted a strategy of 'talking up' the significance of amending section 51(xxvi) by representing their demand for the Commonwealth to take greater responsibility for Aboriginal affairs as a reasonable expectation, even a necessary outcome, of the referendum being passed, and, in turn, constructed a scenario whereby this would result in the adoption of major programs to tackle Aboriginal people's inferior status.[36] One should note, however, that for many of the campaigners this was a matter of genuine, unreflective belief on their part, an unquestioned assumption inherited from earlier generations of campaigners for Commonwealth intervention.

Thus Gordon Bryant, one of FCAATSI's referendum campaign directors, told voters that 'the Referendum would not solve everything, but it would be a start on a national problem'; the 'Yes' vote information of FCAATSI stated: 'Aborigines are a national responsibility. We must see to it that the National Parliament is able to accept that responsibility', and a national press release, answering the question, 'what will be the positive results if the referendum is passed', answered: 'the Commonwealth will be able to pass laws relating to Aborigines'; Jack Horner, secretary of FCAATSI's campaign in New South Wales, told the readers of one newspaper that upon amendment of section 51(xxvi) 'the Federal Government will take formal responsibility for Aborigines'; the director of the Council's campaign in the same state, Faith Bandler, told the press: 'by voting yes, you give this responsibility to the national Parliament and make possible a real programme of equal rights and equal opportunity for Aboriginals'; a FCAATSI poster, showing an Aboriginal humpy, was captioned 'End Discrimination – Vote "Yes" on 27 May'; and the Leader of the Opposition, Gough Whitlam, told Parliament: 'The fact is that with the excision of the words from paragraph (xxvi) of section 51 the members of this Parliament will be able for the first time to do something for Aboriginals.'[37] While these statements are not false in a literal sense, they are nevertheless misleading inasmuch as they imply that the only thing preventing greater Commonwealth intervention was a few words in the Constitution; by their silence on the crucial matter of the government's intent, FCAATSI gave the impression that the outcomes they desired would occur as a matter of course.

This strategy was successful to the extent that influential opinion-makers came to represent the referendum in much the same manner as the campaigners for a Yes vote. For example, in mid-May 1967 the *Age* was cautious in its suggestion that the referendum 'may not go far, but it is

an essential first step towards any programme for measured improvement in their status', yet ten days later it was proclaiming that 'A Yes vote
will pave the way for improving their health, education and housing; it
will give them opportunities to live normal lives'.[38] And the *Sydney
Morning Herald* stated baldly: 'In simple terms the object of these constitutional changes is to provide the Commonwealth with more definite
power to give positive and practical aid to the Aboriginal people whose
plight, in some places, has been rightly described as [...] "disgusting
and inhuman".'[39]

The talking-up process is also evident in the representation of section
127. For some time Aboriginal people had been counted more or less
accurately by governments seeking evidence that their numbers were
declining, and so, as one FCAATSI leader remarked in 1965, it was a
measure which would 'do little for the Aboriginal people'.[40] It gained
significance only because FCAATSI and others represented it (as well as
section 51(xxvi)) as being discriminatory and thus a matter of citizenship
and equal rights for Aborigines. In the campaign they argued that
section 127 'made [Aborigines] feel a race apart in the land of their
birth', and 'insulted' them by implying that they were 'not people' and
'not worth counting'. 'Today, we count sheep, but not the original Australians', voters were told.[41] Importantly, FCAATSI's narrative characterised
this not only as an issue of 'equal recognition' in a cultural sense, but also
as a matter of political status. Section 127 was interpreted as denying full
citizenship to Aboriginal people, and so its repeal would mean that they
would 'be recognised [...] as Australian citizens by right', no longer
'excluded from Commonwealth benefits on account of race' but 'treated
equally with other Australians'.[42]

The Sydney–Melbourne press represented this constitutional change
in the same manner. For example, the *Age* spoke of 'The case for allowing
the Commonwealth to treat Aborigines as a people', and of Aboriginal
people's 'right to be called Australians', the *Sydney Morning Herald*
referred to 'the referendum on the status of the Aborigines' and 'the
referendum on Aborigines', the Melbourne *Herald* wrote of 'the referendum on whether discrimination against the aboriginals should be
ended', and a *Bulletin* column was headed 'When Aborigines become
people'.[43]

FCAATSI's inflation of the significance of repealing section 127 is
nowhere more apparent than in the language it used during the
campaign of April and May 1967. The very name of the organisation
FCAATSI created for the referendum campaign – Aboriginal Rights 'Vote
Yes' Committee – indicates the manner in which it approached the
referendum: not as a matter of constitutional change so much as a
general issue about the status of Aboriginal Australians. This is strikingly

evident in the materials the committee prepared for the campaign. Leaflets called upon voters to simply 'Vote Yes for Aborigines', which was the slogan chosen for the campaign.[44] One poster called upon voters to 'Right wrongs: Write Yes for Aborigines on May 27'; another read: 'Vote Yes for Aboriginal Citizenship Rights'.[45] In calling on newspapers for support, FCAATSI suggested they urge electors 'to vote yes to the question of Aboriginal rights', and at public meetings the referendum was also cast in terms of 'full citizenship' for Aborigines. FCAATSI made use of a song recorded by folk singer Gary Shearston called 'We are Going to Freedom', which stressed 'freedom' and 'equal rights'.[46] And so, even though FCAATSI's civil rights agenda had all but been accomplished by 1967 – the vote in federal elections had been restored to Aboriginal people in 1962,[47] all Aboriginal people had become eligible for all Commonwealth social welfare benefits by 1966, and the previous decade had seen the dismantling of legal discrimination in nearly all States[48] – its publicity campaign gave the impression that this was not so.

It is quite evident that voters were confused by the representation of the referendum in terms of equal rights, citizenship and the Commonwealth's responsibility for Aboriginal affairs. For example, one voter told a journalist: 'I'll be voting yes on the Aboriginal question. They're real Australians'; many were reputedly saying 'The Aborigines are all right. I will give them a tick'; and others spoke in terms of 'a referendum on Aboriginal rights'. A Morgan Gallup Poll of 19 May reported that twenty-two per cent of those polled believed the 'chief effect' of the referendum would be 'equal rights' for Aboriginal people as citizens, and a further fourteen per cent expected that it would produce, among other outcomes, improved 'status' and 'Aboriginal freedom'.[49] Many voters had come to believe that the referendum was concerned with what was, for settler Australians at any rate, the most symbolic of citizenship rights: the right of Aboriginal people to vote (even though the pamphlet of the official Yes case delivered to all households had pointed out that Aboriginal people had been entitled to vote in federal elections 'for some years now').[50]

In trying to persuade the voters to support the referendum, FCAATSI and its supporters appealed to a set of liberal principles that emphasised individual rights and equality, and presented a vision of a homogenous 'modern' and 'progressive' society that integrated all peoples as citizens, casting the referendum as a means of continuing this project. For example, one senior church member characterised it as a 'proposal [that] can only advance the Aborigines and make them completely Australian', a sentiment ringingly endorsed by the *Sydney Morning Herald*, the newspaper most supportive of the Yes campaign.[51] More particularly, though, FCAATSI and its allies vigorously exploited a sense of

'Australianness' in order to rally voters to their cause. As the political scientist and historian Charles Rowley observed soon after the event, this meant that what was eventually at issue in the referendum was 'the kind of nation Australians wanted to be part of, the view of themselves which Australians were developing'.[52] This was evident, for example, in some of the other slogans mooted for the campaign – 'Towards an Australia Free and Equal: Vote Yes', and 'Let's Be Counted – Vote Yes' – and in statements to the media; for instance, Bandler suggested to voters that 'When you write Yes [...] you are holding out the hand of friendship and wiping out nearly 200 years of injustice and inhumanity'; Horner encouraged the use of this rhyming slogan: 'If to Aborigines you would be fair, put a YES in the bottom square'; and Whitlam argued that 'The people of Australia should and must, in all humanity and, for their own honour, support [the referendum] overwhelmingly'. It was, he claimed, essential for 'the interests of our nation and [...] the conscience of all of us'.[53] By talking up the constitutional changes in this fashion the referendum effectively became a plebiscite on Australia as much as one concerning the status of indigenous people.

FCAATSI's attempt to turn the referendum into an issue about Australian national identity and reputation, and to shame the voters into supporting it, seems to have been enormously successful, if the editorials of the major metropolitan newspapers are any guide. The *Age* told its readers during the campaign:

> Voting Yes to these proposals is a simple matter of humanity. It is also a test of our standing in the world. If No wins, Australia will be labelled as a country addicted to racist policies. In spite of our increasing involvement with Asia, in spite of our protestations of good will towards all men of all colours and creeds, this label would have a millstone's weight around the neck of Australia's international reputation.[54]

And, on the day before voters went to the polls, it reminded its readers that 'a No vote [...] will [...] bring this country into international disrepute'.[55] For its part, the *Sydney Morning Herald* was, if anything, more fervent in arguing this. In early May, it forecast that defeat of the referendum 'would be a signal humiliation for Australia [... which] would not go unnoticed' in the world. 'Australia', it warned, 'cannot risk the spectacle of a national affront to her native race'.[56] Ten days later, it gave notice that: 'Its rejection by the people [...] would be a disgrace unmatched in the history of a nation whose treatment of its native people already mars a proud tradition of social enlightenment.'[57] Less than a week later, it declaimed: 'If we do not vote Yes on Saturday on the question affecting Aborigines, we will be endorsing our shameful, ignorant neglect of Aborigines – and proclaiming that we do not care enough even now.'[58] And, finally, on the day of the poll: 'Today's vote will be a measure of the responsibility of our attitude towards Aborigines'.[59] The *Australian* concurred, telling its readers that 'on no account can this be refused [...] If it is not carried the nation should be ashamed of itself'.[60]

As part of the strategy of talking up the referendum in order to place pressure upon the Government, FCAATSI and its allies repeatedly called for a 'massive' or an 'overwhelming' vote in the plebiscite.[61] Whitlam, for example, had argued that 'The good name of Australia demands that it be carried overwhelmingly', and an Anglican Primate greeted the result for it 'show[ed] the world that we believe in racial equality'.[62] In the wake of the poll, the campaigners (not surprisingly) highlighted the large vote. As one metropolitan newspaper observed: 'By itself, the vote is a statement of intent rather than a solution to any problems. Its very size, however, will be a valuable weapon for the proponents of reform in Aboriginal welfare.'[63] Thus, FCAATSI leaders drew attention to the 'overwhelming' response to the referendum in urging 'immediate action in a number of fields'.

On 27 May and immediately after, FCAATSI and its allies and supporters were euphoric[64] but it soon became evident that the talking-up of the referendum had not yielded the results anticipated by the proponents of change. If we turn to the immediate outcome of the referendum, we can observe that its sweeping 90.77 per cent approval by the electorate barely affected the Coalition Government's attitude to the Commonwealth's role in Aboriginal affairs. Although the government was eventually forced to respond to the Yes vote, it is clear that considerations of national and international opinion were once again uppermost in its decision-making. Holt told the Cabinet in August 1967: 'we must take into account the place the Aborigine question occupies in Australia's international relationships, and also the fact that the electorate will undoubtedly look increasingly to the Commonwealth Government as the centre of policy and responsibility on Aborigine questions'. Yet the Prime Minister and the Cabinet were also concerned that the government 'should not magnify the Aborigine problem out of its true reality', and remained of the opinion that it should not take any large-scale initiatives in either policy or administration; indeed, that it would be best to avoid creating any impression of the Commonwealth's newly won authority in the area and continue to leave administration of Aboriginal affairs to the States. However, the Cabinet recognised that it had to appear to be doing something and so it agreed to 'a small office', an Office of Aboriginal Affairs, 'perhaps [with] only two or three people', whose function would be merely advisory.[65] In the period immediately following 27 May, then, FCAATSI's narrative about the referendum came face to face with another representation of the constitutional changes it comprised – that of the federal government – and so it foundered.

Yet, in the longer term, the FCAATSI narrative was not without significance: expectations for change had been raised and many people believed that a mandate for a greater and more positive Commonwealth role in Aboriginal affairs had been given and remained to be utilised. In the white community, within the context of a political groundswell favourable to reform, the narrative of the 1967 Referendum served to act as a focal point. In particular it was used to legitimise the Whitlam Government's agenda and, later, to deter opposition from the States; thus in 1972 the electoral platform of the Australian Labor Party stated that if elected to government it would 'assume responsibility for Aborigines and Islanders accorded to it by the Referendum of 1967'. The campaigners' strategy eventually facilitated the process of change, authorising a new role for the Commonwealth, just as they had hoped it would in 1967.[66]

Reviewing the referendum historically leads us, then, to a conclusion that is now counter-intuitive. In the context of the policies of the Liberal–Country Party Government the constitutional changes proposed were of only minor importance. They acquired significance at the time because the referendum was talked up so much by proponents who joined the text of the constitutional changes to another, richly symbolic narrative for change. This was FCAATSI's achievement. It was its act of *con*textualising – of joining together these narratives – that bestowed immense significance upon the referendum. The historical significance of the referendum, we conclude, ultimately rests upon the myth-making of 1967. And yet, as we have also shown, this myth was, necessarily, ephemeral, a signifier that was ultimately dependent upon another force if it was truly to make history rather than remaining just a story. It awaited a government which, in 1972, had the authority and the will to tie the two narratives of the referendum together.

Remembering the referendum, 1977–1997

With the exception of the first decade after the referendum, when there was much disillusionment about its value among its proponents, particularly Aboriginal people whose expectations had been raised enormously by 1967, the passing of time has seen its precise terms disappear from historical consciousness, only to be replaced by other myths about it, many of which uncannily resemble the earlier one. The referendum has once again come to be considered very significant, as betokened by descriptions of it as 'historic', 'momentous', a 'turning point', and a 'landmark' event;[67] whereas the first decennial was more or less ignored, by 1987 it was regaining significance, and by the twenty-fifth anniversary it was the subject of much commemoration.[68]

Why the referendum is commemorated depends, of course, on who is reconstructing it. For conservatives in search of an event to celebrate in the field of desolation that is the history of Aboriginal–white relations, the referendum is undoubtedly attractive. Since it can be held up as a 'massive' vote for Aboriginal people by the Australian people, it can readily be made to stand for the beginning of the much vaunted reconciliation between Aboriginal and settler Australians, and is all the more valuable in the continuing absence of a 'compact'. It is also reassuring because it seemingly represents 'Australian' principles, such as equality before the law, as well as the ideal of 'one people, one nation', rather than notions of 'special rights' and a vision of a pluralistic future. Presumably this is why it can be suggested that 27 May become Australia Day: 'on that date in 1967 by referendum, all Australian citizens, indigenous or otherwise, became equal under the Constitution with the same rights and responsibilities. True nationhood was born on the day.'[69]

The referendum, thus remembered, is all the safer as a moment of reconciliation when one considers the alternative political arrangements between Aboriginal and non-Aboriginal people mooted today, such as a treaty that recognises indigenous sovereign rights, or merely a new preamble to the Constitution that acknowledges the prior Aboriginal presence. The referendum, one might say, is talked up in order to counter the remembrance of another event whose anniversaries march in tandem – that of the Aboriginal Tent Embassy (of 27 January 1972). Similarly the referendum holds none of the dangers of something like a republican constitution which would entrench citizenship rights, or even the much more important 1975 Racial Discrimination Act which focuses on racial prejudice, the commemoration of which might only serve to highlight the ongoing need for it.

By representing the referendum as the moment when Aboriginal people were granted 'full equality before the law and equality of opportunity',[70] celebrating it also serves the function of drawing a sharp if artificial distinction between the past and the present, allowing conservatives to acknowledge the unfortunate events of the past at the same time as they can proclaim that these are no longer present in contemporary Australia and are instead 'just history'.

In a somewhat similar fashion, the referendum may well serve a redemptive function for small 'l' liberals, an 'historic' moment when Australia's 'racist past' is purged once and for all.[71] It can also stand as living proof of the correctness of their assumptions about their fellow Australians' humanity, all the more so given the 'overwhelming' vote. Simultaneously, the referendum can be invoked as a benchmark of

Australian goodwill towards Aboriginal people from which there should be no regression; thus, liberals and radicals alike often measure so-called backlashes against the referendum. In the course of all this commemoration, one must note that the relatively large No vote in the referendum in the rural areas (as high as 29.04 per cent in the case of Kalgoorlie), where there were the highest or most visible populations of Aboriginal people, is conveniently forgotten.[72]

More pointedly, the last decade has seen Aboriginal leaders and their sympathisers treating the twentieth and twenty-fifth anniversaries of the referendum in an ironic mode, as occasions to contrast the dreams of 1967 with a nightmarish contemporary reality, drawing attention to present-day problems and the lack of progress, and calling for greater commitment and resources to tackle Aboriginal people's inferior status.[73] Thus, in 1987 Charles Perkins spoke of the slowness of progress; and in 1992 Lois O'Donoghue spoke of how little had been achieved, Patrick Dodson of the urgent need for further change, and Pat O'Shane of how far 'the quest for real citizenship has [...] to go'. They were joined by the Labor Prime Minister Paul Keating who commented upon Australia's failure to rise to 'the challenge which the triumphant referendum required us to meet'.[74]

More puzzling are those commonly uttered assertions by Aboriginal people (most evident in south-eastern Australia) that they 'got the rights in 1967' or were 'given the vote in 1967'. Historians are often inclined to reject such oral testimony when it is contradicted by a reliable documentary record. However, if we follow Heather Goodall's advice and go beyond the literal meaning of these statements, looking for interpretation rather than information,[75] we can gain rich insights into the historical reality of racial relations.[76]

Anthropologist Peter Sutton has usefully compared these modern Aboriginal historical constructions with traditional Aboriginal myths. Not only are both 'charged with strong feelings' and lacking in 'empirical rigour', but they also 'focus on [...] events without giving central importance to generalisations about processes or external factors'.[77] In these myths of the referendum 'getting the rights' is condensed (as history in the form of memory and, more particularly, myth, so often is) into a single moment in time. As in traditional myth, too, these narratives are highly symbolic; the vote has become for Aboriginal people, as it had previously been for others, 'a shorthand statement, used [...] to represent the wider range of citizens' rights' they have lost or been denied.[78]

To understand more fully these Aboriginal myths of the referendum, though, we need to know the circumstances of their utterance. Goodall has suggested that myths of this nature owe something to the fact that 'when they have spoken out, Aborigines have been met not simply with arguments to the contrary, but usually by flat denials of their accusations, accompanied by denigration of Aboriginal truthfulness and of their ability to judge their own conditions'. This, she argues, 'has influenced the form of recollections'; they have been distilled into symbolic elements or become 'balder and more simplistic', 'the subtleties and complexities worn away over the years of trying to put a case in the face of indifference and denial'.[79] In this particular case, Barry Morris has argued that 'getting the rights' is a statement made in a context where Aboriginal people have the rights in a formal sense but are actually denied these by the prevailing social and cultural practices of racism. Asserting that they 'got the rights in 1967' is, therefore, a speech act, a performative narrative whose purpose (like that of FCAATSI's) is to re-negotiate the status quo and effect changes to it. Here, myth works as a charter to bolster rights that exist on paper but not in reality. As with the myths of Aboriginal leaders, these narratives are linked to the struggle for political advantage.[80]

For Aboriginal people, as well as for many settler Australians, then, myths of the referendum are still being exploited to good effect, and might serve as a vehicle for changing the course of history.

Conclusion

In general terms, a study of the 1967 referendum and its myths highlights the importance of representation – of presenting and re-presenting Aboriginal issues in order to achieve what Tim Rowse has called 'moral community'.[81] Since Aboriginal people constitute only a very small minority of the Australian populace, their political influence is 'largely based on an appeal to abstract matters – social justice, equality, righting the wrongs of history', as ATSIC chairperson Lois O'Donoghue noted in her commemoration of the referendum in 1992. This was not to 'disparage the symbolic', she remarked; on the contrary, 'as the 1967 Referendum shows, the larger gestures may have to underpin other forms of progress'.[82]

And so one might also conclude that what originally puzzled us – that small constitutional changes could be represented as a matter of major political and cultural change – is by no means peculiar, and thus should no longer baffle us. In the context of the contemporary debates concerning the republic, for example, it is evident that its champions attribute broad, mythic and symbolic meanings to seemingly minor textual changes – meanings that they hope will prove powerful and far from minimalist in the outcomes they might realise.

One can also conclude that other scholars have been in error inasmuch as their histories – confusing textual with contextual signifiers and documentary with performative functions of language – imply or assert that the referendum simply bestowed citizenship on Aboriginal people and responsibility for Aboriginal affairs on the Commonwealth; but that their meta-narrative, by analogising the referendum with these significant outcomes, does have a historical truth once it has been re-contextualised.

Notes

1 See, eg, Holmes and Sharman 1977: 87; Barry Cohen, 'Dreaming of reconciliation', *Australian*, 27 May 1992 (Cohen was assistant campaign director of the Aboriginal Rights Vote Yes campaign (New South Wales branch) in 1967). Bennett 1989: 64 notes other examples.

2 Mike Secombe, 'Aboriginal advances threatened: Perkins', *Australian*, 27 May 1987; Robert Haupt, 'White nightmare after a 20-year dreamtime', *Sydney Morning Herald*, 26 May 1987; P P McGuinness, 'Turn back the pages of history', *Australian*, 27 May 1992; *Sydney Morning Herald* (editorial), 27 May 1992; John Lahey, 'Memories of an Aboriginal victory', *Age*, 27 May 1992; Gary Hughes, 'Blacks assess 25 years of basic rights', '25 down', *Australian*, 27 May 1992; Paul Heinrichs, 'Stolen lives', *Age*, 2 December 1995; Tim Colebatch, 'The hemline that shocked the nation', *Age*, 1 January 1996; Jamie Walker, 'Black Australia's game plan', *Australian*, 6–7 January 1996; Tim Bowden, 'The man from Mer', *Australian*, 12–13 October 1996; *Australian* (editorial), 26–27 October 1996; Bill Bunbury, 'Unfinished business, part v', *Hindsight*, ABC Radio National, 3 November 1996; James Button, 'A land that time forgot', *Age*, 5 April 1997; Tony Stephens, 'Dynamic duo turned the tide on justice', *Sydney Morning Herald*, 12 April 1997.

3 *Commonwealth Parliamentary Debates, House of Representatives*, 33rd Parliament, 1st Session, 1983: 3493; see also Holding 1987. A decade earlier, Peter Howson, Minister for Environment, Aborigines and the Arts in the McMahon Ministry, was unsure whether the Commonwealth had 'acquired the power to deal with land for Aborigines in the States' (Aitken 1984: 911).

4 Sykes 1989: 1, 7, 9, 19; Smith and Sykes 1981: 72; see also Gary Foley, 'The 1967 referendum to ATSIC: a Koori perspective', seminar, the Australian Centre, University of Melbourne, 30 July 1991; McGinness 1991: 82; O'Donoghue 1992: 5–16; Patrick Lawnham, 'Perkins warns of Sydney 2000 turmoil', *Australian*, 15 May 1996.

5 See, eg, *Age* (letters to the editor), 20 September 1990.

6 See, eg, *Australian*, 10–11 February 1996; Stretton and Finnimore 1993: 521, 534.

7 Winton 1991: 411; see also 405, 406. By 1962 Aborigines in Western Australia had the right to vote in both federal and State elections.

8 Macintyre 1985: xxi, cf 130, 134; Grimshaw et al. 1994: 279, winner of the 1994 Human Rights Commission Award for non-fiction; Goodall 1995: 108; Broome 1982: 178; see also Gale 1990: 222–3; Engel 1993: 169.

9 Morris 1989: 157, 175, 185, 193, 204, 211. More convincing is Morris's suggestion that the referendum's 'political significance was blown up into a rejection of exclusionary practices against Aborigines' (Morris 1989: 157). Morris would have had a point had he written (in the passage we have cited in the text) of 'practices' instead of 'laws' (see Attwood and Markus 1997: ch. 8).

10 See Markus 1994: ch. 5.
11 Another section of the Constitution was relevant to Aborigines: section 41, which guaranteed the right to vote in federal elections to those who had that right in their State of residence. See also parallel provisions for allocation of seats and qualification or membership of parliament:
    Section 24: The number of members [of parliament] shall be in proportion to the respective numbers of their people [...]
    Section 25: [...] if by the law of any State all persons of any race are disqualified from voting at elections for the more numerous House of Parliament of the State, then, in reckoning the number of people of the State or the Commonwealth, persons of that race resident in that State shall not be counted.
    Section 30: Until the Parliament otherwise provides, the qualification of electors of members of the House of Representatives shall be in each State that which is prescribed by the law of the State as the qualification of electors of the more numerous House of Parliament of the State [...]
12 Sir Robert Garran to Professor A P Elkin, 22 July 1944, A P Elkin Papers, University of Sydney Archives, series 1/12/205.
13 See Sawer 1966: 17–30; Chesterman and Galligan 1997: 70–73; Hanks 1984: 20–21; Attwood 1996: 112.
14 Bennett 1989: 64.
15 See Attwood and Markus 1997: ch. 3.
16 Cabinet Minutes, 22 February & 11 May 1965, Australian Archives, CRS A5827, vol. 22, agendum 660, vol. 23, agendum 741.
17 Cabinet Minutes, 22 February & 23 August 1965, Australian Archives, CRS A5827, vol. 31, agendum 1009.
18 *Commonwealth Parliamentary Debates, House of Representatives*, 25th Parliament, 1st Session, 1965: 2639, 2640. It should be noted that these sentiments were expressed on both sides of the House (ibid. 1965: 3070–2, 3078–9).
19 *Commonwealth Parliamentary Debates, House of Representatives*, 25th Parliament, 1st Session, 1965: 3950, 3951.
20 Markus 1994: 190.
21 *Commonwealth Parliamentary Debates, House of Representatives*, 26th Parliament, 1st Session, 1967: 47, 107, 113.
22 Cabinet Submissions, nos 46 & 64, January 1967, and Cabinet Decision no. 79, 22 February 1967, Australian Archives, CRS A5425 & A5840.
23 Voters were asked: 'Do you approve the proposed law for the alteration of the Constitution entitled – An Act to alter the Constitution so as that the Number of Members of the House of Representatives may be increased without necessarily increasing the Number of Senators?'
24 *Age*, 17 & 22 May 1967.
25 *Commonwealth Parliamentary Debates, House of Representatives*, 25th Parliament, 1st Session, 1965: 2639; 26th Parliament, 1st Session, 1967: 263; television and radio address opening the campaign, 15 May 1967, *Age*, 16 May 1967.
26 *Age*, 27 May 1967.
27 *Commonwealth Parliamentary Debates, House of Representatives*, 26th Parliament, 1st Session, 1967: 107, 113, 115, 263; Holt, address, *Age*, 16 May 1967; Commonwealth of Australia 1967: 11.
28 *Age*, 22 May 1967.
29 *Smoke Signals* 1967, vol. 6 (2): 6; *Sydney Morning Herald*, 27 May 1967.
30 *Age*, 16 May 1967; *Sydney Morning Herald*, 16 May 1967.

31 *Australian*, 26 May 1967; *Sydney Morning Herald*, 22 May 1967. See also *Commonwealth Parliamentary Debates, House of Representatives*, 26th Parliament, 1st Session, 1967: 107; *Age*, 26 & 27 May 1967.

32 Kim Beazley (Sr), for example, realised that there were 'many things that future Commonwealth Governments *may* do if these prohibitory words are eliminated', and that it was insufficient to pass the referendum since this was only the first of the steps that had to be taken (*Commonwealth Parliamentary Debates, House of Representatives*, 26th Parliament, 1st Session, 1967: 286, our emphasis).

33 Editorial, *Smoke Signals* 1967, vol. 6 (2): 1.

34 See Markus 1990: 1–2, 161–2.

35 Vote Yes Information, 31 March 1967, FCAATSI Papers, Mitchell Library, Mss Y604; *Age*, 16 & 20 May 1967; *Sydney Morning Herald*, 26 May 1967; *Commonwealth Parliamentary Debates, House of Representatives*, 26th Parliament, 1st Session, 1967: 279; *Smoke Signals* 1967, vol. 6 (2): 1, 7; FCAATSI Press Release, cited in Bandler 1989: 110.

36 Bennett 1989: 64, also makes this point.

37 *Australian*, 8 & 17 May 1967; Vote Yes Information, 31 March 1967, Jack Horner to the Editor, *The Bridge*, 22 April 1967, FCAATSI Papers, Mitchell Library, Mss Y604; cited in Bandler 1989: 107; *Sydney Morning Herald*, 22 & 25 May 1967; *Smoke Signals* 1967, vol. 6 (1): 29; *Commonwealth Parliamentary Debates, House of Representatives*, 26th Parliament, 1st Session, 1967: 279.

38 *Age*, 17 & 24 May 1967, our emphasis.

39 *Sydney Morning Herald*, 10 May 1967.

40 *Commonwealth Parliamentary Debates, House of Representatives*, 25th Parliament, 1st Session, 1965: 3074.

41 *Commonwealth Parliamentary Debates; House of Representatives*, 25th Parliament, 1st Session, 1965: 3077; Vote Yes for Aboriginal Rights (Leaflet), Circular Letter, April 1967, FCAATSI Papers, Mitchell Library, Mss Y604; *Australian*, 17 May 1967; *Age*, 16 May 1967.

42 Horner, radio talk for Station 2GZ; Operation Referendum, Recommendations on Campaign Structure, 25 March 1967; Vote Yes Information, 31 March 1967, FCAATSI Papers, Mitchell Library, Mss Y600, Y604; *Age*, 16 May 1967.

43 *Age*, 11 & 25 May 1967; *Sydney Morning Herald*, 16, 17, 22 & 24 May 1967; Melbourne *Herald*, 26 May 1967; *Bulletin*, 20 May 1967: 27.

44 Operation Referendum, Recommendations on Campaign Structure, 25 March 1967, FCAATSI Papers, Mitchell Library, Mss Y604.

45 Leaflets reproduced in Attwood and Markus 1997.

46 Horner to the Editor, *The Bridge*, 22 April 1967, FCAATSI Papers, Mitchell Library, Mss Y604; *Age*, 3 May 1967.

47 See Stretton and Finnimore 1993.

48 Markus 1994: 177, summarises this situation.

49 Morgan Gallup Poll, 19 May 1967.

50 Commonwealth of Australia 1967: 12.

51 *Australian*, 9 May 1967; *Sydney Morning Herald*, 10 May 1967. A year earlier, in a protest in Sydney, Bandler had held a placard which read 'Count us together: make us one people' (Bandler 1989: 4).

52 Rowley 1970: 310, 343.

53 *Australian*, 17 May 1967; Horner, Radio Talk, FCAATSI Papers, Mitchell Library, Mss Y604; *Smoke Signals* 1967, vol. 6 (2): 7; *Australian*, 25 May 1967.

54 *Age*, 22 May 1967.

55 *Age*, 26 May 1967.
56 *Sydney Morning Herald*, 6 May 1967.
57 *Sydney Morning Herald*, 16 May 1967.
58 *Sydney Morning Herald*, 22 May 1967.
59 *Sydney Morning Herald*, 27 May 1967.
60 *Australian*, 5 May 1967; see also Melbourne *Herald*, 26 May 1967.
61 Vote Yes for Aboriginal Rights (leaflet), Circular Letter, 10 May 1967, FCAATSI Papers, Mitchell Library, Mss Y604; *Smoke Signals* 1967, vol. 6 (2): 7; *Australian*, 25 May 1967.
62 *Age*, 17 May 1967; *Sydney Morning Herald*, 29 May 1967.
63 *Australian*, 30 May 1967.
64 See photographs in Bandler 1989: 118–19, 211.
65 *Age*, 29 May 1967; *Australian*, 29 & 30 May, 5 June 1967; *Sydney Morning Herald*, 29 & 30 May 1967; Bandler 1989: 116, 121; Cabinet Submission, no. 432, 14 August 1967, Cabinet Decision, no. 507, 15–16 August 1967, Australian Archives, CRS A5245 & A5840; *Commonwealth Parliamentary Debates, House of Representatives*, 26th Parliament, 1st Session, 1967: 185-7, 196, 297, 384, 767, 768-70.
66 This is not to ignore the context in which Labor did so. The late 1960s and early 1970s saw the emergence of black and indigenous power, climaxing in the Aboriginal Tent Embassy which placed enormous pressure on the Australian state to address Aboriginal people's demands for change.
67 *Sydney Morning Herald*, 27 May 1992; Hughes, 'Blacks assess 25 years', *Australian*, 27 May 1992; Lahey, 'Memories of an Aboriginal victory', *Age*, 27 May 1992.
68 eg, see O'Donoghue 1992 and other papers in this ATSIC volume.
69 *Age* (Access Age), 23 January 1996. Another caller corrected this historical romance, but in doing so also misinterpreted the referendum (*Age*, 24 January 1996).
70 McGuinness, 'Turn back the pages of history', *Australian*, 27 May 1992.
71 cf Rowley 1971: 394
72 See Bennett 1985: 28–9
73 Beckett 1988: 214, endnote 17.
74 *Australian*, 27 May 1987, 27 May 1992; see also *Sydney Morning Herald*, 26 May 1987, 27 May 1992; *Age*, 27 & 28 May 1987, 27 May 1992; Sykes 1989: 3; 'Twenty Years On', *Land Rights News* 1987, vol. 2 (3): 18.
75 Goodall 1987: 17–20 (Our argument here draws heavily on this article).
76 We should not ignore the possibility that Aboriginal people *were* able to exercise certain 'citizenship rights' as a consequence of the referendum – not in the sense that it bestowed these rights upon Aboriginal people legally but rather because it drew attention to discriminatory practices in Australia and Aboriginal people's rights as Australian citizens. It thus persuaded or forced local governmental authorities and shopkeepers to abandon long-standing administrative and commercial practices (such as refusing access to swimming pools and hotels) on the one hand, and making Aborigines more aware of their rights or giving them the confidence to assert them on the other. Indeed, there is evidence that suggests this is what happened as a result of the referendum (see Attwood and Markus 1997: documents 53–5).
77 Sutton 1988: 263, 265.
78 Goodall 1987: 23, 24.
79 Goodall 1987: 22, 23, 24, 28.

80 Morris, conversation with Bain Attwood, 12 February 1996; Sutton 1988: 252, 254, 265.
81 Rowse 1993: ch. 1.
82 O'Donoghue 1992: 13, 14.

References

Aitken, D. (ed.) 1984. *The Life of Politics: The Howson Diaries.* Ringwood, Victoria: Penguin.
Attwood, B. 1996. Mabo, Australia and the end of history. In *The Age of Mabo: History, Aborigines and Australia,* ed. B. Attwood. Sydney: Allen & Unwin, pp. 100–16.
Attwood, B. and Markus, A. (in collaboration with D. Edwards and K. Schilling) 1997. *The 1967 Referendum, or When Aborigines Didn't Get the Vote.* Canberra: Aboriginal Studies Press.
Bandler, F. 1989. *Turning the Tide: A Personal History of the Federal Council for the Advancement of Aboriginals and Torres Strait Islanders.* Canberra: Aboriginal Studies Press.
Beckett, J. 1988. The past in the present; the present in the past: constructing a national Aboriginality. In *Past and Present: The Construction of Aboriginality,* ed. J. R. Beckett. Canberra: Aboriginal Studies Press, pp. 191–217.
Bennett, S. 1985. The 1967 referendum. *Australian Aboriginal Studies* 2: 26–31.
Bennett, S. 1989. *Aborigines and Political Power.* Sydney: Allen & Unwin.
Broome, R. 1982. *Aboriginal Australians: Black Response to White Dominance 1788–1980.* Sydney: Allen & Unwin.
Chesterman, J. and Galligan, B. 1997. *Citizens Without Rights: Aborigines and Australian Citizenship.* Cambridge: Cambridge University Press.
Commonwealth of Australia. 1967. *Referendums to be Held on Saturday, 27th May 1967.* Canberra: Government Printing Office.
Engel, F. 1993. *Christians in Australia, Volume 2: Times of Change 1918–1978.* Melbourne: Joint Board of Christian Education.
Gale, F. 1990. Aboriginal Australia: survival by separation. In *Shared Space: Divided Space. Essays on Conflict and Territorial Organization,* eds M. Chisholm and D. M. Smith. London: Unwin Hyman, pp. 217–34.
Goodall, H. 1987. Aboriginal history and the politics of information control. *Oral History Association of Australia Journal* 9: 17–33.
Goodall, H. 1995. New South Wales. In *Contested Ground: Australian Aborigines under the British Crown,* ed. A. McGrath. Sydney: Allen & Unwin, pp. 55–120.
Grimshaw, P. et al. 1994. *Creating a Nation.* Ringwood, Victoria: Penguin.
Hanks, P. 1984. Aborigines and government: the developing framework. In *Aborigines and the Law,* eds P. Hanks and B. Keon-Cohen. Sydney: Allen & Unwin, pp. 19–49.
Holding, C. 1987. *A Renewed Commitment: The 20th Anniversary of the 1967 Referendum.* Canberra: Australian Government Publishing Service.
Holmes, J. and Sharman, C. 1977. *The Australian Federal System.* Sydney: Allen & Unwin.
Macintyre, S. 1985. *Winners and Losers.* Sydney: Allen & Unwin.
McGinness, J. 1991. *Son of Alyandabu: My Fight for Aboriginal Rights.* St Lucia: University of Queensland Press.

Markus, A. 1990. *Governing Savages*. Sydney: Allen & Unwin.

Markus, A. 1994. *Australian Race Relations 1788–1993*. Sydney: Allen & Unwin.

Morris, B. 1989. *Domesticating Resistance: The Dhan-Gadi Aborigines and the Australian State*. Oxford: Berg.

O'Donoghue, L. 1992. One nation: promise or paradox? In ATSIC, *25 Years On: Marking the Anniversary of the Aboriginal Referendum of 27 May 1967*. Canberra: ATSIC, pp. 5–16.

Rowley, C. D. 1970. *Outcasts in White Australia*. Canberra: Australian National University Press.

Rowley, C. D. 1971. *The Remote Aborigines*. Canberra: Australian National University Press.

Rowse, T. 1993. *After Mabo: Interpreting Indigenous Traditions*. Melbourne: Melbourne University Press.

Sawer, G. 1966. The Australian Constitution and the Australian Aborigines. *Federal Law Review* 2 (1): 17–36.

Smith, S. and Sykes, B. 1981. *Mum Shirl: An Autobiography*. Richmond: Heinemann.

Stretton, P. and Finnimore, C. 1993. Black fellow citizens: Aborigines and the commonwealth franchise. *Australian Historical Studies* 25 (101): 521–35.

Sutton, P. 1988. Myth as history, history as myth. In *Being Black: Aboriginal Cultures in 'Settled' Australia*, ed. I. Keen. Canberra: Aboriginal Studies Press, pp. 251–65.

Sykes, R. B. 1989. *Black Majority*. Hawthorn: Hudson.

Winton, T. 1991. *Cloudstreet*. Melbourne: McPhee Gribble.

CHAPTER 7

Citizenship and the Community Development Employment Projects Scheme: Equal Rights, Difference and Appropriateness

Will Sanders

Discussions about citizenship and indigenous Australians are character-ised by two divergent sets of ideas. On the one hand there are ideas about equality, equal rights and sameness. On the other, there are ideas about difference, indigenous rights and uniqueness. Relationships between these two sets of ideas are inevitably rather complex and may also be changing over time. One common way of analysing discussions of recent years, for example, has been to suggest that an emphasis on equality and equal individual rights for indigenous Australians that prevailed from the 1930s to the 1960s began in the early 1970s to give way to an emphasis on difference and group indigenous rights.

Although there is considerable truth in this analysis, the reality of recent discussions about citizenship and indigenous Australians is in fact more complex. Considerations about indigenous group difference, if not quite indigenous group rights, were already being articulated in the 1960s and before, while considerations about equality and equal individual rights continue to be articulated to the present day. What has, perhaps, changed is the relative prominence given to these two sets of ideas and the precise ways in which they are balanced and reconciled with each other.

This chapter examines how these two broad sets of ideas have been implicated in the development of what has become, in dollar terms, the largest single program of the Commonwealth's Aboriginal and Torres Strait Islander affairs portfolio, the Community Development Employ-ment Projects (CDEP) scheme. Both sets of ideas have had a significant role to play in the development of this scheme, despite being somewhat in tension. In this chapter I argue that, in the context of the scheme, the two sets of ideas have been balanced or reconciled with each other through a third set of ideas focusing on the notion of appropriateness.

Origins of the CDEP scheme

The origins of the CDEP scheme are firmly based in the push for equal rights for individual indigenous Australians that reached its high point during the 1950s and 1960s. The scheme relates, in particular, to the push for equal rights for indigenous Australians within the Commonwealth social security system.

As already mentioned in earlier chapters, in the first half of the twentieth century, Aboriginal people were legislatively excluded from the social security system. In the 1940s, this legislative exclusion began to be broken down. Some Aboriginal individuals who were exempted from State and Territory Aboriginal laws could now be included, and child endowment began to be paid in respect of Aboriginal children, though not always to their parents. In 1959 the complex of exclusionary references to 'aboriginal natives' in the Social Services Act was largely removed and in 1966 one last exclusionary reference to 'nomadic and primitive' Aboriginal people was also removed. The Commonwealth's Social Services Act became devoid of any references to indigenous Australians; they were now legislatively included in the social security system in the same way as others.

During the 1960s and the early 1970s, the precise terms and nature of the inclusion of indigenous Australians within the social security system were matters of considerable administrative and policy debate. One of the most contentious issues was the extent to which Aboriginal people living in remote areas might be eligible for unemployment benefit (UB). Initially, the Department of Social Security (DSS) was not granting eligibility for UB to virtually any Aboriginal people in these areas. It regarded them, rather than unemployed, as outside the work force; or alternatively as unemployed but being unavailable or unwilling to undertake suitable work. These interpretations of the eligibility criteria for UB, as applied to Aboriginal people in remote areas, were gradually challenged and broken down. By the mid-1970s, eligibility for UB among Aboriginal people in remote areas was becoming slightly more widespread.[1]

Reactions against this spreading eligibility were, however, also considerable. In March 1974, for example, the Minister for the Northern Territory in the Whitlam Government argued that, while he accepted the 'philosophy of equality' within the social security system for indigenous Australians, he had in recent times become increasingly aware of the possible impact of such payments 'from a social welfare point of view' when applied to Aboriginal people in remote areas and he urged great sensitivity in implementation. More specifically, while he was not opposed to UB being made available to Aboriginal people in remote areas, he did note that 'in our national economy' UB 'is paid against the background of relatively full employment' while in Aboriginal communities in remote areas 'it will be paid in circumstances of general unemployment'.[2]

In 1976, the DSS's first two Aboriginal liaison officers, one of whom was himself Aboriginal, portrayed social security payments to Aboriginal people in remote areas as creating a 'dilemma'. While these people were 'officially recognised as equal', social security payments to them were, these officers argued, contributing to their 'continued dependence and inertia' and placing them 'at a greater disadvantage than ever before'.[3] Of UB they wrote:

> Unemployment Benefit is not understood – it is termed 'sit -down money' – and the payment of it is a sensitive issue [...] There is truth in the opinion that unemployment benefit plays a part in breaking down the tribal structure by giving influence, through the possession of buying power, to younger men.[4]

H C Coombs, who was at that time working with the Pitjantjatjara people in Central Australia, was another who was critical of the spread of UB payments. In early 1977 he argued that it was 'irrational' to pay UB to Aboriginal men 'to be idle' when 'socially valuable works' remained unfunded and undone in Aboriginal communities.[5]

These arguments, coming from a number of different quarters, all in various ways relied on the idea that the circumstances of Aboriginal people in remote communities were substantially different from the circumstances in which UB was normally paid in Australian society. Because of this difference, the arguments also contended that UB payments in these communities were inappropriate. But if UB payments were inappropriate because of the different circumstances of indigenous people in remote areas, what would be a more appropriate arrangement? And would a more appropriate arrangement be able to be reconciled with Aboriginal people's recently recognised equal rights within the social security system?

Coombs believed that it would be 'rational and practical to resolve this policy issue' by having the Commonwealth Department of Aboriginal Affairs (DAA) make quarterly payments to Aboriginal community organisations 'equivalent to the Unemployment Benefit which would have been received by those assessed as likely to be unemployed'. These payments would be for the purposes of employing these community members three or four days a week on 'approved work projects'. Coombs also suggested that the DAA should 'supplement these employment grants to cover material and equipment costs' and that 'Aborigines from these communities should [...] be regarded as ineligible for Unemployment Benefit'.[6]

H C Coombs was not the only force behind this idea of a UB-equivalent employment grants scheme. In 1976, an interdepartmental working party on Aboriginal employment, convened by the newly elected Fraser Coalition Commonwealth Government, made it their central concern. Reactions to the idea within the working party were, however, rather mixed. The DSS, for example, having in recent years been successfully challenged over its past application of UB eligibility criteria to Aboriginal people in remote areas, was concerned that it may face 'charges of discrimination [...] if an attempt was made to redirect payment of the unemployment benefit to the Community Council without the approval of individual beneficiaries within the community.'[7]

The Department of Employment and Industrial Relations (DEIR) also had concerns about possible charges of discrimination in its areas of responsibility, such as the payment of award wages and stipulated conditions of employer–employee relations. Reflecting these concerns, the report of the 1976 working party came to the conclusion that the 'only real long term solution' was to create 'useful employment' opportunities for Aboriginal people against which a 'realistic application' of the eligibility criteria for UB could then be made.[8] To this end, the report recommended that major upgrading and program expansion should occur within the Aboriginal Employment Section of the DEIR.[9] The idea of redirecting UB to Aboriginal community councils as employment grants was, at this stage, rejected.

In the months following the submission of this working party report to the relevant ministers in July 1976, it became evident that both the Fraser Government and the DAA were still enthusiastic about the idea of a UB-funded employment program, despite the reservations of the DSS and the DEIR. In May 1977, as part of its response to the working party report, the Fraser Government announced that for 'Aboriginals who live in remote or separate communities who do not form part of the open labour market' a new program was to be established called the Community Development Employment Projects (CDEP) scheme. The scheme was to be run by the DAA and would involve the payment of grants to Aboriginal community councils to provide employment to individual community members on a part-time basis. Funding to communities involved in the scheme would 'not exceed the total entitlement of individual community members to unemployment benefit', but could include 'specific grants' for the purchase of 'materials and equipment'. The guidelines for the CDEP scheme went on to state that:

> Each community will be encouraged to establish its own method of remuneration for its members who participate in the project provided that:
> (a) all unemployed community members, eligible to apply for unemployment benefits will be given the opportunity to participate;

(b) each contributing member, provided he contributes the required minimum hours or satisfies other minimum criteria determined by the community, will be guaranteed a minimum income approximating his normal
unemployment benefit entitlement.[10]

These elements of the CDEP scheme's guidelines linked it clearly to
eligibility for UB. They were attempting to balance ideas about equal
rights to UB for Aboriginal people with ideas about different circumstances and needs in remote areas. Some recognition of equal rights was
being made, while at the same time the CDEP scheme was attempting to
put in place a more appropriate arrangement for remote Aboriginal
communities than standard individualised UB payment. This more
appropriate arrangement was being justified by an analysis of difference.
Whether this balancing exercise between equality, difference and
appropriateness would indeed work, only time would tell. However, by
1977, the idea of attempting such an exercise had attracted the Fraser
Government's support.

Early years

The CDEP scheme began in May 1977 and within just over a year it
involved twelve communities and 800 individual participants. A year
later, in the face of strong demand from communities for inclusion, the
scheme had expanded to eighteen communities and 1300 individual
participants. From 1979 to 1983, however, the scheme did not expand at
all, despite continuing strong demand. The table on the following page
shows full details of participation and expenditure. This lack of
continued expansion related to a number of 'problems' with the scheme
that had become evident during the first couple of years of its operation.

Perhaps the greatest problem during these early years was that, unlike
UB and other DSS programs, the scheme did not have an open-ended
budgeting arrangement. Like other DAA programs, the scheme had a
fixed annual budget which it allocated at the beginning of each financial
year to participating communities. If more people in a community came
to participate in the CDEP than had been budgeted for, the fixed budget
allocation soon ran out. This happened a number of times in the early
years of the scheme and led either to supplementary budget claims on
the DAA from participating communities or the lodgement of UB claims
with the DSS. The first course of action strained relations between the DAA
and participating communities, while the second caused confusion in
relations between the DSS and CDEP communities. Was CDEP a thoroughgoing alternative to UB within participating communities or was it not?

A second problem with the CDEP scheme during its early years, at least
as viewed by the Commonwealth Auditor General and Department of

CDEP participant numbers and expenditure

Year	Communities participating	Participants (workers)	CDEP expenditure ($ million)	CDEP as % of Aboriginal affairs portfolio expenditure
1976/77	1	100	0.1	0.1
1977/78	10	500	2.0	1.6
1978/79	12	800	2.9	2.1
1979/80	17	700	3.8	2.7
1980/81	18	1,300	6.9	4.3
1981/82	18	1,300	7.0	4.1
1982/83	18	1,300	7.4	3.7
1983/84	32	1,700	14.2	5.8
1984/85	33	2,900	23.5	8.3
1985/86	38	4,000	27.2	9.2
1986/87	63	6,000	39.5	12
1987/88	92	7,600	65.5	17
1988/89	130	10,800	98.8	22
1989/90	166	13,800	133.2	25
1990/91	168	18,100	193.1	34
1991/92	185	20,100	204.5	32
1992/93	186	19,900	234.4	28
1993/94	222	24,100	251.9	27
1994/95	252	27,000	278.3	29

Sources: Sanders 1988, ATSIC and DAA Annual Reports various years since.

Finance, was that there was no precise identification of individuals involved in the scheme. Because of this, there was no capacity within the administration of the scheme for cross-checking with DSS records relating to UB. There could, as a consequence, be no guarantee that the scheme was, in fact, operating as a direct UB alternative. Potentially eligible people could be missing out on both, or participating in both. The latter, in particular, worried the Auditor General considerably and the Department of Finance to a lesser extent. Without the support of these two key bureaucratic actors, the CDEP scheme was unlikely to prosper and further expand.

A third set of problems for the CDEP scheme at this time was criticism of it in relation to International Labour Organisation conventions and domestic industrial awards. Was the scheme breaching these conventions and awards, either by paying below award wages, by forcing participants to work, or by denying participants UB? The Fraser Government and the DAA defended the CDEP scheme, arguing that it breached no conventions or awards. However, in time and in response to these sorts of criticisms, a provision was written into the scheme's guidelines that part-time pro-rata award rates had to be paid to participants.[11]

These early problems may seem a somewhat disparate array. However, they can arguably be linked, conceptually, to the question of whether the CDEP scheme was dealing adequately with the rights (and responsibilities) that individual participants in the scheme shared equally with others in the Australian community. Was the scheme adequately respecting these individuals' equal rights to UB and award wage conditions? Was it achieving a level of individualised administrative precision that could ensure protection of these rights and compliance with associated responsibilities? The problems and criticisms all suggested that there was at least some doubt about whether enough attention was being paid to these rights (and responsibilities). All suggested that the CDEP scheme's equivalence with UB was only loose and that individuals could, potentially at least, either miss out on or participate in both. The right balance between individual equal rights concerns and group difference and appropriateness did not yet appear to have been struck.

Re-adjusting the balance

From 1980, the DAA began to engage in some re-assessment of the CDEP scheme in conjunction with other Commonwealth government departments. The primary focus of this re-assessment process was the budgetary arrangement for the CDEP scheme. For a time the DAA pursued the idea of funding the wages/income support component of the scheme through the 'special benefit' provisions of the Social Security Act. By 1982, however, this had foundered and the DAA turned instead to the idea of simply gaining an open-ended budget for the scheme. The key to gaining this budgetary arrangement was convincing the Commonwealth Department of Finance that it could be justified by the links between the CDEP scheme and UB. This the DAA did finally achieve in late 1982 and early 1983. However, in doing so the DAA also had to agree that it would in future attempt to identify, precisely and regularly, individual participants in the scheme. As a result of collaboration with the DSS to determine fairly precise notional individual UB entitlements, improved identification of individual participants was also to become the basis for calculating CDEP funding levels. Potentially the arrangement could meet the concerns of not only the Department of Finance but also the Auditor General.

These changes to administrative and budgetary arrangements can be seen as a re-adjustment of the balance between considerations of individual equal rights and those of appropriateness based on arguments of indigenous group difference, the shift being strongly in favour of the former. They aimed to ensure that there would be in the scheme's budget sufficient funds to provide the equivalent of UB to all people in a CDEP community who came forward to participate. They also aimed to ensure that people listed on CDEP participant schedules could be cross-referenced against DSS records.

That the previous balance between considerations of individual equal rights and those of indigenous group difference and appropriateness had come to be seen as unacceptable was in some ways not surprising. Back in 1977, the DAA and the Fraser Government had pushed ahead with the idea of the scheme without the support of the DSS and the DEIR and largely without their input. These organisations did have both legitimate concerns and considerable expertise in issues relating to individual equal rights and individualised administration of government programs. The DAA, however, had glossed over these concerns and expertise, since its own commitments were more to community-level Aboriginal programs. Yet once the CDEP scheme was up and running, it became hard to ignore these persistent concerns. Re-adjustment of the initial balance took some time to emerge, but it was in many ways inevitable from the outset.

Expansion

When the Hawke Commonwealth Labor Government was elected to power in March 1983, these bureaucratic processes of re-adjusting the administrative and budgetary arrangements of the CDEP scheme were just being concluded. The new government allowed the open-ended budget for the CDEP scheme to proceed and also allowed some modest expansion of the scheme to additional communities which had, for some time, been seeking participation (see table, page 146). For the longer term, the Hawke Government in 1984 appointed a review committee, chaired by prominent north Queensland Aboriginal Mick Miller, to examine not just the CDEP scheme but all Aboriginal employment and training programs.

When it reported in 1985, the Miller Committee strongly supported the CDEP scheme.[12] At one level this was not surprising, since H C Coombs, still a great advocate of CDEP, was among the members of the Miller Committee. However, Labor had been quite critical of the CDEP scheme while in Opposition and, rhetorically at least, the Miller Committee was highly committed to the need to pursue an approach to Aboriginal employment policy that was quite different from those of earlier governments.[13] None of this seemed to count against the CDEP scheme. Indeed in 1986/87, further expansion of the CDEP scheme became a central element in the Hawke Government's response to the Miller Committee, its Aboriginal Employment Development Policy (AEDP).

The AEDP envisaged that the CDEP scheme would expand by 1600 participants per year for the next five years. It also suggested that the scheme could expand beyond remote communities into 'other situations where Aboriginal people have no alternative employment prospects'.[14] Annual growth in the scheme over the next five years in fact averaged something closer to 3000 participants and the scheme did spread very significantly into more settled southern Australia. By 1992 there were around 20,000 individual participants in the CDEP scheme, in 185 indigenous communities, with approximately a fifth of these communities being in more settled southern Australia (see table, page 146).

Expansion of the CDEP scheme from the mid 1980s brought its own problems. One of these was that the capacity of the DAA to effectively administer the scheme was stretched to the limit. One particularly problematic area was maintaining up-to-date individualised scheme participant schedules that were sufficiently detailed to allow the DSS to calculate individual notional UB entitlements, if indeed this was ever really achieved. Aware of this incapacity, the DAA in 1989 initiated a further interdepartmental review of the funding and administration of the CDEP scheme. Within this working party, the idea was floated of having the DSS undertake the task of managing CDEP participant schedules on the DAA's behalf.[15] However, many within the DAA were reluctant for the staffing resources and control of this central aspect of *their* program to be handed to another government agency. In the end, another approach altogether was developed under which the Aboriginal affairs administration would continue to identify people in the CDEP scheme who were on participant schedules, but would no longer attempt to provide sufficient information to allow the DSS to calculate precise notional individual UB entitlements. A simpler average-per-participant funding formula would be used. This formula was to be worked out through a 'profiling' exercise of existing CDEP participants carried out in conjunction with the Department of Finance.

At around the time when these new arrangements for CDEP participant schedules and the average-per-participant funding formula were being negotiated, the DAA ceased to exist. Its role in administering the CDEP scheme was being assumed by the newly created ATSIC. A year later, UB also ceased to exist and was replaced by two new payments under the Social Security Act: Job Search Allowance (JSA) and Newstart Allowance (NSA). In the process of amending the Social Security Act for the introduction of JSA/NSA, the Commonwealth government chose, for the first time, to spell out legislatively the relationship between CDEP and the social security benefits on which it was notionally based.

Provisions of the Social Security Act now stated that if a community or group was funded for a Commonwealth employment program on the basis of 'the number of people in that community or group who are, or are likely to be, qualified for job search or newstart allowance', then JSA/NSA would *not* be payable to persons within that community or group.[16] This legislative move was prompted by a realisation in the late 1980s that, without such provisions, it was theoretically quite legal for indigenous Australians both to participate in CDEP and, if their income was low enough, still to derive some income from UB.[17] Practically, however, it is highly doubtful that any CDEP participants who applied to the DSS ever succeeded in also gaining access to UB. The DSS seemed, administratively, quite clear on the mutual exclusiveness of CDEP and UB, even if the legislation till then had not been.

These changes to the legislative and administrative arrangements of the CDEP scheme in the early 1990s present a complex picture in relation to the analytic schema of equal individual rights and indigenous group difference. On the one hand, the equivalence of CDEP payments with individual rights to JSA/NSA was, for the first time, being legislatively specified, if only to prevent the theoretical possibility of perceived 'double dipping'. On the other hand, administrative arrangements for participant schedules and budgeting were moving away from a direct individualised equivalence to average-per-participant rates for the whole group. It might, in fact, be best to think of these outcomes of the 1989/91 review process as not so much a re-adjustment of the balance as a re-alignment of policy and legislation so as to better reflect extant administrative capacities and practices. The balance between individual equal rights and indigenous group rights did not greatly shift, but it was finally specified in a way that was more in line with the scheme's actual on-the-ground administration.

Re-emerging individual equal rights issues

These budgetary, administrative and legislative arrangements for the CDEP scheme, settled in the early 1990s, have since endured. At the general program level, they have proven reasonably satisfactory. Expansion of the scheme has continued, albeit at a rate slower than in the late 1980s (see table, page 146) However, at the level of individual CDEP participants, issues of equal rights continue to be raised and have indeed experienced something of a re-emergence.

The Human Rights and Equal Opportunity Commission (HREOC) has in recent years received a number of complaints alleging discrimination against individual CDEP participants in comparison with JSA/NSA recipients. These allegations appear to have significant credibility. CDEP participants are failing to qualify for a number of benefits, both within the social security system and outside it, for which comparable JSA/NSA recipients are qualifying. These forgone benefits include beneficiary tax rebates and, in some instances, social security rent assistance and/or health care cards. CDEP participants are also not qualifying for some State and local government concessions and rebates granted to equivalent JSA/NSA recipients.

The root cause of this apparent discrimination against individual CDEP participants in comparison with JSA/NSA recipients appears to be that, other than in the provisions of the Social Security Act added in 1991, CDEP participants are not being formally recognised as the equivalent of JSA/NSA recipients. Consequently, while they receive a rough equivalent of the basic JSA/NSA entitlement through CDEP, participants appear at times to be missing out on some of the flow-on benefits associated with being a JSA/NSA recipient.

More empirically, the growing numbers of complaints to the HREOC seem to be related to the CDEP scheme's move into southern, more settled areas of Australia. Over a quarter of CDEP participants (some 7800) were, according to ATSIC, in 'non-remote' areas as at June 1995.[18] In these areas the flow-on benefits associated with being a JSA/NSA recipient, such as rent assistance, health care cards and State and local government concessions, may be of greater relevance and importance than in remote areas. Also, interaction with similar indigenous or non-indigenous social security recipients living near them might make CDEP participants in these areas more conscious of the possibility of missing out on such benefits.[19]

Future balances: indigenous rights without remoteness

The HREOC has not yet reported on these allegations of racial discrimination on the part of the CDEP scheme. One reason is that the Commission recognises the value of the scheme as an appropriate group-based program for the delivery of social security-type payments in Aboriginal communities and does not, therefore, want to undermine this indigenous group basis of the scheme by over-zealous pursuit of equal individual rights concerns. Indeed, in dealing with these charges of discrimination, the HREOC will have to develop a quite sophisticated and subtle approach that carefully balances considerations of individual equal rights and indigenous group difference

One change that the Commission, along with others who wish to support the CDEP scheme, is now having to make is shifting its arguments away from ideas about indigenous group difference *based on remoteness*. In the past, the different circumstances of remote indigenous communities could figure prominently in arguments about the CDEP scheme's appropriateness. But now that the scheme has spread extensively into southern, more settled Australia, arguments about difference and appropriateness can no longer be cast in terms of this remoteness. Those arguments must now be cast in terms of indigenous group difference and rights, irrespective of remoteness. This is a new challenge for the CDEP scheme as it is developing at the turn of the century.

Notes

1 See Sanders 1985 for a more extensive discussion.
2 Sanders 1985: 26.
3 Harris and Turner 1976: 1.
4 Harris and Turner 1976: 3. It should perhaps be noted that Harris and Turner's contribution did provoke a reply from a more senior DSS officer, who defended equal legal entitlement provided by the social security system for indigenous Australians and argued that any new move away from it would be 'regressive'. This DSS officer argued for supplementary 'special assistance', such as interpreter services and welfare rights programs, to help overcome specific problems (Beruldsen 1976–77: 1–2).
5 Coombs 1977: 4.9.
6 Coombs 1977: 4.9–4.10.
7 Interdepartmental Working Party on Aboriginal Employment 1976: 31.
8 Interdepartmental Working Party on Aboriginal Employment 1976: 31.
9 Interdepartmental Working Party on Aboriginal Employment 1976: 4–5.
10 Commonwealth Parliamentary Debates, House of Representatives, 26 May 1977: 1922.
11 For an elaboration of all these problems during the early years of the scheme see Sanders 1988: 37–8.
12 See Miller et al. 1985: 100–1, 344–66.
13 See Miller 1985: 181–92; also Altman and Sanders 1991a.
14 Australian Government 1987: 6.
15 CDEP Working Party 1990: 29–32.
16 The relevant sections of the Social Security Act are 23(1), 532A and 614A.
17 This was pointed out during a review of the social security system in the late 1980s. See Cass 1988: 251; Altman and Sanders 1991b.
18 ATSIC Annual Report 1994/95: 70.
19 Where CDEP has been introduced in more settled areas, it has not usually completely replaced JSA/NSA in those areas. Hence the possibility of interaction with similar indigenous, as well as non-indigenous, social security recipients.

References

Altman, J. C. and Sanders, W. G. 1991a. Government initiatives for Aboriginal employment: equity, equality and policy realism. In *Aboriginal Employment Equity by the Year 2000*, ed. J. C. Altman. Research Monograph 2. Canberra: Centre for Aboriginal Economic Policy Research, Australian National University, and Academy of Social Sciences in Australia.

Altman, J. C and Sanders W. G. 1991b. The CDEP scheme: administrative and policy issues. *Australian Journal of Public Administration* 50 (4): 515–25.

Australian Government, 1987. *Aboriginal Employment Development Policy Statement, Policy Paper No. 3. Community-Based Employment, Enterprise and Development Strategies.* Canberra: Australian Government Publishing Service.

Beruldsen, J. 1976-77. The Aboriginal dilemma: a reply. *Social Security Quarterly* (Summer): 1–4.

Coombs, H. C. 1977. *The Pitjantjatjara Aborigines: A Strategy for Survival.* Canberra: Centre for Resource and Environmental Studies, Australian National University. A working paper.

Cass, B. 1988. *Income Support for the Unemployed in Australia: Towards a More Active System,* Social Security Review, Issues Paper No. 4. Canberra: Australian Government Publishing Service.

CDEP Working Party 1990. Community Development Employment Projects: Review of Funding and Administration. Unpublished report to the Review Steering Committee, February, pp. 1–97.

Harris, G. and Turner, L. 1976. The Aboriginal dilemma. *Social Security Quarterly* (Autumn): 1–4.

Interdepartmental Working Party on Aboriginal Employment. 1976. Report (unpublished), 31 July. Canberra, pp. 1–37.

Miller, M., Bin-Sallik, M. A., Hall, F. L., Coombs, H. C. and Morrison, J. 1985. *Report of the Committee of Review of Aboriginal Employment and Training Programs.* Canberra: Australian Government Publishing Service.

Sanders, W. 1985. The politics of unemployment benefit for Aborigines: some consequences of economic marginalisation. In *Employment and Unemployment: A Collection of Papers,* eds D. Wade-Marshall and P. Loveday. Darwin: North Australia Research Unit, pp. 137–62.

Sanders, W. 1988. The CDEP scheme: bureaucratic politics, remote community politics and the development of an Aboriginal 'workfare' program in times of rising unemployment. *Politics* 23 (1): 32–47.

Sanders, W. 1993. *The Rise and Rise of the CDEP Scheme: An Aboriginal 'Workfare' Program in Times of Persistent Unemployment.* Canberra: Centre for Aboriginal Economic Policy Research, Discussion Paper No. 54.

CHAPTER 8

Citizenship and Indigenous Responses to Mining in the Gulf Country

David Trigger

Certain literature on notions of citizenship in societies such as Australia posits a sense of collective commitment to the nation as crucial to being a citizen. A good example is Robert Birrell's argument that:

> Citizenship involves a social contract in which members of a society accept mutual rights and obligations towards each other. This contract is unlikely to flourish if members do not feel a sense of affinity towards one another. In this sense [...] the two ideals of nationhood and citizenship tend to fortify each other.[1]

In this chapter, I consider the relevance of this proposition to the place of indigenous people as citizens in the Australian nation. Is the 'sense of affinity' that Aboriginal people feel with the wider society such that appeals to a common citizenship (underpinned by shared interests) can be embraced? I pose this question in the context of indigenous responses to a large-scale mining development in the Gulf Country of north-west Queensland. More specifically, I address two issues. First, I look at how the discourses and practices of large-scale mining enterprises encompass a particular vision about what being a good Australian citizen entails, this vision mirroring Birrell's sense of a close connection between citizenship and commitment to what is seen as a 'national good'. Secondly, I seek to contrast such pro-development notions, which posit mining as a good thing for the nation and therefore as implicating one of the responsibilities of citizenship, with various responses to mining among the indigenous communities of the Gulf Country with whom I have conducted research for almost two decades.

To pose the question about the extent to which Aboriginal people share in sentiments generally celebrated by the broader nation is to connect with several recent theoretical issues concerning citizenship.

The ideal Western model of the polis has 'fellow citizens' sharing a common language, culture and identity, yet indigenous (and other) minority groups may well assert separate identities that confound the notion of 'a high level of mutual concern' among citizens.[2] While nation-states seek to establish citizenship as a general identity that subordinates all other identities,[3] groups like Aboriginal Australians may well reject such a notion as eroding locally cherished rights to be different. Thus, if a 'leap of faith' is required to accept that there is a 'national community committed to constituting a common good',[4] we may well ask whether indigenous citizens of the late 1990s are prepared to make it .

To address this matter, in this chapter I broach a particular instance in which identity politics has disrupted established ideologies of civic unity and moral solidarity – something that has happened in various contemporary settings across the world.[5] In this case, the ideology at issue is one that has arguably been central to the formation of the Australian nation – the proposition that large-scale natural resource development is unambiguously beneficial for all of the citizenry and thus deserves routine support.

My approach is to consider such pro-development ideology as a taken-for-granted set of assumptions about what constitutes appropriate and expected social goals for Australia, even though these assumptions are increasingly subject to challenge from various quarters, including people embracing an indigenous rights perspective. In this sense, I am investigating citizenship as a 'contested concept',[6] one that entails struggle over the *meaning* of 'membership' in societies such as contemporary Australia.

Natural resource development and what it means to be Australian

There is a growing body of work that addresses the way contemporary Australian discourses and practices in industries such as mining valorise the project of wringing material wealth from the land.[7] The moral standing of large-scale mining enterprises is framed in terms of economic productivity, as well as notions of excellence in technical accomplishment and achieving social progress through honest hard work. The latter sentiment is commensurate with a broader (and perhaps older) 'frontier ethos' in Australian society 'which places a high premium on taming harsh, unsettled northern environments'.[8] Indeed, to the extent that a very general ideology throughout Australian history has rested on the imperative to make the land productive, this notion can be read as a fundamental trope in the construction of national identity. [9]

While such convictions about mining are certainly contested in particular sectors of Australian society (for example, among those identifying with the environmentalist or Aboriginal social movements), it is not uncommon for these challenges to be regarded as intellectually un-Australian, almost outside of the historical trajectory of the national society and culture. To take an example from Western Australia, during the early 1990s several conflicts over large mining developments prompted industry spokespeople to rue the 'crisis' facing what had until recent times been a 'development consensus'. By this view, the consensus about the value of resource development has been of a moral nature in that it has been historically central to the 'nation-building ethos' that has, in the reported words of one industry executive, 'made Australia'.[10] From this perspective, then, for land to remain 'undeveloped' is considered counter to its essential moral purpose. As the Premier of Western Australia put the matter in 1976, the development of resources 'gives individuals and nations a chance to rise to the stars'; and again in 1978: 'A modern community stripped of minerals is virtually stripped of civilisation'.[11]

More recently, Wayne Goss as premier of Queensland spoke just as enthusiastically about a new 'massive mining and industrial province the size of France' in the north-west of his State.[12] This is a region designated the 'Carpentaria Mineral Province'; it straddles the Queensland–Northern Territory border and already contains five new large mines. A report released in 1993 on the 'prospects' of this area[13] agrees with the view of development as heroic and constituting Australian culture and economy. The report presents what is termed a 'vision' that looks forward to 'an ideal result' of large-scale growth in the economy and society of the region, and, by extension, to a significant positive impact on the nation.[14]

Not surprisingly, it was this 'vision' that the Queensland Premier appropriated publicly in depicting his government's achievements, clearly regarding as electorally beneficial any sentiments that support large-scale mining. Thus, to quote Goss's address to an industry conference in May 1992, Queensland is still, in the 1990s, 'a new frontier' promising great material wealth. Furthermore, 'we' (referring to some encompassing category of Australian citizens) are compelled to create this 'era of prosperity', not just for economic reasons but also for the 'more basic' and 'fundamental' reason of 'self-respect'. This rationale, he said, was related to constructing Australian identity, for it was: 'really a question of how we as Australians [...] want to see ourselves, how we want others to see us, how we want to be remembered'.[15]

My argument, then, is that in such texts we can read an underlying proposition: not to support (or in fact, not to be enthusiastic about) large-scale mining developments amounts to a type of betrayal of a national project that is paramount in moral-cum-cultural, as well as economic, terms. Hugh Morgan, a spokesperson for the mining industry during the 1980s, phrased it as a kind of traitorship towards the 'nation building ethos' that 'gave us purpose, gave us legitimacy, gave us confidence to explore, to develop, to see ourselves as taking part in the great enterprise of building an Australia which would take its place among the great nations of the world'.[16] In this type of expression of pro-development ideology, it would seem that part of the responsibility of being a good citizen encompasses the expectation that wealth-producing mining projects be supported.

Indigenous responses

Among the indigenous responses to such pro-development sentiments are those of several Gulf Country communities in north-west Queensland, especially Doomadgee and Mornington Island. I would like to focus on these here. The communities are located within the Carpentaria Mineral Province that has been the subject of so much public celebration given prominence by Wayne Goss, other politicians and commentators. However, the ebb and flow of discussion among Aboriginal people has proved much more ambiguous on the matter of support for the notion of a new 'era of prosperity' based on large-scale mining.

The communities of Doomadgee and Mornington Island began to hear about the biggest mine of the Mineral Province in 1991. Known as Century Mine, it is located some 100 kilometres south of Doomadgee and is to include a slurry pipeline to the Gulf coast. This pipeline will enable zinc ore to be loaded onto ocean going ships, which, with the beginning of the project, will enter these waters regularly for the first time. During 1991, I was engaged as a consultant to prepare two reports on initial Aboriginal responses to these plans.[17] Both listed a range of local concerns; in particular, there was little immediate positive comment. Initial indigenous responses to the discovery and subsequent celebration of the potential Carpentaria Mineral Province did not encompass, let alone rest upon, unqualified enthusiasm for 'development'.

The point I want to focus on here is the clear lack of any sense among residents of communities such as Doomadgee and Mornington Island, that they were, from the beginning, bound to support mining because it is good for the Australian nation. Furthermore, as negotiations have continued through the 1990s, there is little evidence of Aboriginal identification with the aspirations of the people building the development enterprise. Put bluntly, while the prospect of the biggest zinc mine in the world has been invested with almost gargantuan value in the media – 'the potential to generate absolutely massive wealth for the State and the nation' being the words chosen by one politician[18] – Aboriginal responses have remained fundamentally distant from and marginal to this discourse. In fact, for those *most* opposed to aspects of the development, appeals to a sense of allegiance to the national interest fare badly in the face of an overriding set of apprehensions about the effects of the mine on local Aboriginal lives. To quote the coordinator of the regional land council, after predicting negative social impacts of the mine such as 'racial' conflicts with 'redneck miners' and the prostituting of 'our young women for alcohol', he challenges directly the notion that indigenous people should prove themselves loyal to dominant sentiments: 'Is that something we should accept, *just in the interests of the nation*, more degradation to our culture?'[19]

On some occasions, pro-development protagonists have sought to link a responsibility to support mining with keeping the economy strong so that Aboriginal communities may continue to receive welfare monies. Industry and government personnel have, at several meetings where I have been present, put the proposition that without the wealth-producing enterprises of industries like mining, government spending on such 'benefits' as social security payments would not flow to any citizens of Australia. Those putting this view may well have been seeking to imply that Aboriginal communities are in fact disproportionately greater consumers of welfare benefits and therefore this matter of strengthening the economy should be acknowledged as important in places like Doomadgee and Mornington Island. However, if this was so, the point seems hardly to have been embraced appreciatively among those with whom I have conducted research. People in the Gulf communities are more likely to think of (and label) welfare entitlements as a form of 'pay' from a government that owes monies to Aboriginal people than to accept the view that this is a form of largesse which will only continue to flow if something called the national economy remains strong.

Furthermore, if there is resistance against taking responsibility for keeping the national economy healthy, there is at least as much scepticism about receiving benefits more directly from large-scale mining. During my work (over the past six years) as a consultant in relation to these matters, some acceptance does seem to have developed that the wealth to be created will benefit the Australian citizenry in general – or, at least, that it will somehow be good for the wider society. However, the extent to which material benefits will flow directly to any of the regional Aboriginal groups, has remained a much more vexed matter.

Aboriginal expectations of a reasonable regime of material benefits

Expectations at Doomadgee have certainly been raised over the past few years as news of jobs and other benefits has circulated. At one point, a poster on a notice board at the council office advertised employment at Macarthur River mine near Borroloola in enticing terms: 'Labourers Needed [...] Are you interested in earning $1000/week'. Nevertheless, given the historical marginality of Aboriginal interests to the mining developments at Mt Isa over a number of decades, considerable wariness has remained about such promising talk.

The dimensions of what might be regarded as a fair trade in return for the mining of locally significant country were introduced only gradually at consecutive meetings from 1991 onwards. After initially positing the type of 'Good Neighbour policy' deal in operation at Argyle Diamond Mine in the east Kimberley, involving relatively modest infrastructure payments annually for approved purposes,[20] a much more substantial offer was made. Over the twenty year life of the mine, Aboriginal groups would receive partial interests in surrounding pastoral properties, employment, training and various other financial benefits. This offer has engendered among some Aboriginal people support for signing an agreement to enable the mine to proceed. For example, in the reported words of the chairperson of one of the many incorporated indigenous associations: 'The reality is this mine is going to go ahead whether we like it or not, and if we are not careful we will lose what they have offered us now'.[21] Similarly, others have advocated the view that the mine will bring 'some good things' for Aboriginal people; at a meeting in August 1996, one woman linked her support for the mine and pipeline to improving the circumstances of young people at Doomadgee: 'I'll support the jobless,' she commented forcefully.

These types of sentiments should be understood as indicating two aspects of community-wide responses. One is the obvious point that such a preparedness to sign an agreement about mining does not necessarily represent open enthusiasm for the project; rather, the people quoted can be regarded as expressing a desire to obtain whatever benefits are possible in the face of what seems inevitable. And secondly, both speakers were likely to have been concerned about the divergent views of other members of the Gulf communities, who have stressed issues about the mine quite apart from the matter of deriving economic benefits. While all have thought it appropriate that the company pay monies (at times referred to as 'compensation') should the mine proceed, and all have certainly been impressed with the capacity of the company to pay – for people have witnessed the purchasing of large areas of land surrounding the mine location – diverse family and interest groups have taken a range of positions on two broader issues, namely concerns about the integrity of country and environmental pollution. In contrast with the expressed viewpoints on negotiating for material benefits, one woman living on Mornington Island was convinced that the development would destroy her people's 'culture' and use of the marine environment: 'we don't want to lose our country for some shitty little jobs!'[22]

Apprehensions about the integrity of country

Many among Waanyi people (those who claim traditional connections with the Century Mine area) have expressed concerns about the apparent effects of a large open cut pit on what is locally conceived as 'country' – that is, the landscape and its material and spiritual properties. As people have gradually become aware of the planned scale of disturbance, their sense of apprehension about the land being so drastically modified has grown. I suspect, for example, that for some of those who visited Argyle, on a trip intended to illustrate the type of mine planned for Century, the very large scale of the pit was a great surprise. Several comments made to me during the visit and immediately afterwards indicated concern that the cultural integrity of the landscape around the Century Mine site would inevitably be threatened by developing this type of project there. To quote one man, such a deep pit would in his view inevitably 'wake up that Rainbow Snake' – that is disturb a major spiritual force present so far underground; from his perspective, this was a danger regardless of whether the pit was to be dug in an area where surface features of topography are particular foci of 'sacred sites'.

This type of boding apprehension has not been incommensurate with individuals occasionally marvelling at the engineering feats evident in such developments; as one older woman commented when inspecting the neat contours of a substantial bulk sample test pit at the Century site, 'marvellous thing isn't it'. Like most Australians, local Aboriginal people have commonly not had the opportunity to witness the precision with which mining technologies can carve neat holes in the landscape. However, among the Gulf communities I have recorded nothing similar to the way tourists (as well as local white residents of mining towns) might express a sense of awe and pride when observing the scale of technical achievement at large open cut mines.[23] I have not found indigenous sentiments that match one commentator's view of mineral exploration as 'exciting and intriguing for most Australians'.[24]

To the extent that this latter sentiment is shared across a sufficiently broad proportion of the Australian population, Aboriginal people (along with some other citizens, it must be noted) may be said to remain marginal to an important focus for civic pride. Their different conception of what I have termed the 'integrity' of country entails a lack of 'affinity' (to use Birrell's term) with Australians who valorise large scale resource development. And, to return to my central argument in this chapter, this can be seen as reflecting the partial non-inclusion of Gulf

Aboriginal communities in a key aspect of the type of 'social contract' involved in citizenship.

Furthermore, the difficulties for many residents of Doomadgee and Mornington Island in embracing the achievements of mining do not follow only from the perspective by which landscape is regarded as encompassing spiritual forces that should not be disturbed in the ways that are typically produced by deep open cut mines. The other major problem is people's entrenched fears and apprehensions about damage to both land and water through potential environmental pollution.

Concerns about environmental pollution

Since the first mention of the mine in the meetings and discussions I have attended (beginning in mid-1991), Aboriginal worries about environmental impacts have been expressed constantly. The Lardil, Yanggal and Kaiadilt people of the Wellesley Islands, as well as the coastal mainland Ganggalida people, have remained quite negative about the proposed pipeline and shipping in the Gulf.[25] Their fears about pollution of the marine environment have not been allayed by any evidence designed to convince them that this is not a major negative feature of the development. For example, a question of continual concern among the groups discussing this matter has been whether the water to be separated from the zinc slurry at the coast will be fit for humans to drink. It has been clear that the company has not been able to give such a guarantee. Assurances that the water, after treatment, will nevertheless be fine for cattle to drink has not lessened worries among the groups of 'saltwater people' about whether marine species would be affected drastically in the event of accidental spillage of the zinc ore.

To a lesser extent, the Waanyi people have also expressed concerns about potential environmental pollution at the inland mine site and along the pipeline route; on one instructive occasion when a group of some twenty people had the opportunity to inspect a bulk sample pit, both the colour of the water at the bottom (unlike ordinary surface water) and the fact that no birds were seen to fly near it were commented upon as causes of unease. It was said to look unfit for human or animal consumption. While the company officer could not dispute that fact, he was at pains to assure everyone present that throughout the life of the mine such water would be kept separate so that it evaporated in a safe fashion. However, people were not persuaded that this type of water would not eventually find its way into the streams used for fishing and hunting.[26]

Waanyi people have also always been aware of the importance of taking into account their relatives' fears about 'saltwater country'. Certainly, there have been some among both the 'saltwater people' and the inlanders who have appeared to overcome any apprehensions about the environmental safety of the mine. Yet the pressure on mainlanders from island people who remain opposed to the development is perhaps well illustrated by a comment from one man after a meeting on Mornington Island. He reported a warning received there that those who voted to accept an agreement about the pipeline aspect of the mine project should be careful not to return to the island as they would be physically attacked ('speared' is the term this man reported, and then commented that 'those people don't muck around', implying that he took the threat seriously).

Some of the more extreme expressions of emergent indigenous fears might be regarded as highly unlikely consequences of the mine; for example, a reported apprehension that deformities would appear in new babies in the event of possible leakage from the slurry pipe or from marine operations. However, other concerns about environmental degradation have arguably been well founded. At the least, they are understandable, given the lack of what might be seen locally as reliable information on such matters as the nature of 'zinc'. 'Is it a poison?' asked one man at a meeting in 1994.[27] The reply from a company consultant was that zinc is a natural substance and that it is used to make the type of galvanised iron roofing we were sitting under. Yet these types of explanation never appeared to reassure everybody about the general question of whether water sources and the ecology of the land in general would suffer because of the mine. To cite the chairperson of the main negotiating body that operated during 1995, made up of representatives of many Aboriginal groups, offers of money are unlikely fully to displace people's concerns about such dangers in relation to the pipeline to the Gulf waters: 'You can have the mine but you can't have the pipeline because when all the money is gone what will we have left if our land is destroyed? You can't eat money'.[28]

Conclusion

In this chapter I have sought to depict the way in which natural resource development projects, particularly large-scale mining, are important culturally, as well as economically, in Australian society. Pro-development ideology implies that support and enthusiasm for mining are part of a type of civic virtue, a responsibility entailed in owning an Australian history and identity. While this view has clearly been challenged from a number of directions, I have suggested that it is dominant in the discourses and practices of industry and government. To the extent that predominant notions of citizenship are 'inscribed in the very logic' of contemporary societies,[29] I would argue that in Australia a major strand of this logic places at the centre of a celebrated national identity the enterprise of wealth creation from the land.

Clearly much talk and action rest on the underlying commonsense idea that 'developing' natural resources is part of being Australian. The quotations from politicians given in the first section of the chapter illustrate this proposition vividly in the context of public discourse in the 1990s. The fact that large companies, including mining companies, at times reflect upon their role in society partly through a notion of 'corporate citizenship' is of further interest. For, in the case of mining companies, the underlying proposition would seem to be that what firms do (in this instance, large-scale mining) can be conceived in terms of concepts of social participation and responsibility that are characteristic of the notion of being a good citizen.[30] If this is so, those who may seek to construct the concept of social responsibility differently (in the context of this chapter, perhaps in terms of some quite overt opposition to the mining project) must argue a case against a powerful nexus between government, industry and a substantial degree of popular sentiment.

Indeed, in this chapter I have examined indigenous marginality to that aspect of the 'logic' of Australian identity that focuses on the idea of responsible wealth creation from the land. If there are to be 'civic duties' owed to the nation in return for citizenship, it appears, in the Gulf Country at least, that Aboriginal people remain peripheral to a prevailing conception of what those responsibilities entail. This is not to ignore the fact that many Aboriginal people in this region may well maintain a sense of commitment, perhaps loyalty in the international arena, to Australia as the country and society they share with millions of others; though it would be equally unwise to over-estimate the extent to which nationalist sentiments hold appeal in indigenous communities.[31]

My point here is that the *nature* of Aboriginal 'affinities' with a national identity, and with an encompassing notion of an Australian citizenry, will rest upon 'logics' that are different from the assumption about 'developing' the land that has been so historically important in the wider society. In the light of mainstream Australia's ongoing commitment to natural resource development, indigenous logics currently find expression in *different* commonsense views about what should be done with land, what the rights and responsibilities of Aboriginal people should be, and what the dimensions of a fair 'trade' are with respect to the flow of benefits from large projects.

Finally, to the extent that such 'logics' can be linked to notions of indigenous 'citizenship' in the communities discussed in this chapter, developments like Queensland's new mineral province prompt the broad question of whether (in a multicultural society) difference is to be nurtured or subordinated.[32] A notion of 'cultural citizenship' for encapsulated minorities such as indigenous Australians may be useful here.[33] Cultural citizenship for Australian Aboriginal people would imply that real moral weight should be accorded to world views and practices that are at times inconsistent with predominant sentiments in Australian society. In the case discussed in this chapter, this would mean accepting that one major dimension of indigenous responses to large-scale mining projects entails considerable resistance to a conception of landscape that rests on its commodification for the production of economic wealth and associated societal 'progress'.

Notes

For helpful comments and reading of a draft of this chapter I wish to thank Bob Tonkinson, Myrna Tonkinson and Lillian Maher.

1   Birrell 1995: 281.
2   Kymlicka 1995: 2, 173.
3   Holston and Appadurai 1996: 187.
4   Holston and Appadurai 1996: 192.
5   Holston and Appadurai 1996: 195.
6   Hall and Held 1989: 175.
7   Edmunds 1995; Howitt 1995; McEachern 1995; Trigger 1995.
8   Harman 1982: 175.
9   Bolton 1992.
10 See the *Weekend Australian*, 21–22 September 1991, p. 29, quoting the executive director of the Business Council of Australia; and Morgan 1993: 1–2.
11 Quoted in Harman 1982: 177, 179.
12 *Courier Mail*, 14 April 1993.
13 The report is entitled 'Carpentaria and Mt Isa Mineral Province Study', external release report. It was prepared by a management committee on behalf of the federal, Queensland and Northern Territory governments and representatives of the five biggest mining companies in Australia, namely Mount Isa Mines, BHP, Western Mining Corporation, CRA and Placer Pacific (copy in author's possession).
14 1993: 8.
15 Goss 1992: 31.
16 Morgan 1993.
17 Trigger 1991a; 1991b.
18 *Sunday Mail*, 31 March 1996.
19 Quoted in Wear 1996: 35; my emphasis.
20 See Dixon and Dillon 1990.
21 *Courier Mail*, 4 April 1996, p. 4.
22 Field notes recorded, Mornington Island, October 1991.
23 My research in progress conducted at a number of large-scale mines in Western Australia suggests this kind of identification with technical achievements on the part of visitors at locations like BHP's huge Mt Newman iron

ore mine (Trigger 1995; 1997). There are several resource developments throughout the Pilbara region of Western Australia which cater specifically to those who wish to observe and marvel at the scale of accomplishment. A good example is the visitor's centre overlooking the massive liquid natural gas plant at Dampier. Interestingly, members of the regional Aboriginal population from Roebourne have reportedly shown little interest in the centre; however, according to an anthropologist who has been working recently with them (personal communication, Michael Robinson), these Ngarluma and Yinjibarndi people have expressed the desire to have an alternative visitor's centre built nearby, one that would encompass an impressive gallery of rock engravings and tell a different story of celebration about specifically Aboriginal achievements and occupation of the landscape.

24 Duffy 1991: 6.
25 See Trigger 1992: 19 for a figurative representation of these linguistic territories.
26 Field notes recorded at Century Mine, April 1995.
27 Field notes recorded at Sweers Island during a two day meeting between Aboriginal representatives and CRA personnel (1994).
28 *Courier Mail*, 25 May 1996.
29 Hall and Held 1989: 176.
30 Moon 1995: 10.
31 Indeed, it would be naive to assume that there are not, and will not be, major challenges to this view from certain sections of the Aboriginal political movement. Consider the blunt statement that may be drawn from a recent 'Principles for a Treaty' document circulated by an organisation calling itself an Aboriginal Provisional Government: 'governments presume we are citizens of the Australian nation, and our rights are accordingly limited. But we have never been given the opportunity to say if we agree'.
32 Kymlicka 1995: 189.
33 Peter Brosius (1993) has eloquently discussed the notion of cultural citizenship in relation to the encapsulated Penan peoples of Sarawak, Malaysia, and their responses to large-scale logging.

References

Birrell, R. 1995. *A Nation of Our Own.* Sydney: Longman.
Bolton, G. 1992. *Spoils and Spoilers: A History of Australians Shaping their Environment.* Sydney: Allen & Unwin.
Brosius, P. 1993. Negotiating citizenship in a commodified landscape: the case of Penan hunter-gatherers in Sarawak, east Malaysia. Paper prepared for the Social Science Research Council conference, Cultural Citizenship in South-East Asia, Honolulu, Hawaii, 2–4 May 1993.
Duffy, M. 1991. The battle for our hearts and mines. *Independent Monthly* 6 August: 6–9.
Dixon, R. and Dillon, M. (eds) 1990. *Aborigines and Diamond Mining: The Politics of Resource Development in the East Kimberley Western Australia.* Perth: University of Western Australia Press.
Edmunds, M. 1995. *Frontiers: Discourses of Development in Tennant Creek.* Canberra: Aboriginal Studies Press.
Goss, W. 1992. Queensland's new directions in mining policies. *The Mining Review* 16 (3): 28–31.

Hall, S. and Held, D. 1989. Citizens and citizenship. In *New Times: The Changing Face of Politics in the 1990s*, eds S. Hall and M. Jacques. London: Verso, pp. 173–88.

Harman, E. 1982. Ideology and mineral development in Western Australia, 1960–1980. In *State, Capital and Resources in the North and West of Australia*, eds E. Harman and B. Head. Perth: University of Western Australia Press, pp. 167–96.

Holston, J. and Appadurai, A. 1996. Cities and citizenship. *Public Culture* 8: 187–204.

Howitt, R. 1995. *Developmentalism, Impact Assessment and Aborigines: Rethinking Regional Narratives at Weipa*. Darwin: Australian National University North Australia Research Unit, Discussion Paper No. 24.

Kymlicka, W. 1995. *Multicultural Citizenship: A Liberal Theory of Minority Rights*. Oxford: Clarendon Press.

McEachern, D. 1995. Mining meaning from the rhetoric of nature – Australian mining companies and their attitudes to the environment at home and abroad. *Policy, Organisation and Society* 10: 48–69.

Moon, J. 1995. The firm as citizen? Social responsibility of business in Australia. *Australian Journal of Political Science* 30 (1): 1–17.

Morgan, H. 1993. Australia and its mining industry: the next generation. Australian Institute of Mining and Metallurgy centenary conference, 1993 Keynote Address (2/4/93).

Trigger, D. 1991a. Report on a Trip to Doomadgee, Mornington Island and Mt Isa, 1–10 June 1991. Prepared for Doomadgee Community Council and Carpentaria Land Council.

Trigger, D. 1991b. Submission concerning Century Mine (north-west Queensland) to the Department of Premier, Economic and Trade Development, arising from consultations with members of Doomadgee Aboriginal community and Mornington Island Aboriginal community, 30 September to 4 October 1991.

Trigger, D. 1992. *Whitefella Comin': Aboriginal Responses to Colonialism in Northern Australia*. Cambridge: Cambridge University Press.

Trigger, D. 1995. *Contesting Ideologies of Resource Development in Australia: Towards an Analysis of Pro-development Sentiments*. Perth: Indian Ocean Centre for Peace Studies, University of Western Australia, Occasional Paper No. 42.

Trigger, D. 1997. Mining, landscape and the culture of development ideology in Australia. *Ecumene* 4 (2): 161–80.

Wear, P. 1996. Loudmouths rule, OK? The *Bulletin* (26 March 1996).

PART III

Emerging Possibilities

CHAPTER 9

Whose Citizens? Whose Country?

Peter Read

In 1935 a fair-skinned Australian of part-indigenous descent was ejected from a hotel for being Aboriginal.[1] He returned to his home on the mission station to find himself refused entry because he was not Aboriginal.[2] He tried to remove his children but was told he could not because they were Aboriginal. He walked to the next town where he was arrested for being an Aboriginal vagrant and placed on the local reserve.[3] During World War II he tried to enlist but was told he could not because he was Aboriginal.[4] He went interstate and joined up as a non-Aboriginal person. After the war he could not acquire a passport without permission because he was Aboriginal. He received exemption from the Aborigines Protection Act – and was told that he could no longer visit his relations on the reserve because he was not an Aboriginal.[5] He was denied permission to enter the Returned Servicemen's Club because he was.[6] In the 1980s his daughter went to university on an Aboriginal study grant. On the first day a fellow student demanded to know, 'What gives you the right to call yourself Aboriginal?'[7]

We can multiply examples of this kind of extinction by legislation to the present day. In the 1960s Charles Perkins was told more than once that he could not be Aboriginal because he was a university graduate.[8] Though supposed under the National Service Act to be exempt from compulsory military service, Stanley Ward of Western Australia was ordered by a magistrate to enrol for National Service even though he was in other respects regarded and defined as Aboriginal.[9] In the 1950s officers of the New South Wales Aborigines Welfare Board were ordered to remove children from their parents, but then if possible, to persuade the Department of Child Welfare to receive the children into its – not the Board's – institutions.[10] That is, a child was to be removed because, and

169

only because, she was Aboriginal; but the moment after removal she was to cease to be Aboriginal.

We can find more subtle examples. In the 1990s Michael Mansell attacked the use by non-Aboriginal people of the phrase 'Aboriginal Australians', which focussed attention on the noun 'Australians', instead of 'Australian Aborigines', which focused attention on the noun 'Aborigines'; he identified the *Encyclopaedia of Aboriginal Australia* as one notable transgressor in this matter.[11] Recently the magazine *Open Road*, published by the National Roads and Motorists Association (NRMA), referred to the 'Guringai' people of New South Wales as 'the Aborigines who were here before the White people arrived',[12] not 'after', nor even 'when' the whites arrived. A tourist guide implied that Sydney Aboriginal people had somehow ceased to exist fractionally before 1788: 'many of the birds, mammals, reptiles and fish of the area were woven into the myths of the Aboriginal people who lived here, before the settlement of Sydney.'[13]

In this chapter I will argue that colonialism – not racism – is responsible for the practice of extinction by legislation. I will look at the national unease caused by issues of belonging that emanate from the demands for *unequal* citizenship now being made by Aboriginal people. As a solution I will suggest that indigenous and non-indigenous Australians accept their shared status as second-class citizens – and that we find ways to benefit mutually from this bond.

Whose definition?

Definitions, whether they were enacted as a rule of thumb by a local constable or station manager, or as a promulgation by Act of Parliament, were clearly rules developed by and for the non-indigenous people. But why such diametrically opposed, and seemingly nonsensical, variations in the definitions? Was it simply a matter of legislative incompetence? We could multiply these examples to fill a book, and at each one we might express anger at the stupidity of officials, horror at the callousness of dividing families arbitrarily, pity at the extraordinarily destructive effect of such bloody-minded ineptitude, despair at a bureaucracy whose right hand never seemed to know what the left was doing. But that would be to miss the point. Surely another appropriate emotion would be awe at the never-ending ingenuity of the colonists to puzzle, divide, and ultimately cause to vanish, the indigenous people who continued to pose a problem by their unwillingness to disappear.

These seemingly mutually excluding definitions, at first sight idiotic, were no accident. Likewise, the divisions in the minds of Aboriginal people as to what exactly they were supposed to be was no coincidence.

Separated Aboriginal children who identified themselves in later life as 'white' were intended to do so.[14] The families who moved off reserves to live in towns (if they were allowed), or hundreds of kilometres from other Aboriginal people (if they were not), were meant to leave these sites of Aboriginal community.[15] Nor was it an accident that the word and concept 'assimilation' was first bestowed not on Aboriginal people but on immigrants to Australia as early as the 1920s.[16] Newcomers from overseas had to fit themselves into Australian society by divesting themselves of previous cultural and intellectual norms. Aboriginal people, by implication, were similarly outside the mainstream. They too had to change as if they were immigrants.

So those earlier official definitions which, seemingly without purpose, divided families into categories like 'half-caste', 'quadroon', 'octoroon' and 'having an admixture of Aboriginal descent', and those seemingly innocuous lines in *Open Road* which 'accidentally' suggested that the Ngunnawal ceased to be Ngunnawal after 1788, are symptomatic of an enduring thread in modern Australian history. Put simply, they are evidence of the national failure to come to terms with the continuing existence of the entrapped indigenous minority.[17] In the far north, since it is impossible to deny the presence of large numbers of indigenous people, the Northern Territory government holds to the position of opposing many indigenous land claims per se. In the south it is more common for local government to offer in-principle support for indigenous rights. But for whom? Dozens of regional and local histories testify that 'once' Aboriginal people were present, but now they are gone.[18] Why, we may ask, are there so few self-identifying indigenous people in so many parts of southern Australia? Because, in part, they have been legislated out of existence, told that they did not exist for so long that in the end their children's children forgot where they had come from, or even that they ever had been Aboriginal people at all.[19]

I think non-indigenous Australians have yet to understand fully that the confusion over definitions of Aboriginality, and hence the absence of a self-identifying Aboriginal presence in so much of southern Australia, stems neither from a well-meaning muddle nor from a malevolent desire for cruelty but from a partially successful attempt at ethnic cleansing through language. Tasmania, of course, did it best. The Tasmanian Government was able to resist demands for land rights for decades on the premise that Tasmania did not have any Aboriginal people.[20] Yet the practice of extermination by legislation was widespread on the mainland too. I think it is unhelpful to continue to describe the practice as racism, since non-Aboriginal Australians seem in fact to be no more racist than the rest of the world's national groups, and less so than some. It is true that many non-Aboriginal Australians have yet to come to terms with

Aboriginality as an element of Australian diversity, but if we think of it as a problem stemming from the deadly relationships inherent in colonialism rather than racism, then we all have a better starting point from which to identify where we have gone wrong.

Whose citizens? Whose country?

It's pretty clear that all the myriad ways that non-Aboriginal Australians have used to diminish the indigenous minority have failed to make them disappear. The decade of the 1960s was an important watershed, for it was in that decade that the Aboriginal demand for 'citizens' rights', 'civil rights' or 'equal rights' was dropped as the sole aim of the protest movement. It was replaced with the demand for the status and privileges of *unequal* citizens with which we are familiar today – that is, Aboriginal people of the 1990s want to be equal citizens *and* have the rights pertaining to their special status as 'indigenous people'.

The shift in demand has brought to non-Aboriginal people problems that are intangible as well as tangible. The tangible issues are legislative, and concern compensation, land rights and social justice. They are well known and there's no point in adding anything here. The intangible issues are much more difficult to resolve.

In the 1990s we have begun to think more about our own status as non-indigenous citizens who do not belong here in the way that Aboriginal people do. This unease, so far as I am aware, is a recent phenomenon, and is not to be confused with the concession, two centuries old, that Aboriginal people have been wrongfully dispossessed.[21] Nor should we confuse this growing crisis in confidence with the melancholy Jindyworobaks, because they too argued from the strength of material possession. Rex Ingamells wrote, 'We who are called Australians have no country'[22] but he was writing out of a kind of spiritual magnanimity. The Aboriginal people, so the 'Jindys' thought, were finished.

In our own time, Judith Wright probably was first to touch the theme of alienation: 'The love of the land we have invaded, and the guilt of the invasion, have become part of me. It is a haunted country.'[23]

H C Coombs, the chair of the Aboriginal Treaty Committee, echoed the same thought in 1983:

> We've become acustomed to think of our occupancy of the land as legal, justified and secure. I think, again, each of those assumptions can be brought into doubt. And therefore I think we have to consider that the kind of security we feel in the occupation of the land at the present time may very well be called into question, certainly by Aborigines. [...] And therefore if we wish to feel secure, and for our children and grandchildren to feel secure, then I

think we have to establish the justification, the legitimacy of our occupation. And that means the legitimacy of our relationship with the original inhabitants, the Aborigines. [24]

Wright and Coombs, through experience and relentless self-examination, made their own advances. Others were more reluctant to ponder the Aboriginal message, which has been plain enough for those prepared to hear it.

In the first instance, it was there by implication: 'We belong to the land; our birth does not sever the cord of life which comes from the land.'[25]

In the second instance, non-belonging has been signalled through the technique, familiar to state governments, of redefining the other out of existence. Archie Roach, in the first song of his first album, contrasted native born Australians – humans, plants and animals – with outsiders, and the humans are Aboriginal people only:

> But no one knows and no one hears
> the way we used to sing and dance
> and how the Gum Tree stood and stretched
> to greet the golden morn
> and mother land still sheds her tears
> for lives that never stood a chance
> And Albert Namatjira cries, as we all cry,
> the Native Born.[26]

In the third instance, non-belonging has been simple assertion. I asked an Aboriginal park ranger whether non-Aboriginal people could ever be as attached to the land as Aboriginal people are. His answer: 'Not in the same context as the Aboriginal people. Australian European people have lost contact with the land over the last 2500–3000 years. There's no comparison.'[27]

The distinction drawn by Aboriginal people between themselves and all other Australians became obvious in the recent discovery that we do not have a word for the latter save for the negative 'non-Aboriginal' or 'non-indigenous.' We have no equivalent of the term 'pakeha', which means 'born in New Zealand, but not Maori'. In Australia, 'white' will no longer serve, nor 'European', since so many Australians are neither. 'Settlers' and 'colonials' may have been appropriate for the nineteenth century, but are not for now; it is equally absurd to cast post-World War II migrants as 'invaders', which in any case is so pejorative as to be self-defeating. The lack of a word which, a short time ago, we did not need – a word for the inheritors of, and latecomers to, former colonies still entrapping indigenous minorities – illustrates how recently we have had to face the issue put so eloquently by Judith Wright:

> So it was late I met you,
> late I began to know
> they hadn't told me the land I loved
> was taken out of your hands.[28]

Citizenship, then, is a two way process. We 'non-Aboriginal Australians' – and perhaps now we can feel how degrading it was to be defined by a negativity like 'quarter-caste' – are finding that it is as difficult for us to be first-class citizens of Aboriginal Australia as it is for Aboriginal people to be first-class citizens of our Australia.

Yet the non-indigenous remain profoundly bonded to the land. For the past three years I have been investigating the attachment that non-Aboriginal Australians feel towards the land they live on,[29] and there can be no doubt how passionately many of them love the bush, or a hill or a farm. Not just 'Australia' or 'gum trees' either, but a particular rural property or suburban block where they were born, or where their children grew up, or where they wish to be buried, or where they have spent their lives. There can be no doubt about the depth of attachment that very many Australians feel to quite specific areas. Now, no sooner do we assert that sense of attachment than the obvious question follows: 'How, if at all, can the rest of us emotionally share the same country from which Aboriginal people have been dispossessed?' To recast the problem, how is it possible to hold this love of the land as legitimate and unproblematic in the knowledge that Aboriginal people have been, and still are, displaced from it?

Many younger indigenous people seem to me to be following Roach's lead. The Aboriginal people involved in politics, the arts and the professions whom I have interviewed recently for a National Library oral history project do not seem to be in much doubt about the strength of the relative attachments.[30] When I have asked the question 'Can non-Aboriginal people ever – now or at any point or in the distant future – feel that they can belong here as you do?' the answer is generally a comprehensive 'No'. After a dozen such interviews I realised with alarm that many younger Aboriginal people believe that we non-Aboriginal people may live here, but that we do not belong here in any profound way. Nor can custodianship, it seems, be shared. Uluru, Jervis Bay and Lake Mungo National Park are supposed to be held in joint legal – and, one hopes, spiritual – equality. But some of the Aboriginal interview subjects, at the risk of patronising the actual elders negotiating the principles of shared management, believed that the so-called agreements were simply an imposition of *force majeure*. While Aboriginal people seem likely to remain second-class citizens *in daily life*, it seems that non-Aboriginal people aware of these issues are destined to remain second-class citizens *of Aboriginal Australia* – we do not belong.

Even while recognising the difference between 'We don't belong' and 'Aboriginal people say we don't belong', there seems no very obvious direction for the discussion to follow. The appalling revelations made daily by the inquiry of the Human Rights and Equal Opportunity Commission into the separation of Aboriginal children from their families may only exacerbate feelings that, as fellow inhabitors of this country, non-Aboriginal citizens have some heavy mileage to make up, way beyond financial compensation and the right to a day in court.

It may be thought odd to begin a discussion with the lacunae of Aboriginal citizenship and finish with those of our own. But it is becoming clearer that non-belonging is the other side of the post-colonial coin, and I wish that the Labor Government had approached the native title negotiations not in the spirit of 'We did you wrong and we seek to make it up', but 'What must we do to earn the right to full spiritual citizenship which you Aboriginal people enjoy?' Or to put the matter within the ambit of the Equal Opportunity Commission inquiry: 'the Link-Up agencies can take you separated Aboriginal people home. But who can – or who is willing – to take the rest of us home?'

Conclusion

Whose citizens? Whose country? A variety of more or less unsatisfactory solutions have been offered. People can, and many already do, simply assert the right to emotional or spiritual belonging irrespective of Aboriginal opinion. Or they assert that we share and are bonded by a common history of dispossession, whether by gunfire, bulldozer, mortgage over-commitment, unemployment, or resumption of the family home by government for a freeway or a dam.[31] Or a few lucky ones have grown up with Aboriginal people, or spend so much of their professional lives with them that they are assured by their Aboriginal hosts that they and their children will belong to that land forever; but that will be of little use to the majority who do not enjoy such a privilege.[32] Richard Flanagan's *Death of a River Guide*, is a powerful mix of love of country and Aboriginal and convict ancestry, but is too eclectic to be shared by others.[33] Cassandra Pybus and other writers have wrestled with a violent past which, to quote Don Graham, threatens like subterranean salt to seep to the surface to pollute relationships of the present and the future.[34]

If there is any negotiated resolution to be made in this generation, it may be in answering this question: Is it possible for non-Aboriginal people to be emotional and spiritual citizens of Australia, by holding to a parallel, not shared, affection and love for their own places? Thus, non-Aboriginal people at Uluru or Lake Mungo would bring to those sites their own emotions, desires, spiritual journeys and senses of belonging; and provided they do not assert that what they felt was what Aboriginal people feel, and provided they made no claim to spiritual kinship with them, the deep emotions evoked at these places in native-born Australians of this land would be legitimised and acceptable. Whatever resolution is found, and perhaps it will not be found at all in this generation, its success will and should depend in no small part on how much progress we make on the other side of the equation.

Let's not, therefore, regard the issue of citizenship and indigenous Australians as one-dimensional. It is bilateral. Neither Aboriginal people nor non-Aboriginal people are full citizens of this land. We lack essential, though different things, for we are both, in our different ways, second-class citizens. It is possible to help each other to achieve our goals once we concede that each of us has something to offer the other.

Notes

1 eg Locky Ingram in Read 1984: 78–9.
2 Read 1983: 75ff.
3 eg Aborigines Protection Act, NSW, Amendment No. 32 of 1936.
4 Australian Military Regulations and Orders, no. 177; however, since judgements of people unknown to the local authorities were made solely on appearance, it was perfectly possible for a person of Aboriginal descent to enlist in another State. For further discussion see Robert Hall 1980: 73.
5 eg Aborigines Act, SA. The Act remained in force until repealed by Don Dunstan, no. 45 of 1962.
6 eg see Read 1990: ch. 4.
7 eg see Sinclair 1989: 74–5.
8 C Perkins, personal communication.
9 Jordens 1989: 131–2.
10 Former Aborigines Welfare Board officer, personal communication.
11 Mansell 1994: 884.
12 July 1995. I am grateful to Jay Arthur for this and the following reference.
13 Raymond 1989: 74.
14 cf Robert Donaldson, later Chief Inspector of the New South Wales Aborigines Protection Board, to the Australian Catholic Congress, 1909: [if the removed children are prevented from returning to the camps, then soon] 'the old people will have passed away, and their progeny will be absorbed into the industrial classes of the colony'.
15 eg unnamed family in Read 1988: 105.
16 Ramson 1988: 16–17 records the first use of 'assimilation' in relation to migrants is 1927 and to Aboriginal people in 1951. However, Gray (see

Chapter 3 of this book) identifies usage of the term 'assimilation' in relation
to Aboriginal people as early as 1940.

17 I was first alerted to the significance of this concept in Rowley 1986: ch. 7.

18 eg Fitzgerald asserts that 'nothing is known of the relevant (Wiradjuri) tribe',
while in fact more than a hundred Wiradjuri people live only thirty
kilometres away in Condobolin.

19 The other major reason is the many thousands of Aboriginal children who
were removed from their families and communities and did not return.

20 cf, for example, Broome 1982: 161.

21 Reynolds 1989: 76–7.

22 Ingamells 1979: 21.

23 Wright 1991: 30.

24 H C Coombs, interviewed in the series 'The Aboriginal Treaty', produced for
public radio, 1983.

25 Dodson in Burger 1990: 20.

26 A Roach, 'Native born', from the album *Charcoal Lane*, 1990.

27 C Mullett, interview, September 1994.

28 Wright 1985: introduction.

29 Read 1996.

30 'Seven Years On', oral history project coordinated by J Huggins and P Read.

31 eg Wollondilly Heritage Centre, New South Wales, exhibition on the flooding
of the Burragorang valley.

32 Read 1977.

33 Flanagan 1994.

34 Pybus 1994: 109.

References

Broome, R. 1982. *Aboriginal Australians*. Sydney: Allen & Unwin.

Burger, J. (ed.) 1990. *The Gaia Atlas of First Peoples*. Ringwood, Victoria: Penguin.

Fitzgerald, M. 1979. Where the line ends. Burcher [NSW]: Jubilee Committee.

Flanagan, R. 1994. *Death of a River Guide*. Ringwood, Victoria: McPhee Gribble
and Penguin.

Graham, D. 1994. No questions please, we're Australians. In *Being Whitefella*, ed.
D. Graham. Fremantle: Fremantle Arts Centre Press, pp. 93–109.

Hall, R. 1980. Aborigines, the army and the Second World War in Northern
Australia. *Aboriginal History* 4: 72–95.

Ingamells, R. 1979. Unknown land. In *The Jindyworobaks*, ed. Brian Elliott.
Brisbane: University of Queensland Press.

Ingram, L. 1984. In *Down There With Me on the Cowra Mission*, ed. P. Read. Sydney:
Pergamon Press, pp. 41–4, 78–9.

Jordens, A. 1989. An administrative nightmare: Aboriginal conscription 1965–72.
Aboriginal History 13: 124–34.

Mansell, M. 1994. Politics of language. In The *Encyclopaedia of Aboriginal Australia*,
ed. D. Horton. Canberra: Aboriginal Studies Press.

Pybus, C. 1991. *Community of Thieves*. Melbourne: Heinemann.

Ramson, W. S. (ed.) 1988. *The Australian National Dictionary*. Melbourne: Oxford
University Press.

Raymond, R. 1989. *Discover Australia's National Parks*, 3rd edn. Melbourne:
Macmillan.

Read, P. 1977. Eleven o'Clock on the last night of the conference. *University of Technology Sydney Review*, May.

Read, P. 1983. A History of the Wiradjuri People of N.S.W. 1883–1969. PhD thesis. Canberra: Australian National University.

Read, P. 1988. *A Hundred Years War*. Canberra: Australian National University Press.

Read, P. 1990. *Charles Perkins: A Biography*. Ringwood, Victoria: Viking.

Read, P. 1996. *Returning to Nothing*. Cambridge: Cambridge University Press.

Read, P. (ed.) 1984. *Down There With Me on the Cowra Mission: An Oral History of Erambie Aboriginal Reserve, Cowra, New South Wales*. Sydney: Pergamon Press.

Reynolds, H. 1989. *Dispossession*. Sydney: Allen & Unwin.

Rowley, C. D. 1986. *Recovery*. Ringwood, Victoria: Penguin.

Sinclair, J. 1989. In *The Lost Children*, eds C. Edwards and P. Read. Sydney: Doubleday, pp. 69–77,144–51,190–93.

Wright, J. 1985. Two dreamtimes. In *Fighters and Singers*, eds I. White, D. Barwick and B. Meehan. Sydney: Allen & Unwin, pp. xix–xxi.

Wright, J. 1991. The broken links. In *Born of the Conquerors*. Canberra: Aboriginal Studies Press, pp. 29–32.

CHAPTER 10

Citizenship and Legitimacy in Post-colonial Australia

Richard Mulgan

Effective citizenship, even among people of diverse interests and values, requires a shared sense of political community, including allegiance to common legal and political institutions and general acceptance of each other's legitimate membership of the community and right to citizenship. In most democratic countries, issues of legitimacy are relatively insignificant, provided the borders are well established and the basic constitutional rules uncontested. In some democracies, however, particularly former settler societies such as Australia, New Zealand, the United States and Canada, the legitimacy of the regime and therefore the legitimacy of its citizens have been called into question. The assumptions that underlay colonial settlement, including the supposed civilising mission and ethnic superiority of Europeans, have been discredited. With this discrediting has come the realisation that the regimes of the settlers were imposed on the indigenous peoples by force and with callous disregard for their cultures and rights. For the indigenous minorities themselves, there is little reason to owe allegiance to a legal and political system to which they have never consented and by which they continue to be dispossessed. While the legitimacy of their residence in the country is beyond doubt, they must question the legitimacy of the imposed regime and the citizenship it confers. Like other colonised peoples, they are seeking restoration of the rights lost through colonisation, particularly the right to their lands and the right to political self-determination.

For the settler and migrant majorities, at the same time, the shift in values can be disturbing. They must face the fact that their own political community rests on unjust colonial conquest, on the type of invasion, even genocide, that is now widely condemned, say, in Tibet or East Timor. This tends to undermine the legitimacy of their citizenship, which they had assumed was securely founded in the supposed benevolence of their settlement and in their liberal and democratic institutions. Not surprisingly, their reaction to indigenous claims and to the morally uncomfortable truths supporting such claims is often impatient and angry.

Can this conflict be resolved? Can indigenous and non-indigenous people come to share a common citizenship that both groups recognise as legitimate? Or are societies such as ours condemned to harbour a continuing legacy of unjust dispossession and illegitimacy in their constitution? These questions lie at the core of the government's reconciliation process which, in the words of Patrick Dodson, chair of the Council for Aboriginal Reconciliation, is intended to help heal the wounds of our past and build the foundations upon which the rights and affairs of indigenous Australians may be addressed in a manner that gives respect and pride to all of us as Australians.[1]

The council's vision statement clearly assumes that a shared legitimacy is possible. Reconciliation is said to aim at 'A united Australia which respects this land of ours, values the Aboriginal and Torres Strait Islander heritage, and provides justice and equity for all.'[2]

This chapter deals with some of the issues raised by this process and casts some doubt on the optimism of the rhetoric, while endorsing the search for legitimacy and the general enterprise of coming to terms with colonial conquest. It concentrates on the situation of the non-indigenous majority, not because members of this majority are more important, but because the dilemmas facing them tend to be neglected in debates about reconciliation and the rights of indigenous peoples. Most of the writing about Aboriginal issues focuses, not unnaturally, on the position of the Aboriginal people themselves and adopts a more or less critical stance towards the non-Aboriginal majority – which is seen, in varying degrees, as indifferent, exploitative and racist. While such criticisms are in general well founded – it is certainly not the intention of this chapter to justify or defend the general treatment of Aboriginal by non-Aboriginal people over the years – they do raise important issues concerning the appropriate response to be expected from the non-Aboriginal majority.

Indeed, the reaction of the non-Aboriginal majority to Aboriginal claims is arguably the most significant political factor determining the extent of possible progress towards Aboriginal justice. Admittedly, the views of Aboriginal people themselves are vital. In the words of Frank Brennan, the Aboriginal people 'have an exclusive power to withhold their agreement to the moral legitimacy of the nation–state built upon their dispossession.'[3]

On the other hand, the attitudes of non-Aboriginal people set the limits of electoral tolerance within which governments, however sympathetic to the Aboriginal cause, must formulate policy. Hence, the response to reconciliation to be expected from non-Aboriginal people is an issue of pressing public importance.

The anti-colonial critique

We may begin with the delegitimising effects of the history of colonial settlement. A central theme of the reconciliation process is that the non-Aboriginal majority must face up to the damaging effects of colonisation on the Aboriginal people. The provision of justice and equity for Aboriginal people and Torres Strait Islanders depends on recognising that their present, well-documented position of socio-economic disadvantage, in terms of health, housing, education, employment and imprisonment, is the result of colonial dispossession of their lands, culture and autonomy. The dispossession of Aboriginal people began with the process of original settlement, during which Aboriginal people were ruthlessly dispersed and murdered as the settlers expanded their holdings, and continued through the period of paternalistic control when Aboriginal people were excluded from many of the legal and political rights of citizenship. The process of dispossession persists into the present; it is 'continuing' and 'ongoing'.[4] Though all of the legal restrictions on Aboriginal people have been lifted, the effects of conquest and discrimination still live on. This connection between present disadvantage and past dispossession was one of the major conclusions of the Royal Commission on Aboriginal Deaths in Custody and is reiterated in the CAR's documents. For example 'The terrible tragedy facing Aboriginal and Torres Strait Islander peoples today is a legacy of history'[5] and

> the disadvantage exists largely because for most of Australia's history since 1788 indigenous peoples have been treated unjustly, deprived of many basic human rights and excluded, through laws and actions of government, from mainstream society and its economic opportunities.[6]

> This disadvantage arises because of long-term failures by Commonwealth, State, Territory or local governments to ensure that indigenous individuals and communities have access to their citizenship rights. Governments have maintained the process of subordination through their policies and strategies in responding to Aboriginal and Torres Strait Islander people's calls for justice and greater control over their lives.[7]

Acceptance of such a history can also be made to carry the implication that non-Aboriginal people and their culture must accept responsibility for current Aboriginal dispossession. That is, it is not sufficient for non-Aboriginal Australians simply to recognise that injustice was done by the settlers and that something must be done about it. They must also accept collective blame for what has occurred. One of the most eloquent expressions of this view was given by the then prime minister, Paul Keating, in his speech at Redfern in December 1992:

> The starting point might be to recognise that the problem starts with us non-Aboriginal Australians. It begins, I think, with that act of recognition. Recognition that it was we who did the dispossessing. We took the traditional lands and smashed the traditional way of life. We brought the diseases. The alcohol. We committed the murders. We took the children from their mothers. We practised discrimination and exclusion. It was our ignorance and our prejudice [...][8]

Such language surely implies that the present generation is being asked to accept at least some degree of personal responsibility. Similar implications of collective responsibility and guilt are present in calls for 'atonement', for an 'apology' or for a 'public expression of regret'.[9]

Few would doubt that the history of colonial conquest must be faced and digested if Aboriginal people are to be accorded justice. However, if colonial settlement was wrong and so seriously wrong that the Aboriginal people are still suffering its ill effects, where does this leave the settlers and their descendants, particularly if the present generations are considered to carry collective guilt? Once the injustice in the origins of the state is recognised, serious doubts are raised about the legitimacy of the present state and its laws as well as about the rightful place in this country of those whose citizenship depends on that state.

Questions about the legitimacy of the citizenship of non-Aboriginal people and of their institutions are implicit not only in the history of colonial settlement but also in the language commonly used to assert distinctively indigenous rights, language which arises out of the anti-colonialist critique. To begin with, the very term 'indigenous', meaning 'at home' or 'native', implies that other members of the population, the 'non-indigenous', do not truly belong to the country and have a home elsewhere to which they could return. Moreover, one of the central rights claimed by Aboriginal people is the right to 'self-determination', which is the term normally used by peoples claiming the right to political independence as a sovereign nation–state. In this way, indigenous peoples align themselves with other colonised peoples who have sought, and often gained, independence from their former colonial masters. Similar implications are conveyed by the demand for 'Aboriginal sovereignty'.[10]

Such language suggests that the non-indigenous descendants of colonial settlers and other migrants in countries such as Australia and Canada have no more right to citizenship than the British had in India or the French in Indo-China. For this reason, many governments initially resisted the claim of indigenous peoples to include the right to self-determination in the Declaration of the Rights of Indigenous Peoples being developed by the United Nations Working Group on Indigenous Populations in Geneva and have preferred less ideologically loaded terms such as 'autonomy' or 'self-government'.[11] Similar concerns about the constitutional implications of 'self-determination' were behind the Fraser Government's preference for the concept of 'self-management'.

The other major right claimed by indigenous peoples, the right to land, is sometimes couched in terms that suggest a claim is being made to all land unjustly taken and that therefore an attack is being made on the legitimacy of all non-Aboriginal property holdings. For instance, Article 27 of the United Nations Draft Declaration on the Rights of Indigenous Peoples states:

> Indigenous peoples have the right to the restitution of the lands, territories and resources which they have traditionally owned or otherwise occupied or used, and which have been confiscated, occupied, used or damaged.[12]

In Australia this could be interpreted to apply to almost all land now under non-Aboriginal ownership, an interpretation that some commentators – for instance the more inflammatory denizens of talk-back radio – have not been slow to adopt.

As is well known to those familiar with Aboriginal policy, what is actually being sought by and for Aboriginal people falls well short of what the more paranoid non-Aboriginal people think is being sought. Virtually all Aboriginal people accept, as does the indigenous people's movement worldwide,[13] that the post-colonial state is here to stay. In Australia at least, self-determination has been understood, since its adoption as a principle by the Whitlam Government, as prescribing levels of autonomy and devolution consistent with the final authority of existing parliaments and courts. Such a modified sense of self-determination can now be seen as 'non-controversial' in an Australian context.[14] The concept of sovereignty may also be subject to qualification, given that sovereignty itself is not necessarily indivisible, in which case Aboriginal people may claim an element of sovereignty within the Australian state.[15]

Similarly, Australian land rights have been tailored to be consistent with the continuation of existing holdings sanctioned by parliament and the courts. Under Mabo, there was never any practical likelihood of people's backyards being threatened.[16] In general, as with most indigenous peoples, the level of resources being sought is not the full value of what was originally taken but rather the much more modest amount necessary for the present material and cultural needs of Aboriginal people.

In practice, then, Aboriginal rights to self-determination and land are being interpreted in ways that do not seriously infringe the rights of other Australian citizens. However, the language being used to justify Aboriginal rights, if not the rights themselves, can be seen to be inimical to the legitimacy of the rights of non-Aboriginal citizens. In so far as Aboriginal arguments explicitly rely on the language of anti-colonialism, they inevitably carry the implication that non-indigenous institutions, including the dominant Australian legal system and the structure of property and other rights supported by that system, have no legitimate basis. Again, recognising the injustice of colonialism seems to require that non-Aboriginal people question the legitimacy of their own citizenship.

Living with guilt

How, then, can non-Aboriginal people come to terms with their past injustice and recognise Aboriginal rights with the 'respect and pride' sought by the Council for Aboriginal Reconciliation? This problem, it may be noted, is not one to which the organisers of the reconciliation process appear to have given much attention. The problems for non-Aboriginal people in dealing with the hostile view of their culture to be found in the history of colonialism does not appear to be a matter for major concern among those organising the reconciliation process. Perhaps understandably, they are more preoccupied with the initial task of educating non-Aboriginal people about the dark side of colonial settlement and of generating respect for the Aboriginal perspective on the land and its history.

Moreover, one suspects, most of those working and writing in this area do not themselves have any difficulty in accepting a hostile view of their own culture and its history. They – I should properly say 'we' – belong to that section of the modern middle class closely associated with the new moralising social movements, such as environmentalism, anti-racism and feminism. These moralising liberals tend to be tertiary educated, to be attracted to humanistic ideals such as autonomy and justice, and to find employment in the public sector and social services rather than in economic production.[17] Sometimes, moralising liberals may belong to the group that claims to be oppressed; for instance, feminists who are women or anti-racists who are black. In this case, their moralising appears in the form of righteous anger and a sense of just grievance. However, they are just as likely to belong to the oppressors, for instance as white anti-racists or male anti-sexists or people of any sex or colour who object to the exploitation of animals or the destruction of the environment. In such cases, the moralising comes out in the acceptance of responsibility and guilt. Moralising liberals are particularly prone to take on moral responsibility for the sufferings of others and are very comfortable with feelings of 'collective self-reproach'.[18] They set themselves apart from other members of their group by their moral revulsion at the values and behaviour of their fellow oppressors and by their support for political movements that seek an end to such oppression. For such people, collective guilt, far from being a problem, is more a badge of honour and a source of self-esteem. Their superior moral sensitivity to the injustice of oppression raises them above the others in their group. At the same time, in relation to the oppressed, the assumption of responsibility for oppression implies greater moral maturity in comparison with the helpless and childlike condition of the victims of injustice. Thus the assumption of collective guilt can be seen as a form of moral elitism dressed up in the guise of apologetic humility.

For such people, there is little difficulty in embracing the Aboriginal view that non-Aboriginal people and their culture are guilty of continuing oppression. The implication that their citizenship lacks legitimacy will be accepted without problem. Any suggestion, such as that being advanced in this chapter, that the undermining of non-Aboriginal legitimacy is a potential obstacle to reconciliation is likely to be interpreted as special pleading on behalf of the racially prejudiced. However, though the moralising liberals are influential in policy-making circles, they do not appear to be representative of non-Aboriginal people as a whole. As Frank Brennan notes, many non-Aboriginal people who are otherwise sympathetic to the Aboriginal cause are unwilling to accept personal responsibility for the plight of Aboriginal people.[19] Most non-Aboriginal people, like most members of most groups, are likely to react negatively and defensively to negative criticism of themselves, their culture and their institutions. Collective self-worth is as important for predominant majorities as it is for marginalised minorities. As Paul Keating himself recognised in the same Redfern speech in which he so eloquently acknowledged collective guilt, such guilt does not provide a secure foundation for non-Aboriginal reconciliation:

> Down the years there has been no shortage of guilt, but it has not produced the responses we need. Guilt is not a very constructive emotion. I think we should open our hearts a bit.[20]

Though the moralising liberals find self-worth through self-abnegation and a sense of their own moral superiority, they appear to be a minority within the majority. Indeed, in so far as their moralising is an elitist reaction against the predominant values of their compatriots, they necessarily represent a minority point of view. In any case, our political problem remains. 'Respect and pride', for most non-Aboriginal people, requires beliefs and values that justify and legitimate their rights to citizenship. But the anti-colonialist critique appears to rob them of such legitimating values and beliefs. Is there a way out of this impasse?

The acquisition of legitimacy

What is needed is a theory of constitutional legitimacy that equally legitimates Aboriginal rights *and* the general citizenship rights of all Australians and the institutional framework that creates and supports these rights. Such a theory implies an acceptance that the existing Australian state and society were unjustly founded by colonial settlers and migrants but, nonetheless, have a right to be recognised, and to recognise themselves, as legitimately located on this continent and entitled to restrict the original rights of Aboriginal people in the name of protecting the rights of non-Aboriginal people. This raises the general issue of unjust origins. We are required to believe that a state can be legitimate though it was founded in injustice.

For some, this proposition is too problematic to accept. It is much simpler to hold that a state unjustly founded must remain irredeemably illegitimate or, conversely, to claim that a state, if it is legitimate, must have had just origins. However, most states have historically murky origins and the transition from de facto coercive power to de jure authority is one which many, indeed most, regimes have made. The main factor in this process is the sheer passage of time. The longer the occupation continues, the harder it is to return to the status quo ante. The difficulties are partly theoretical, requiring increasingly complicated counterfactual assessments of people's likely situation if the original occupation had not occurred; partly practical, calling for massive disentangling and upheaval of people's lives; and partly moral, imposing penalties on innocent beneficiaries of other people's wrong doing.[21] With the passing of time, the question of the legitimacy of a regime turns less on its origins than on its present behaviour. If it acts lawfully and upholds the rights of its existing citizens, then there is no need to deny its legitimacy or that of its citizens. This point is acknowledged, for instance, in international law, which has to deal with the question of recognising regimes that are based on original usurpation. International law accepts two logically inconsistent maxims. One is *ex injuria jus non oritur:* law does not arise out of wrong – that is, unjustly founded regimes are not lawful and legitimate; but the other is *ex factis jus oritur:* law arises out of facts – that is, regimes that are well established can be lawful and legitimate. Though the logical and philosophical problems still remain, there can be no doubt of the practical political imperative of coming to terms with de facto situations.[22]

Similar arguments can be used to justify the limitation of land claims where land has long since been transferred into other hands. Most legal systems eventually respect the rights of de facto possession through statutes of limitation or other such devices. For Aboriginal people to repossess freehold land would require the dispossession and dislocation of people who have acquired the property they hold in good faith. If there is to be redress, the more appropriate means becomes public compensation from public funds, rather than restitution from individual property holders. But here, too, in setting the level of compensation, the relevant criterion is not the supposed present value of what was originally taken. Given the passage of time and the manifold consequences of the original dispossession, such a standard involves the same practical and moral difficulties as the attempt to overturn the regime itself. The counterfactual calculations involved in assessing the likely present value of land and other resources supposing they had remained in Aboriginal hands and not been developed by the settlers are impossibly complicated.[23] The more appropriate test for compensation is not the present value, actual or hypothetical, of what was taken, but rather the level of means necessary to meet the current needs of the current Aboriginal people to recover and maintain their culture. This, after all, is the main substance of what the Aboriginal people are claiming themselves – the main political basis of their claims is usually their relative deprivation with regard to other Australians.

Thus, the test of legitimacy for the present-day Australian state becomes whether it upholds the rights of its present citizens, whatever they may be. There is room for disagreement, of course, about these rights and therefore about the content of the test of legitimacy. Indeed, we can now expect that these rights should include additional distinctive rights for Aboriginal citizens as descendants of the original inhabitants. A state that denies these rights is no longer legitimate while acknowledgement of Aboriginal rights can become a means of confirming the legitimacy of the state and all its citizens. However, these rights need to be seen to coexist with the equally legitimate rights of all citizens. That is, the limitations on Aboriginal self-determination and land rights due to recognition of the rights of all Australian citizens and their state are to be seen not as practical concessions to *force majeure* but as the proper recognition of legitimate citizenship rights. At the same time, the rationale for distinctive Aboriginal rights may need to be disconnected from the anti-colonial critique and linked more to the historical priority and present minority status of indigenous people rather than to the injustice of their original dispossession.[24]

Non-Aboriginal reconciliation

Given acceptance of the arguments from the passage of time, then, the descendants of settlers, as well as later migrants and their descendants, can be legitimate citizens of a legitimate state, provided that they and their state recognise certain reasonable rights for the Aboriginal minority. These rights are based on the Aboriginal people's prior occupation of the territory now known as Australia but their implementation involves recognition of the legitimate rights of non-Aboriginal people – for instance, their right to equal citizenship and the protection of their property. Where does this leave the issue of collective guilt for colonialism? According to one approach, the arguments from the passage of time may be said to remove, or rather shift, the onus of responsibility and scope for guilt. What is morally reprehensible for the present generation is not what was done by others in the past so much as failure to provide present remedies for what was done in the past. To quote Frank Brennan again:

> This is not to argue that we must pay for the sins of our forbears perpetrated on others' forbears. It is to say that we have a duty to share the fruits of those sins with those who suffered by them and who continue to suffer. We must compensate them for their loss.[25]

According to this argument, the concept of compensation invokes the memory of past injustice but need not imply the direct responsibility of the present generation for that injustice. The reason why the present generation owes compensation for what was done in the past is not that it is actually responsible for the dispossession but rather that it benefits from such dispossession.[26] In this respect, the duty to compensate arises from the present enjoyment of the rights of Australian citizenship and is incumbent on all non-Aboriginal Australians regardless of ethnic origin or of how recently they, or their ancestors, migrated to this country.

On the other hand, some non-Aboriginal Australian citizens, particularly those of the dominant Anglo-Celtic culture largely responsible for colonial settlement, may still identify with the history of their colonising ancestors and thus accept a share in this responsibility. After all, if they choose to take pride in noteworthy achievements of the colonisers – for instance, the Eureka Stockade, the Australian ballot or votes for women – they must also draw shame from the disreputable aspects of this past. These non-Aboriginal people will therefore accept the assumptions of guilt implicit in acts of public apology or atonement.

However, the main purpose of such acts is not so much an acceptance by present citizens of continuing guilt as an expression of moral condemnation of such dispossession and a determination to deal justly in the future. In this respect, non-Aboriginal people are to take on guilt in order to be exonerated from guilt. Such acts of public atonement recall similar acts of post-war apology and compensation by Germany to the Jews or by Japan to fellow Asians. The political function of such acts is to improve relations with former victims by openly repudiating the principles on which such victimisation was based. Though such acts of apology and expressions of regret may be largely symbolic, they are highly significant as an indication of the degree to which former aggressors have genuinely rejected the imperialist and nationalist assumptions on which their former conquests were based. Thus the difficulty that Japanese governments have had in formulating statements of thoroughgoing apology for wartime aggression reveals the continuing hold of militaristic nationalism on the Japanese people. At the same time, the continuing pressure to apologise puts pressure on the Japanese to confront these values in their own tradition.

In an Australian context a statement of public apology for Aboriginal dispossession could have similarly beneficial effects in forcing non-Aboriginal people to recognise the injustice of the past and confront lingering assumptions of ethnic superiority. In such circumstances, Paul Keating's use of the collectively guilty 'we' may be justifiable as working towards a public repudiation of past assumptions. But, it should be emphasised, such apologies are not necessarily expressions of individual personal guilt. Moreover, in so far as they are statements of generalised collective guilt, they imply that the guilt can be successfully expiated. They are not an invitation to assume the moralising liberals' mantle of sanctimonious responsibility for all the world's ills. They are more a means for the non-Aboriginal people of laying the unjust past to rest and building a new foundation for guilt-free legitimacy.

Expiation, it should be noted, is a two-way process. Acts of atonement and apology all require for their satisfactory completion that the injured party accept the admission of guilt as in some sense wiping the slate clean and marking a new start. Only then can guilt be left behind. If non-Aboriginal Australians publicly admit to the wrongs done to Aboriginal by non-Aboriginal people in the past and publicly endorse Aboriginal rights to limited self-determination and limited land rights, they will expect the Aboriginal people, as a quid pro quo, to agree to give up blaming them for the sins of colonial conquest. The apology will be seen formally to seal the renewed legitimacy of the Australian state based on a new dispensation that recognises Aboriginal rights in balance with the equal rights of all Australian citizens. (In relation to the reluctance of the Japanese to offer public apologies, it may be not without significance that the concept of 'apology' in Japanese does not carry the same connotations of forgiveness and expiation as it does in Christian cultures[27] and thus does not offer the same prospect of a balanced ledger and a new beginning for both aggressor and victim.)

A rationale for a non-Aboriginal acceptance of Aboriginal rights can therefore be seen to involve four elements. The first is recognition of the priority of Aboriginal occupation as a basis for Aboriginal rights to self-determination and land rights, such rights to be limited by respect for the overall authority of a single nation–state and for the property rights of non-Aboriginal people. The second is recognition of the injustice of colonial dispossession as a basis for compensation that is sufficient to enable the recovery and maintenance of Aboriginal culture and identity. The third is public apology for past injustice as a means both of acknowledging non-Aboriginal responsibility for past injustice and of marking a new guilt-free relationship between Aboriginal and non-Aboriginal people. The fourth is Aboriginal acceptance of such an apology and willingness to enter into a new guilt-free relationship.

Such a rationale, it can be argued, is implicit in the reconciliation process, which is aimed at a united Australia with equality and justice for all. Though the publications of CAR do not usually give such explicit emphasis to the problems faced by non-Aboriginal people in coming to terms with colonial dispossession and guilt, their frequent use of terms such as 'pride', 'equality' and indeed 'reconciliation' itself, imply a similar approach to these problems.

However, the non-Aboriginal rationale, though it may settle the issue of non-Aboriginal legitimacy, may do so at a price that Aboriginal people and their supporters are unwilling to pay. It must be open to doubt whether all the elements in this rationale are in fact generally acceptable to Aboriginal people, or at least to Aboriginal opinion leaders. For example, not all Aboriginal people are ready publicly to accept that their rights to self-determination and land are to be so limited by respect for the authority of the nation–state; those associated with the Aboriginal Provisional Government still wish to assert their own sovereignty against that of the Australian state and their right to do so has been vigorously upheld by CAR.[28] Though such claims can be criticised as impractical and utopian,[29] they have significant rhetorical and political effect as part of the wider politics of shame and embarrassment practised by Aboriginal people and other indigenous minorities.[30] Claims to independent sovereignty and to freehold land make good political protest, precisely because they are challenging and unsettling to the non-indigenous majority and thus more readily gain media attention.

The ability to disturb the conscience of the nation and unsettle its government is one of the few weapons available to Aboriginal people and one they are unlikely to surrender lightly. Even if relatively moderate Aboriginal leaders tend to distance themselves from the more radical rhetoric that directly threatens the legitimacy of the state, their cause often benefits from such rhetoric. The publicity gained by more radical protesters tends to encourage governments into serious and constructive negotiations with the moderates as a means of defusing embarrassing public protests. This is a classic example of the potential partnership between insider and outsider interest groups, which has been equally effective in other areas of protest such as the environment. A striking instance of such a de facto partnership in Aboriginal policy occurred during the protracted negotiations over the native title legislation in which the more conciliatory 'A' team negotiated directly with the government while the more radical 'B' team extracted further concessions through the intervention of the minor parties in the Senate.[31]

The political value for Aboriginal people in appealing to the conscience of the nation suggests that they will be most reluctant to countenance the official end to non-Aboriginal guilt for past injustice implied by the acceptance of a public apology. Given that the socio-economically disadvantaged position of Aboriginal people is likely to continue for many years to come,[32] there will be continuing need for public assistance to Aboriginal people to help them make effective use of their rights. There will also be continuing incentives for the Aboriginal leadership in ATSIC and elsewhere to argue politically for the highest possible level of public funding for Aboriginal people. In such a context, it is most unlikely that they will cease using one of the most potent arguments in favour of assistance to Aboriginal people, namely the appeal to white guilt about the injustice of colonial settlement. By the same token, any proposal to expiate white guilt will be seen as an attempt to reduce the political leverage of Aboriginal people and is likely to meet with fierce resistance. (The recent upsurge in ethnic tension in New Zealand is largely attributable to the government's attempt to settle Maori grievances once and for all through a final payment of compensation.)[33]

Indeed, the issue of guilt, and the blame that gives rise to guilt, is much deeper than simple political expediency. It is also intimately linked to the whole issue of Aboriginal identity. For Aboriginal people, as for other conquered peoples, the fact that they originally possessed land and territory that was subsequently unjustly taken from them is a central and defining part of their history.[34] Recalling this past is essential to making sense of their present marginalised and demoralised condition, while maintaining anger at what has happened helps to provide moral self-respect and a basis for demanding redress as a matter of right rather than charity. Thus, so long as their relatively disadvantaged position continues, a sense of just grievance may be said to be functional for their identity. Any attempt by the non-Aboriginal people to rob them of their right to continued just grievance can be interpreted as an attack on their very existence as a people.

Contested history

There is thus a deep-seated conflict between the Aboriginal and non-Aboriginal attitudes to the colonial past. For Aboriginal people, as victims, it is the source of continuing anger and resentment that shows no sign of abating so long as their current predicament continues. Memory of the colonial past must be kept fresh and alive as part of their present identity. However, for non-Aboriginal people, as perpetrators, colonisation is a potential source of guilt that needs to be expiated as part of a genuine commitment to Aboriginal rights. The moral horror of the colonial past can only be squarely faced if a moral distance is interposed between the colonisers, who are condemned, and their descendants, who condemn and are thereby exonerated. In so far as the past is a source of cultural embarrassment for the descendants of colonisers, they will naturally tend to want to put it behind them, to look forward rather than back, while the descendants of the colonised will naturally want to keep the past alive.

Moreover, when the descendants of the settlers do look back, as they surely must, they or their spokespeople[35] will seek to resurrect the more reassuring aspects of their cultural history – for instance, the fact that many Aboriginal people embraced aspects of western technology and western culture, the good intentions behind many of the failed policies of assimilation, and the extent to which concern for human rights and the rights of indigenous peoples is as much a product of the European Christian tradition as colonialism itself. While the injustice of colonial settlement and its damaging effects on the Aboriginal people should properly be emphasised it may be too much to expect non-Aboriginal people to have a wholly or even largely negative view of their past. Such a view may be acceptable to the moralising liberals who are influential in education policy-making. But it is likely to provoke a backlash among the non-Aboriginal rank and file, particularly those of Anglo-Celtic background, who may be seeking cultural affirmation in their history.

In this respect, the reconciliation project of 'sharing history' is more complex than sometimes envisaged – for instance, in the somewhat bland and inevitably one-sided publications of CAR. To be sure, the council's key issue paper on the subject does recognise that 'neither indigenous nor non-indigenous are above criticism'[36] but the point is not developed. There is a brief acknowledgement that colonial settlement did produce some situations in which 'some kind of understanding was reached that led to mutual dependence and violence-free relationships'.[37] But there is little sense of the need for the non-indigenous to find some positive elements in their culture's past to help them get their bearings in this country and provide a secure basis from which they can confidently embrace the concept of Aboriginal rights.

Conclusion

So long as Australian society contains (at least) two ethnic cultural traditions, one identifying with those who were colonised and one with those who did the colonising, then there will inevitably be conflicting attitudes towards the colonial past.[38] This suggests that the hope of true reconciliation, in the sense of a genuine consensus on cultural values between Aboriginal and non-Aboriginal people, may be over-optimistic. Certainly, if Aboriginal and non-Aboriginal people are to share a common citizenship this needs to be anchored in some shared values, such as justice, and some shared traditions, such as egalitarianism and the 'fair go'. However, such agreement cannot be expected to cover all aspects of the past, including the perspective to be adopted towards colonial settlement. If consensus means agreeing on a view of colonisation that robs one side of all legitimacy and self-respect, then it is probably not worth aiming for because it will not provide a stable basis for a just society. Just as the ideology of benevolent colonialism and assimilation failed the Aboriginal people so, too, will the ideology of anti-colonialism and colonial guilt fail the non-Aboriginal people. A more sensible, if less tidy, path is to admit the continuing existence of some conflicting cultural perspectives but to moderate and accommodate them through shared commitment to certain political values, such as democratic principles and human rights, including Aboriginal rights. In such a context, the key terms should not be words like 'reconciliation' and 'consensus', which imply the transcending of disagreement, so much as 'accommodation' and 'compromise', terms that recognise, and legitimate, the existence of conflicting values and interests, though within a framework of peaceful mutual adjustment.

Notes

1 Parliament 1994: vii.
2 Parliament 1994: viii.
3 CAR 1994c: 37.
4 CAR 1995: 7; CAR 1994c: 17.
5 Parliament 1994: 5.
6 CAR 1994b: 3.
7 CAR 1995: 26–7.
8 ATSIC 1993.
9 Nettheim 1988: 123; Brennan 1994: 87; CAR 1994b: 34.
10 Brennan 1994: 18–22.
11 Nettheim 1988: 118–20; Brennan 1994: 111–20.
12 United Nations Working Group on Indigenous Populations 1993, Annex 1.
13 Werther 1992.
14 CAR 1994c: 27.

15 Rowse 1994: 200–1.
16 Brennan 1995.
17 Offe 1985; Pakulski 1991: 170–83; Burgmann 1993: 6–7.
18 Minogue 1963: 197.
19 Brennan 1995: ix.
20 ATSIC 1993.
21 cf Waldron 1992.
22 Mulgan 1989, ch. 2.
23 Waldron 1992.
24 cf Kymlicka 1995: 108–20.
25 Brennan 1994: 32.
26 cf Lucas 1993: 77.
27 J Kubota, *Australian,* 9 August 1995.
28 CAR 1995: 35–6.
29 eg Brennan 1994: 18–22.
30 Dyck 1985: 15; Jennett 1990: 252.
31 Brennan 1995, ch. 2; Jennett 1995: 68–71.
32 Altman and Sanders 1991: 9–10.
33 Mulgan 1996.
34 Brilmayer 1992.
35 eg Hirst 1993.
36 CAR 1994a: 30.
37 CAR 1994a: 41.
38 cf Kymlicka 1995: 189.

References

Aboriginal and Torres Strait Islander Commission (ATSIC). 1993. *International Year of the World's Indigenous People, Speeches.* Canberra: ATSIC.
Altman, J. C. and Sanders, W. G. 1991. Government initiatives for Aboriginal employment. In *Aboriginal Employment Equity by the Year 2000,* ed. J. C. Altman. Canberra: Centre for Aboriginal Economic Policy Research, pp. 1–18.
Brennan, F. 1994. *Sharing the Country,* 2nd edn. Ringwood, Victoria: Penguin.
Brennan, F. 1995. *One Land, One Nation.* St Lucia: University of Queensland Press.
Brilmayer, L. 1992. Groups, histories and international law. *Cornell International Law Journal* 25: 555–63.
Burgmann, V. 1993. *Power and Protest: Movements for Change in Australian Society.* Sydney: Allen & Unwin.
Council for Aboriginal Reconciliation (CAR). 1994a. *Sharing History: A Sense for all Australians of a Shared Ownership of their History.* Key Issue Paper No. 4. Canberra: Australian Government Publishing Service.
Council for Aboriginal Reconciliation (CAR). 1994b. *Addressing Disadvantage; a Greater Awareness of the Causes of Aboriginal Disadvantage.* Key Issue Paper No. 5. Canberra: Australian Government Publishing Service.
Council for Aboriginal Reconciliation (CAR). 1994c. *Agreeing on a Document: Will the Process of Reconciliation be Advanced by a Document or Documents of Reconciliation?* Key Issue Paper No. 7. Canberra: Australian Government Publishing Service.
Council for Aboriginal Reconciliation (CAR). 1995. *Going Forward: Social Justice for the First Australians.* Canberra: Australian Government Publishing Service.

Dyck, N. 1985. Aboriginal peoples and nation–states: an introduction to the analytical issues. In *Indigenous Peoples and the Nation–State: 'Fourth World' Politics in Canada, Australia and Norway*, ed. N. Dyck. St John's, Newfoundland: Institute of Social and Economic Research, pp. 1–26.

Hirst, J. 1993. Australian history and European civilisation. *Quadrant.* May: 28–38.

Jennett, C. 1990. Aboriginal affairs policy. In *Hawke and Australian Public Policy*, eds C. Jennett and R. Stewart. Melbourne: Macmillan, pp. 245–83.

Jennett, C. 1995. Indigenous peoples in Australia: the Keating record. In *Equity and Citizenship under Keating*, eds M. Hogan and K. Dempsey. Sydney: Public Affairs Research Centre, University of Sydney, pp. 38–54

Kymlicka, W. 1995. *Multicultural Citizenship*. Oxford: Clarendon Press.

Lucas, J. R. 1993. *Responsibility*. Oxford: Clarendon Press.

Minogue, K. 1963. *The Liberal Mind*. London: Methuen.

Mulgan, R. 1989. *Maori, Pakeha and Democracy*. Auckland: Oxford University Press.

Mulgan, R. 1996. A race relations lesson from across the Tasman. *Australian Quarterly* 68: 77–87.

Nettheim, G. 1988. Peoples and populations – indigenous peoples and the rights of peoples. In *The Rights of Peoples*, ed. J. Crawford. Oxford: Clarendon Press, pp. 107–26.

Offe, C. 1985. New social movements: challenging the boundaries of institutional politics. *Social Research* 52: 817–68.

Pakulski, J. 1991. *Social Movements: the Politics of Moral Protest*. Melbourne: Longman Cheshire.

Parliament. 1994. *Walking Together: The First Steps. Report of the Council for Aboriginal Reconciliation 1991–4*. Canberra: Australian Government Publishing Service.

Rowse, T. 1994. Aborigines: citizens and colonial subjects. In *Developments in Australian Politics*, eds J. Brett et al. Melbourne: Macmillan, pp. 182–201.

United Nations Working Group on Indigenous Populations. 1993. *Report of the Working Group on Indigenous Populations on its Eleventh Session.* Document E/CN.4/Sub.2/1993/29.

Waldron, J. 1992. Superseding historic injustice. *Ethics* 103: 4–28.

Werther, G. F. A. 1992. *Self-Determination in Western Democracies*. Westport, London: Greenwood Press.

CHAPTER 11

The International Law Context

Garth Nettheim

Anglo–Australian law has long had connections with international law. This is scarcely surprising, given the Eurocentric basis of modern international law, and the importance of England within Europe during the period of its evolution.

In this chapter I will place national law in the wider context of international law, and will explore how recent developments in international law relate to Australia's Aboriginal people.

The relationship between international law and national law

In classical theory international and national law represented two quite distinct domains. International law was concerned with the relationship between states (*inter nationes*) as represented by their governments, and it had little concern for matters internal to such states. It was national law alone that addressed relationships among people and relationships between government and people.

There were, however, exceptional areas in which international law did concern itself with the rights of people, either as individuals or as groups. Such topics included aliens; diplomatic representatives; slavery; piracy; and, in wartime, civilians, the sick and wounded, and prisoners of war.

International law's concern with people, as distinct from states, has increased enormously since World War II, largely through the development of a substantial body of standards and processes relating to human rights. This evolution has developed a growing area of overlap between the international and national systems and raises questions as to the influence of international law within national law.

The approach of the English common law system (from which Australian law derives) has been the 'dualist' approach – that international

law as such has no operation within national law except to the extent that
it is incorporated by national law. This, indeed, reflects the notion of the
'sovereignty' of states – that is, that the international community consists
of totally autonomous and notionally equal players who are not subject to
any supra-national governing structures or obligations in law to other
states unless they voluntarily undertake to be so.

The primary sources of international law are custom and treaty.
Customary international law is based on the actual practice of states,
provided that such practice is itself based on a sense of obligation (*opinio
iuris*). This is similar to the customary basis of English common law still
evident in the area of constitutional conventions under the Westminster
system. It is, of course, also similar to the customary law system of
indigenous peoples.

A rule of customary international law may be automatically part
of Australian law unless national law provides to the contrary, either
by a clear rule of unenacted common law or by the terms of statute
law.

Treaties have become the more important source of international law.
But, while they may appear similar to legislation within a national law
system, they are more akin to contracts in so far as treaties bind only
those states that choose to become parties to them by processes of
ratification or accession.

A treaty as such is taken not to have any effect on Australian law unless
or until it is implemented in Australian law by legislation. Thus, the
International Convention on the Elimination of All Forms of Racial
Discrimination had no effect on Australian law, even when ratified by
Australia, until it was implemented by enactment of the *Racial Dis-
crimination Act 1975* (Cwlth) (RDA).

In a major case concerning indigenous Australians, *Koowarta* v. *Bjelke-
Petersen*,[1] the High Court rejected a challenge by Queensland to the
validity of the RDA. Three judges upheld the Act on a wide interpretation
of the Commonwealth's legislative power with respect to 'external
affairs', notwithstanding that the subject matter of the convention concerned matters occurring entirely within the State. Justice Stephen took
a narrower view of the 'external affairs' power as being confined to
supporting legislation only on matters of 'international concern', but he
held that racial discrimination was such a matter. He stated that the RDA
could be supported both by the convention and by a customary international law principle of non-discrimination. The wide view of the
external affairs power has been affirmed in later High Court decisions as
not requiring that a treaty be on a subject of 'international concern' in
order for the Commonwealth parliament to have power to implement it
in Australian law.

The High Court has also held in several cases that an international treaty ratified by Australia may have an indirect influence in Australian law. In particular, it is a legitimate aid to a court in declaring the common law, when it is unclear, and in interpreting ambiguous legislation.[2]

The Mabo decisions, racial discrimination and equality

In *Mabo* v. *Queensland* (No. 2)[3] the High Court drew attention to the close correlation between, on the one hand, principles of English law concerning the legal regime operating within new British colonies and, on the other hand, the principles of international law concerning acquisition by European powers of sovereignty over colonies. The international law principles relating to acquisition of colonies by 'discovery' and 'occupation' were linked to the classification by English law of some colonies as 'settled', as distinct from colonies acquired by 'conquest' or 'cession'.[4] Indeed the High Court needed to distinguish the international law doctrine of *terra nullius* (confining it to the matter of acquisition of colonies) from the supposed extension of the doctrine, under common law, to the legal consequences of that acquisition of sovereignty for the pre-existing land rights of the indigenous inhabitants.[5]

Modern international law on human rights was highly influential in assisting the High Court to declare Anglo–Australian common law as accommodating the land rights of indigenous peoples. Particularly significant were international law standards against racial discrimination:

> Whatever the justification advanced in earlier days for refusing to recognize the rights and interests in land of the indigenous inhabitants of settled colonies, an unjust and discriminatory doctrine of that kind can no longer be accepted. The expectations of the international community accord in this respect with the contemporary values of the Australian people. The opening up of international remedies to individuals pursuant to Australia's accession to the Optional Protocol to the International Covenant on Civil and Political Rights [...] brings to bear on the common law the powerful influence of the Covenant and the international standards it imports. The common law does not necessarily conform with international law, but international law is a legitimate and important influence on the development of the common law, especially when international law declares the existence of universal human rights. A common law doctrine founded on unjust discrimination in the enjoyment of civil and political rights demands reconsideration. It is contrary both to international standards and to the fundamental values of our common law to entrench a discriminatory rule which, because of the supposed position on the scale of social organization of the indigenous inhabitants of a settled colony, denies them a right to occupy their traditional lands.[6]

The principle against racial discrimination is referred to in the United Nations Charter (1945), the Universal Declaration of Human Rights (1948),[7] the International Covenant on Civil and Political Rights[8] and the International Covenant on Economic, Social and Cultural Rights.[9] Australia has ratified the two covenants and, thus, accepted obligations under international law to implement their terms within Australia.

The International Convention on the Elimination of All Forms of Racial Discrimination (1965)[10] takes the topic as its sole focus and lays down very specific obligations on states parties. Australia has ratified this convention and has enacted the *Racial Discrimination Act 1975* (Cwlth)[11] to implement its terms in Australian law.

Without the RDA the Mabo litigation would not have reached the High Court for final determination. Queensland enacted the *Queensland Coast Islands Declaratory Act 1985* specifically to abort the litigation by declaring, retroactively to 1879 (the year when the Murray Island group was formally annexed to Queensland), that, on the acquisition of the islands, any native title was extinguished, with no entitlement to compensation. In 1988, in *Mabo v. Queensland*[12] a High Court majority held that the RDA served to make the Queensland Act ineffective. The Queensland Act was held to violate the right to own property and the right to inherit under Article 5(d) of the convention, also the right to own property and not to be arbitrarily deprived of property under Article 17 of the Universal Declaration of Human Rights.

The RDA was thus vindicated as a federal 'safety net' against state or territory governments attempting any extinguishment of native title after the date of its commencement (31 October 1975). *The Native Title Act 1993* (Cwlth) (NTA) provided a more specific federal 'safety net' and one that was not predicated on a finding of discrimination. In 1995 in *Western Australia v. Commonwealth*,[13] the High Court held that both the RDA and the NTA served to invalidate 1993 Western Australian legislation which extinguished native title throughout the State and substituted inferior and vulnerable statutory rights of 'traditional usage'.

The international law principle against racial discrimination, as implemented within Australia by the RDA, has been of immense importance on the issue of native title. It has also been of great importance in protecting the interests of indigenous Australians in other areas.

But necessary though the equality principle in the RDA and international law may be for indigenous Australians, it has also been acknowledged to be insufficient.

The limits to the equality principle

The RDA can serve as a federal 'safety net' against state and territory governments that attempt to extinguish or impair native title. Does it

also strike at State and territory governments that set out to acknowledge the indigenous relationship to land? Are state land rights Acts
discriminatory against non-indigenous Australians, so as to violate RDA
principles?

In *Gerhardy* v. *Brown*[14] a majority of the High Court formed the view
that provisions of the *Pitjantjatjara Land Rights Act 1981* (SA) were, prima
facie, discriminatory. The High Court held that the provisions were saved
from invalidity only by the 'special measures' exemption in RDA s. 8,
which cross-refers to Article 1(4) of the convention:

> Special measures taken for the *sole purpose* of securing adequate advancement
> of certain racial or ethnic groups or individuals requiring such protection as
> may be necessary in order to ensure such groups or individuals equal enjoy-
> ment or exercise of human rights and fundamental freedoms shall not be
> deemed racial discrimination, *provided, however, that such measures do not, as a
> consequence, lead to the maintenance of separate rights for different racial groups and
> that they shall not be continued after the objectives for which they were taken have been
> achieved.* [Emphasis supplied.]

The High Court was criticised for reaching the right decision for the
wrong reasons; namely, for finding that the provisions were discriminatory so as to need to be saved by the special measures exemption.
The concept of 'discrimination' in international law is more sophisticated than differentiation as such.[15] In *Western Australia* v. *Commonwealth*
the High Court appears to have accepted this proposition:

> if there were any discrepancy in the operation of the two Acts, the NTA can be
> regarded either as a special measure under s8 of the RDA *or as a law which,
> though it makes racial distinctions, is not racially discriminatory so as to offend the RDA
> or the Convention*'. [Emphasis supplied.][16]

The *Native Title Act 1993* (Cwlth) (NTA) purports in its preamble to be
consistent with the RDA as (together with other initiatives) a 'special
measure', despite the validation provisions (ss. 14–18), which prioritise
post-RDA grants of interests over lands that may have been subject to
surviving native title. The Aboriginal and Torres Strait Islander Social
Justice Commissioner has difficulty in accepting this characterisation:

> I do not believe it is accurate to characterise the NTA as a whole as a 'special
> measure'. That is not to say that legislation which establishes a general scheme
> for the recognition of indigenous land rights cannot constitute a special
> measure. Both the *Pitjantjatjara Land Rights Act 1981* (SA) and the *Aboriginal
> Land Rights (Northern Territory) Act 1976* (Cwlth) could be described as 'special
> measures' because, at the time of enactment, they were considered to be the
> only means by which Aboriginal rights to land could be legally acknowledged.
> *Mabo [No. 2]* altered that position, and the subsequent NTA lacks that rationale:

it regulates rather than confers rights. In addition, because of the validation provisions, it is arguable that the NTA is not a 'special measure' as it is not for the sole purpose of securing the advancement of indigenous people – a requirement which would appear essential under both s. 8(1) of the RDA and the Convention.

Whether specific provisions can be construed as special measures is another question. In my view however, the issue will not arise in most cases, as I believe that the majority of the provisions of the NTA do not need to be construed as special measures as they operate to protect indigenous people from having the equal enjoyment of our human rights impaired. They are therefore not discriminatory.[17]

The problem with reliance on the 'special measures' exemption is that it is tightly circumscribed by the 'sole purpose' requirement and by the provisos to Article 1(4). While the circumscription of the exemption is understandable and cogent if the sole concern is with the equality principle and individual rights, it is inadequate to deal with the longer term, collective interests of indigenous peoples to retain their distinctiveness as peoples.[18]

Differential and collective rights

Elsewhere[19] I have attempted to group the claims being advanced by indigenous peoples worldwide, on both international law and national law, under four headings: peoplehood, autonomy, territory and equality. The equality/non-discrimination principle is well accepted in both international law and Australian law. The other sets of claims involving specifically indigenous rights, based on difference and collective identity, are more problematic and therefore require some discussion here.

Peoplehood

The claim to physical survival of a people is one of the few collective rights clearly established in international law, notably in the Convention on the Prevention and Punishment of the Crime of Genocide (1948).[20] The definition in the convention includes 'forcibly transferring children of the group to another group', and references to genocide currently recur in litigation and inquiries about 'the stolen generation'.

Cultural survival is partly accommodated in the International Covenant on Civil and Political Rights (ICCPR), Article 27:

In those States in which ethnic, religious or linguistic minorities exist, persons belonging to such minorities shall not be denied the right, in community with the other members of their group, to enjoy their own culture, to profess and practise their own religion, or to use their own language.

Article 27 has been invoked by indigenous people in a number of communications to the Human Rights Committee established under the convention.

Autonomy

Arguably, the claim of indigenous peoples to control over matters affecting them is also met in international law as another collective right clearly accepted. The United Nations Charter refers to the right of self-determination of peoples. The right is spelled out in the common Article 1 in the two covenants – the International Covenant on Civil and Political Rights, and the International Covenant on Economic, Social and Cultural Rights:

> 1. All peoples have the right of self-determination. By virtue of that right they freely determine their political status and freely pursue their economic, social and cultural development.

> 2. All peoples may, for their own ends, freely dispose of their natural wealth and resources without prejudice to any obligations arising out of international economic co-operation, based upon the principle of mutual benefit, and international law. In no case may a people be deprived of its own means of subsistence [...]

The problem has been the reluctance of governments to treat the principle of self-determination as applicable to indigenous peoples within states that have become independent under the dominance of non-indigenous people. The particular fear arises because the principle of self-determination became closely identified in the 1950s and 1960s with the decolonisation process which, in most cases, led to the former colonies achieving independence. While few indigenous peoples may aspire to secession as independent states, states generally oppose any threat to the 'territorial integrity' of existing states. The effort has been to develop principles whereby indigenous peoples may achieve a substantial degree of self-government and autonomy *within* states. In theory, self-determination has been Commonwealth government policy in Australia since the early 1970s. It has been perceived by indigenous organisations and by inquiries such as the Royal Commission into Aboriginal Deaths in Custody as a key to improving the position of Aboriginal people and Torres Strait Islanders.

Territory

Issues of land and waters and resources have already been referred to, and find support in international law, particularly in Article 17 of the

Universal Declaration of Human Rights and Article 5 of the International Convention on the Elimination of All Forms of Racial Discrimination. Article 27 of the International Covenant on Civil and Political Rights is also relevant.

UN draft Declaration of the Rights of Indigenous Peoples

A working group on indigenous populations was established in 1982 by the UN Sub-commission on Prevention of Discrimination and Protection of Minorities. In 1985 it embarked on one of its primary functions, the evolution of standards. It proceeded with the full and active participation of indigenous peoples from around the world. By the time the working group had completed its task and referred its draft through the sub-commission to the full Commission on Human Rights, the draft substantially reflected the aspirations of the world's indigenous peoples. Whether it will survive unscathed the attentions of states, as represented by their governments in the Commission, remains to be seen. But, in the meantime, various articles of the draft declaration are relevant to the theme of citizenship and indigenous Australians. There is some overlap and cross-referencing but, broadly speaking, the concerns of Articles 1 and 2 and Part IV are with equality, Parts II and III are about physical and cultural identity, Articles 3 and 4 and Parts V and VII are concerned with political rights, and Part VI addresses territorial rights.

Advancing the agenda

It is possible for indigenous Australians to communicate directly with the Human Rights Committee alleging violations by Australia of its obligations under the International Covenant on Civil and Political Rights. (The first such communication against Australia under the covenant's first optional protocol was the Toonen case concerning laws of Tasmania relating to homosexual conduct.)

It is also possible for indigenous Australians to communicate directly with the Committee on the Elimination of Racial Discrimination under the International Convention on the Elimination of All Forms of Racial Discrimination.

Such communication procedures normally require the prior exhaustion of domestic remedies. Some domestic remedies are available in the equality/discrimination area under the RDA. There are no specific national procedures set up to deal with the rights under the ICCPR other than the limited inquiry and report functions of the Human Rights and Equal Opportunity Commission.

As noted, the equality aspirations of Aboriginal people and Torres Strait Islanders are better recognised in law than the differential indigenous aspirations. But even the equality aspirations are not achieved in the broad area of socio–economic disadvantage. Statistics continue to show gross disparities between indigenous and non-indigenous people in the areas of health, housing, education, employment and so on. Various governmental strategies and funding commitments have, to date, failed to eliminate such disadvantage.

Indigenous Australians in 1994–95 had an opportunity to put forward proposals for a social justice package as the third stage of the Keating Government's response to Mabo. Proposals were put forward, after consultation, by ATSIC, the Council for Aboriginal Reconciliation and the Aboriginal and Torres Strait Islander Social Justice Commissioner.[21]

The various recommendations put forward include matters such as constitutional protection of indigenous rights, indigenous participation in the structure of government, revision of inter-governmental financial arrangements, cultural heritage, regional agreements, self-government, compensation, and progress towards a 'treaty' or (a) document(s) of reconciliation.[22]

Throughout these attempts by Aboriginal people and Torres Strait Islanders to secure acceptance in national law of their aspirations, both for equality and for indigenous collective differences, increasing reliance is being placed on international law principles and processes.

Prospects and processes

Prospects for achieving full recognition of these aspirations within Australian law appear less positive since the federal election of 2 March 1996 which saw a Coalition government take office after thirteen years of Labor government. Past Coalition governments made positive contributions to the recognition of indigenous people's rights; one example is the landmark *Aboriginal Land Rights (Northern Territory) Act 1976* (Cwlth). But in its first year of office the Howard Government reduced funding for the Aboriginal and Torres Strait Islander Commission and sought to restrict its powers.[23] It cut the budget for the Council for Aboriginal Reconciliation by nearly a quarter. It proposed major changes to the *Native Title Act 1993* (Cwlth), particularly after the High Court decision on 23 December 1996 in *The Wik Peoples* v. *Queensland*;[24] the more significant changes would allow upgrading of pastoral leases at the cost of extinguishing any underlying native title and would substantially dismantle the 'right to negotiate' processes in relation to mining on native title land and compulsory acquisitions.[25] The government also made it clear that it is not interested in pursuing the 'social justice package' proposals.

What, then, are the prospects for significant advances with the agenda?

The Howard Government has spoken strongly of the need for improvement on the equality issues, notably health and other areas of socio–economic disadvantage. In a period of massive budget cuts, imaginative administrative re-arrangements will be needed to achieve progress in these areas. And, as ever, the critical need is to secure better fulfilment by state and territory governments of their responsibilities. This applies in areas such as reducing Aboriginal deaths in custody and the over-representation of indigenous Australians in the criminal justice system. It is feasible that State and Territory governments (all but one of which are Liberal or Coalition) may respond more readily to a federal Coalition government. There is the example of the 1996 national agreement to reduce the availability of a range of guns, following the massacre of thirty-five people at Port Arthur. But clear and firm proposals will be needed.

Prospects seem less positive for progress on collective indigenous rights such as autonomy and land rights. Indeed, the period since the March 1995 election has seen leading members of the Commonwealth government seeming to endorse proposals for a return to policies of assimilation which represent the antithesis of what indigenous peoples in Australia (and elsewhere) are seeking.

Failing progress on the specific indigenous rights within the Australian legal and political system, we are likely to see Aboriginal and Torres Strait Islander organisations making increasing use of such processes as are available under international law to advance the agenda.

Unless the Howard Government's proposals to amend the *Native Title Act 1993* (Cwlth) are substantially altered before, or during, Senate consideration, they appear to represent a violation of Australia's international law obligations under a number of headings: property rights, cultural rights, participation rights and equality rights.

The international instruments in question include the Universal Declaration of Human Rights, the International Convenant on Civil and Political Rights, the International Covenant on Economic, Social and Cultural Rights and the International Convention on the Elimination of All Forms of Racial Discrimination.

However, rather than resorting to the several international treaty committees, it would be preferable and more beneficial for Australia as a whole if due regard were paid to the relevant international law standards within Australia in the development of legislation and policy.

Notes

1 1982: 153 *Commonwealth Law Reports (CLR)* 168.
2 Kirby 1993: 363.
3 1992: 175 *CLR* 1.
4 Brennan J at 32, Deane and Gaudron JJ at 77–8.
5 Brennan J at 31–40, 43–5; Deane and Gaudron JJ at 78–83; Toohey J at 179–82.
6 1992: 175 *CLR* 1 at 42, Brennan J; G Nettheim 1995: 36.
7 United Nations General Assembly Resolution (A/RES)/217 A (III), 10 December 1947.
8 A/RES/2200 A (XXI), 16 December 1966.
9 A/RES/2200 A (XXI), 16 December 1966. These and other key human rights instruments are reproduced in the Department of Foreign Affairs and Trade's *Human Rights Manual* (Canberra: AGPS. 1993).
10 A/RES/2160 A (XX), 21 December 1965.
11 Commonwealth, the RDA.
12 *Mabo (No. 1)* 1988: 166 *CLR* 186.
13 1995: 183 *CLR* 373.
14 1984–85: 159 *CLR* 70.
15 Sadurski 1986; McRae, Nettheim & Beacroft 1991: 140–3.
16 1995: 183 *CLR* 373: 483–4.
17 Aboriginal and Torres Strait Islander Social Justice Commissioner, *Native Title Report. January–June 1994.* Canberra: AGPS. 1995: 68.
18 See Pritchard 1995: 183, 233.
19 Nettheim 1987 (61): 291. See also ATSIC *Recognition, Rights & Reform. Report to Government on Native Title Social Justice Measures.* Canberra: ATSIC. 1995: ch. 3.
20 A/RES/260 A (III), 9 December 1948.
21 Jull 1996; see also pp. 67 & 75.
22 Land issues had primarily been addressed in stages 1 and 2 of the Keating Government's response to *Mabo – the Native Title Act 1993* (Cwlth), and the *Land Fund and Indigenous Land Corporation (ATSIC Amendment) Act 1995* (Cwlth).
23 *Aboriginal Legal Service Ltd* v. *Minister for Aboriginal and Torres Strait Islander Affairs* 1996: 139 *ALR* 577; 1996: 1 (4) *AILR* 579.
24 1996: 141 *ALR* 129.
25 *Aboriginal and Torres Strait Islander Social Justice Commissioner, Native Title Report, July 1995–June 1996* (Canberra: AGPS. 1996); proposed *Amendments to the Native Title Act 1993. Issues for Indigenous Peoples* (Canberra: ATSIC. 1996).

References

ATSIC, 1995. *Recognition, Rights and Reform. Report to Government on Native Title Social Justice Measures.* Canberra: ATSIC.
Aboriginal and Torres Strait Islander Social Justice Commissioner. 1995. *Native Title Report. January–June 1994.* Canberra: Australian Government Publishing Service.
Jull, P. 1996. An Aboriginal policy for the millennium: the three social justice reports. *Australian Indigenous Law Reporter* 1 (1): 1–13.

Kirby, M. 1993. The Australian use of international human rights norms: from Bangalore to Balliol – a view from the antipodes. *University of New South Wales Law Journal* 16 (2): 363–93.

McRae, H., Nettheim G. and Beacroft, L. 1991. *Aboriginal Legal Issues.* Sydney: Law Book Company.

Nettheim, G. 1987. *Indigenous Rights, Human Rights and Australia.* London: Australian Studies Centre, Institute of Commonwealth Studies.

Nettheim, G. 1995. Native title and international law. In *Mabo: The Native Title Legislation,* ed. M. A. Stephenson. Brisbane: University of Queensland Press, pp. 36–48.

Nettheim, G. 1995 Special measures, a response. In *The Racial Discrimination Act: A Review,* ed. Race Discrimination Commissioner. Canberra: Australian Government Publishing Service, pp. 233–48.

Pritchard, S. 1995. Special measures. In *The Racial Discrimination Act: A Review,* ed. Race Discrimination Commissioner. Canberra: Australian Government Publishing Service, pp. 183–231.

Sadurski, W. 1986. *Gerhardy* v. *Brown* v. the concept of discrimination: reflections on the landmark case that wasn't. *Sydney Law Review* 5 (11): 5–43.

CHAPTER 12

Sovereignty

Henry Reynolds

The conventional story is straightforward enough. It was like this: the Aboriginal people and Torres Strait Islanders became British subjects when the Crown progressively asserted sovereignty over the Australian continent in 1788, 1824, 1829 and 1879. However, the new Australian Commonwealth defined citizenship in such a way as to exclude indigenous Australians as well as non-European residents. This situation was remedied by a series of measures culminating in the constitutional referendum of 1967. Aboriginal people and Torres Strait Islanders are now citizens on an equal footing with everyone else. But underpinning this story are the assumptions about sovereignty, about nations and states and about the course of Australian history. In this chapter I will discuss these assumptions, all of which need rigorous examination.

As we have seen (in Chapter 11) until the Mabo judgment of 1992 Australian law rested upon the doctrine of *terra nullius* which depicted Aboriginal Australia as a place without people or settled law, to use the words of the Privy Council's Lord Watson in *Cooper* v. *Stuart* in 1889. Australia was a legal desert without land tenure, politics or sovereignty. The British Crown became the first sovereign and the first proprietor. From the moment of annexation there was 'only one sovereign, namely the King of England, and only one law, namely English law'.[1]

The High Court modified the story in the Mabo judgment overturning *terra nullius* as it related to property but reserved it in respect of sovereignty. The Crown did not become the beneficial owner of the land at the point of annexation but did become the sovereign over the entire land mass. Because it was not acquired from the indigenous people the sovereignty was original rather than derived. Justices Deane and Gaudron observed that 'it must be accepted in this court' that the whole of the territory designated in Governor Phillip's commission was, from the formal declaration of annexation on 7 February 1788, 'validly established as a settled British Colony'.[2] Their colleague Justice Dawson declared that the claim of sovereignty over Murray Island in 1879 was equally effective, explaining that:

> Whatever the justification for the acquisition of the territory by this means (and the sentiments of the nineteenth century by no means coincide with current thought), there can be no doubt that it was, and remains, legally effective.[3]

Aboriginal litigants who have sought to lessen the iron grip of this thesis have been confronted with an impenetrable barrier known as the 'act of state' doctrine, which holds that the extension of sovereignty is a matter of the prerogative powers of the Crown which cannot be questioned by the courts. The argument was restated in the High Court by Justice Gibbs in the *Sea and Submerged Lands* case in 1975 when he declared that the acquisition of territory by a sovereign state was 'an act of state which cannot be challenged, controlled or interfered with by the Courts of that state'.[4]

Even if the act of state doctrine can be circumvented, two other theories protect legal orthodoxy. The first is that Aboriginal society was too primitive to exercise even the most rudimentary form of sovereignty, a view enunciated by Justice Burton in 1836 when he declared that:

> although it might be granted that on the first taking possession of the colony, the Aborigines were entitled to be recognised as free and independent, yet they were not to be considered free and independent tribes. They had no sovereignty.[5]

The second is the traditional English view of sovereignty, which was described by the celebrated eighteenth century jurist William Blackstone as deriving of necessity from one 'supreme, irresistible, absolute, uncontrolled authority'.[6]

The logic of these ideas leads irresistibly in one direction. Because Australia was a land without sovereignty the supreme and absolute power of the Crown occupied every bit of jurisprudential space from the moment of annexation. By implication it can be assumed that indigenous Australians must be declared to be totally outside the circle of citizenship or inside it on the same basis as everyone else. There is no other space from which they could negotiate a separate and distinctive relationship with the Australian state. There can be no escape by way of inherent rights rooted in a pre-European past. Any special status could only come as a grant – made by the sovereign authority and therefore vulnerable to subsequent extinguishment.

Despite their seeming invulnerability, Australian theories about sovereignty rest on shifting, uncertain foundations. They do not measure up to long recognised principles of international law, nor do they provide a realistic account of the actual course of Australian history. I will consider these two aspects in turn.

International law provides three principal means by which territory can be acquired: by conquest, by cession and by settlement. The first two can be demonstrated by specific events at particular times – by battles and by the signing of treaties. They both assume the transference of a pre-existing sovereignty from one party to the other. But there can be no such certainty about acquisition by settlement. Originally it was meant to apply to uninhabited territories, an 1834 textbook on colonial law declaring that colonies were acquired:

> 1. by conquest; 2. by cession under treaty; or 3. by occupancy, viz. where an uninhabited country is discovered by British subjects, and is upon such discovery, adopted or recognised by the crown as part of its possessions.[7]

Because both the British and colonial authorities endeavoured to maintain the myth of an empty land – a land without any sovereignty at all – they never dealt with the jurisprudential problems inherent in the planting of colonies in an already inhabited land. In New Zealand the Crown negotiated the Treaty of Waitangi with Maori chiefs. In the United States the Supreme Court developed the doctrine of domestic dependent nations as early as the 1830s to explain the residual sovereignty exercised by Indians on their reserve lands. In more recent times the Canadians have enunciated the theory of the first nations' inherent right to self-government based on their pre-existing sovereignty.

Australian jurisprudence makes sense only if the Aboriginal people were traditionally so primitive as to be almost totally without law, politics or authority – a conclusion at odds with modern anthropological knowledge and with principles of human rights upheld vigorously by the High Court in the Mabo judgment. If the opposite case is accepted – that the Aboriginal tribes exercised a form of sovereignty that could have been recognised by the international law of the late eighteenth century and early nineteenth century – then the history buttressing the jurisprudence does not make sense.

The argument that, from the moment of annexation, there was only one sovereign and one system of laws in Australia was often questioned in the colonial courts during the 1830s and 40s. Perth barrister E W Landor defended Aboriginal people on trial for crimes committed on compatriots and, in doing so, poured scorn on the already orthodox view of Australian settlement:

your laws had been imposed upon this people as a conquered nation, or if they had annexed themselves and their country by anything like a treaty, all these proceedings would be right and proper. But as it is, we are two nations occupying the same land, and we have no more right to try them by our laws for offences committed *inter se*, than they have to seize and spear an Englishman, according to their law.

He went on to examine the question even more deeply, asking theoretically:

Is jurisdiction a necessary incident of sovereignty? Do a people become subject to our laws by the very act of planting the British standard on the top of the hill? [...] We claim the sovereignty yet we disclaim having obtained it by conquest; we should be very sorry to allow that it was by fraud; and how, in the name of wonder, then, can we defend our claim ?[8]

How would a more realistic historical account run? The British claim to sovereignty over the whole of Australia was exaggerated but, because no other power challenged it, the Crown eventually came to possess the external sovereignty. But internal sovereignty was another matter altogether. Because of the vast size of the continent and the slow expansion of British settlement there were many systems of law and many sovereignties in nineteenth century Australia. Many Aboriginal tribes did not see Europeans until the twentieth century.

What Britain oversaw was basically three zones of territory each with a status that would have been commonly understood elsewhere in the Empire. In the initially very small areas directly under British control sovereignty was fully asserted. Outside those areas there was a shifting zone of varying size where the colonial authorities exercised some authority for some of the time. What Britain had in this case was, in effect, a protectorate. Farther away from white settlement was another zone where colonial authority had never been exercised but which Britain would have strenuously defended against any other power. This was what, elsewhere in the Empire, would have been called a sphere of influence.

Over time the first zone expanded, impinging on the second, as did the second on the third. But just as British authority expanded gradually, Aboriginal sovereignty was eroded slowly. The same process was apparent in relation to native title and political authority. If, as the High Court declared in Mabo, native title was extinguished in a piecemeal fashion over a long period of time, the same clearly happened with sovereignty. If native title survives in some places then remnant sovereignty must also still exist among communities that still recognise, exercise and accept their traditional law.

While Australia re-examines the extension of British sovereignty over the continent, the concept of sovereignty itself is undergoing intense scrutiny in many parts of the world. This is particularly so in Europe where national sovereignty is being ceded upwards to the European institutions – the commission, the parliament and the court – and downwards to the regions. This process has been accompanied by a serious rethinking about the concentration of sovereignty that occurred historically with the creation of strong centralised states. The leading British politician Sir Geoffrey Howe has questioned the traditional view of indivisible and all powerful sovereigns, arguing:

> I believe sovereignty is not some pre-defined absolute, but a flexible, adaptable, organic notion that evolves and adjusts with the circumstances [...] sovereignty constitutes a resource to be used, rather than a constraint that inhibits or limits our capacity for action [...] In exactly the same way as the property rights of an individual, sovereignty may be seen as divisible, and exploitable in the interests of the nation whose sovereignty it is in a thousand different ways and circumstances.[9]

A leading English political scientist has called for a 'decentring' of power, a scattering of authority among a variety of smaller political units, with a return to the situation of the early modern period when Western Europe contained five hundred political units of varying types and sizes.[10] In the introduction to a recent collection of interviews with prominent European intellectuals, Irish philosopher Richard Kearney observed that the emerging Europe had 'a unique opportunity to foster new notions of sovereignty' which were 'inclusive rather than absolute, shared rather than insular, disseminated rather than closed in upon some bureaucratic centre'.[11]

Much recent discussion about sovereignty and the relations between cultural and national minorities and the world's states has embraced a new and intense interest in federalism as a means to manage inter-ethnic conflict. In a recent book *Federalism: The Multi-Ethnic Challenge* John Agnew noted how radically the context for examining federalism had changed because:

> in much contemporary writing on federalism the federal form of governance is firmly tied to the management of inter-ethnic conflict. Previously differences of language, religion or nationality were not privileged relative to considerations such as dissimilarity of social institutions or forces of geographical separation such as mountain barriers or great distance between communities. Discussion of federalism is today much more strongly related to the 'politics of identity' than was formerly the case.[12]

In 1901 Australia divided sovereignty between State and federal governments to overcome the tyranny of distance and the existence of six colonial governments with their own constitutions, institutions and traditions. The challenge for the new century is to use the accumulated experience of federalism to accommodate the growing demand for indigenous self-government. If sovereignty could be divided one way in 1901 there can be no reason, in principle, why it cannot be cut again to create a new level of government that would allow Aboriginal and Islander communities to run their own internal affairs in ways already apparent in the external territories of Cocos–Keeling, Christmas and Norfolk Islands.

Aboriginal and Islander calls for self-government arise both from purely Australian circumstances and the universal desire of indigenous people to claim their right to self-determination. They rest their case on existing international covenants, treaties and agreements. Of particular importance are the twin international covenants of 1966 – on civil and political rights and on economic, social and cultural rights – which share the same clause: 'All peoples have the right to self-determination, by virtue of that right they freely determine their political status and freely pursue their economic, social and cultural development.'[13]

Many existing governments deny that reference to 'all peoples' includes indigenous minorities. They in turn counter-attack with the proposition that not only are they 'peoples' but that their survival as distinctive cultures is clearly linked to the right to self-government. This was the view taken by Jose Cobo in his UN sponsored paper of 1987 entitled 'Study of the Problems of Discrimination Against Indigenous Populations'. Cobo argued that self-government was:

> an inherent part of their cultural and legal heritage which has contributed to their cohesion and to the maintenance of their social and cultural tradition [...] Self-determination, in its many forms, is thus a basic pre-condition if indigenous peoples are to enjoy their fundamental rights and determine their future, while at the same time preserving, developing and passing on their specific ethnic identity to future generations.[14]

The right to self-determination is a central theme in the recently completed draft Declaration of the Rights of Indigenous People which is currently being considered by the UN Commission on Human Rights. Article 31 is the section most relevant to the question in hand. It reads:

> Indigenous peoples, as a specific form of exercising their right to self-determination, have the right to autonomy or self-government in matters relating to their internal and local affairs, including culture, religion, education, information, media, health, housing, employment, social welfare, economic activities, land and resource management, environment and entry by non members, as well as ways and means of financing these autonomous functions.[15]

Indigenous self-government may require some re-distribution of sovereignty within states while falling far short of secession. But there are increasing calls for some form of international representation for indigenous people. In a recent article in the journal *Foreign Affairs*, American scholar Gideon Gottlieb argued that nations that do not have a state of their own should be granted a 'formal non-territorial status and a recognised standing internationally, albeit one that differs from the position of states.'[16] Similar calls are currently heard from many parts of the world. Danish jurist Frederick Harhoff has linked indigenous cultural survival with both internal self-government and international standing which would:

> involve the indigenous peoples themselves directly in the international society as entitled and obliged parties for all purposes of their optimal cultural survival. Thus, it seems clear that self determination is more than just an internal, national rearrangement of domestic powers. It reflects new dimensions in the international society and requires new thinking in international law.[17]

Conclusion

Consideration of the future status of Aboriginal people and Torres Strait Islanders raises questions about the distribution of power within Australian society, the domestic impact of international law, the future of the federal system and the nature of sovereignty itself. And what of citizenship? How is it possible to reconcile the equal rights accorded to all citizens with the special group rights increasingly demanded by indigenous people? The problem can best be tackled by prising apart the two concepts of state and nation. The unique status sought by Aboriginal people and Islanders relates to their membership of the first nations, not to special rights acquired from the state. They are citizens of the state, not of the nation; theirs is a civic, not an ethnic, loyalty. But the paradox is that their commitment to the state may be enhanced by the fact that it alone can underwrite and protect indigenous nationalism and self-government from inimical forces both within Australia and without.

Notes

1 Lord Watson quoted by Justice Roth in *R* v. *Wedge, 1976 New South Wales Law Reports* 1976: 584.
2 *Australian Law Reports* (ALR) 192: 79.
3 ALR 1992: 121.
4 *New South Wales* v. *The Commonwealth, 1975 Commonwealth Law Reports* (CLR) 1975, 135: 388.

5 Quoted by Justic Roth in *R* v. *Wedge, 1976 New South Wales Law Reports* 1976: 586
6 Blackstone 1823 (1): 9.
7 Clark 1834: 4.
8 Landor 1847: 192–3.
9 Quoted by Clark in 'Sovereignty: the British experience', *Times Literary Supplement*, 29 November 1991: 15.
10 J Keane, 'Democracy's poisonous fruit', *Times Literary Supplement*, 21 August 1992: 11.
11 Kearney 1995: 3.
12 Smith 1995: 294.
13 Quoted by Reynolds 1996: 163.
14 Quoted by SJ Anaya 1990: 842.
15 Quoted by Reynolds 1996: 163.
16 G Gottlieb, 'Nations without states', *Foreign Affairs*, May–June 1994: 107.
17 Harhoff 1988: 290.

References

Anaya, S. J. 1990. The capacity of international law to advance ethnic or nationality rights claims. *Iowa Law Review* 75(4): 837–44.
Blackstone, W. 1823. *Commentaries on the Laws of England* (two volumes, 18th edn). London: Sherwood Jones.
Clark, C. 1834. *A Summary of Colonial Law*. London: Sweet.
Harhoff, F. 1988. Constitutional and international legal aspects of Aboriginal rights. *Nordic Journal of International Law* 57: 289–94.
Kearney, R. (ed.) 1995. *States of Mind*. Manchester: Manchester University Press.
Landor, E. W. 1847. *The Bushman: Or, Life in a New Country*. London: R. Bentley.
Reynolds, H. 1996. *Aboriginal Sovereignty*. Sydney: Allen & Unwin.
Smith, G. (ed.) 1995. *Federalism: The Multi-Ethnic Challenge*. London: Longman.

Index

INDEX
221